Hope

SUNY series in Italian/American Culture

Fred L. Gardaphé, editor

Hopelessly Alien

The Italian Immigration Experience
in Chicago Heights

LOUIS CORSINO

Cover: (1) Workers, of all ages, posed outside the Flintkote manufacturing plant. Courtesy Chicago Heights Library Collection. (2) Man in front of houses. Personal collection of Louis Corsino. Immigrants and their children looked upon homeownership as a way of demonstrating their commitment to America. (3) Children standing in two rows. Personal collection of Angelo "Sam" Ciambrone. Children were valuable sources of cultural capital. Front row (l to r): William Wright, Arthur Potts, John Narcisi, Angelo Ciambrone, John Bianconi. Back row (l to r): Percy Griffin, Norman Swiderek, Andrew Mark, Augie Bamonti.

Published by State University of New York Press, Albany

© 2024 State University of New York

All rights reserved

Printed in the United States of America

No part of this book may be used or reproduced in any manner whatsoever without written permission. No part of this book may be stored in a retrieval system or transmitted in any form or by any means including electronic, electrostatic, magnetic tape, mechanical, photocopying, recording, or otherwise without the prior permission in writing of the publisher.

For information, contact State University of New York Press, Albany, NY
www.sunypress.edu

Library of Congress Cataloging-in-Publication Data

Name: Corsino, Louis, 1948– author.
Title: Hopelessly alien : the Italian immigration experience in Chicago Heights / Louis Corsino.
Description: Albany, NY : State University of New York Press, [2024] | Series: SUNY series in italian/american culture | Includes bibliographical references and index.
Identifiers: LCCN 2023039275 | ISBN 9781438497648 (hardcover : alk. paper) | ISBN 9781438497631 (ebook) | ISBN 9781438497617 (pbk. : alk. paper)
Subjects: LCSH: Italian Americans—Illinois—Chicago Heights—Social conditions. | Italian Americans—Ethnic identity. | Immigrants—Illinois—Chicago Heights—Social conditions—20th century. | Chicago Heights (Ill.)—History—20th century.
Classification: LCC E184.I8 C6537 2024 | DDC 977.3/10045107304—dc23/eng/20231213
LC record available at https://lccn.loc.gov/2023039275

10 9 8 7 6 5 4 3 2 1

Contents

List of Illustrations		vii
Preface		ix
Introduction	Hope in a Sociological and Community Context	1
Chapter 1	Hope, Cultural Capital, and Habitus within an Italian Community	19
Chapter 2	Drawn into the Social Spaces of Hope: The Italian Social Journey from Italy to America	41
Chapter 3	Purchasing an Acceptance in American Society: Occupational Mobility as Cultural Capital	65
Chapter 4.	Purchasing an Acceptance in American Society: Homeownership as Cultural Capital	87
Chapter 5	Purchasing an Acceptance in American Society: Children as Cultural Capital	103
Conclusion	Individualized Hope and Communal Hopes	123
Notes		135
Index		173

Illustrations

Figures

1.1	Hope produced a physical presence that was orderly, measured, and dignified.	35
1.2	Formal, traditional dress of Italian culture.	37
2.1	As one of the leading shipping companies in Italy, Navigazione Generale Italiana had a particular interest in encouraging emigration on the part of Italian citizens.	46
2.2	This emigrant guidebook presents a flowery, pastoral picture of life in South America.	47
2.3	The riches and hopes of different worlds and travel were often displayed in colorful, dramatic posters that brought together blue skies, the open seas, and modern technology.	48
2.4	Title: The Corsino family photo (with boarders as well) in the early 1950s.	57
2.5	Boarding houses in Chicago Heights were sometimes private homes, sometimes owned by industries, sometimes hotels.	58
3.1	Workers Outside the American Manganese Steel Company, circa 1920s.	69
3.2	The Chicago Heights Octopus: At the beginning of the last century, the octopus was a common image for something alien, malevolent, and insidious.	70

3.3 Occupational Trajectories, Male, Unskilled/Semiskilled Italian, Polish, and Native-Born Workers, 1910–1940. 76

4.1 The Chicago Heights Land Association promoted the benefits of living in and establishing industrial plants in the city as early as 1893. 89

4.2 Chicago Heights East Side Street. 91

4.3 In the Chicago Heights suburban environment, renting was increasingly disvalued for financial, political, and personal reasons. 99

5.1 Daughters had a more difficult time achieving success outside the home, but the Pancrazio family was one of the exceptions. 111

Tables

3.1 Occupational Ranking of Italian, Adult Males, Chicago Heights, 1900–1930 (in Percent) 72

3.2 Occupational Mobility, Italian, Polish, and Native-born Male Sample, Chicago Heights, 1910–1920, 1910–1930, 1910–1940 (in Percent) 78

4.1 Homeownership among Italians: Chicago Heights, Chicago, Illinois, and the United States, 1900–1930 (in Percent) 91

5.1 Fathers' Life Work and Job Choices of Sons as Reported by 336 Eighth-, Tenth-, and Twelfth-Grade Students (in Percent) 112

5.2 Son's Occupation from Father's Occupation. Inflow Mobility, Chicago Heights Italian Immigrants, 1910 to 1930–1940 (in Percent) 114

Preface

My first book, *The Neighborhood Outfit: Organized Crime in Chicago Heights,* was a long time coming. I worked at it for fifteen years on and off. When I finished, I was relieved. However, the academic (and personal) side of me was still uneasy. Why was it that some Italian immigrants were successful and others not so much—and thus resorted to the opportunities organized crime provided. This was especially poignant for me since my grandfather, father, and many of our family friends had Outfit connections and jobs. The most common explanations suggested that people who worked in these criminal organizations were pathological, lazy, or just "bad apples." In slightly more acceptable language: they lacked the appropriate hopes and desires, if not hopes and desires altogether.

The consistent assumption in the studies on Italian immigration, if not formally stated at least in the background, was that the hope for a better life was the main motivating force that explained immigration and a successful adjustment in the American context. Giovanni Schiavo's characterization put this boldly—in the face of a series of omnipresent sorrows and humiliations, the Italian immigrant had an internal desire "far much stronger than any obstacle he was to overcome."[1] This distinctive description of desire permitted the separation of the apples into good and bad piles. Some Italian immigrants had deep reserves of desire and hope—others not so much.

Yet, the characterization of the inner lives of these immigrants appeared too convenient. Personal experience in Chicago Heights, my hometown, and sociological doubts led me to question the motivating power of hope not only with respect to immigration but more broadly in different spheres of life. Is hope in fact a form of mental energy that propels action forward? Do some people, like my father and grandfather, run low on this energy and thus take an easier path? Does hope reside deep inside the person, or is it something that can be manipulated from the outside? And why is it that some people have to rely upon hope for a better life going forward, while others with resources can bypass hope, simply making a better life happen for themselves? These seem uniquely sociological questions more than the personal, idiosyncratic ones normally associated with hope.

In thinking about these possibilities, I came to realize that in the American context hope has taken on a sacred, divinelike character, especially in connection with immigration but also in different secular spheres of contemporary life. Hope is often viewed as omnipresent, transcendent, and infallible. Hope is something that rises above and is set apart from the mundane world. And to challenge its sacred character is likely to invite strong negative reactions. Thus, early on when I was formulating my ideas, my wife and I were out to dinner with several friends when I mentioned that hope was quite possibly as much a problem to overcome as it was a remedy. Their reactions ranged from bewilderment, disbelief, and disapproval. "You mean, 'hope sucks'?" asked one of our friends. Inelegant, perhaps, and not always the case, but a concise and perceptive characterization of my thoughts and the reluctance of others to view hope from a critical perspective. Another time, I made a presentation at a conference where once again I put hope into doubt. In a most sincere manner, one of the respondents warned against using the word "hope" in an ungracious fashion. He suggested that I use a different word, for "hope was a virtue."

Not long afterward, the neighborhood where I lived held one of its annual block parties. Along with the food and games for some of the children, my wife suggested that we reserve an hour out of the day for a "hope seminar." I had been in casual conversation with several of our neighbors about some of the issues surrounding hope, and though I was dubious as to whether such a seminar would fit well with the bouncy house down the block, we went ahead. At the scheduled time, we set up several chairs in a circle under the tree in front of our house. One by one, however, the group began to grow; and all fifteen or so of our neighbors joined in the free-flowing discussion on hope. In this casual get-together and in others through the year, I learned a lot and found some of my thoughts too broad or found myself attacking hope as a strawman. These were smart, engaged conversations with smart, engaged people. Still, the core argument still held: that hope can be used in a social and ideological sense to manipulate people.

One discussion best captured this idea. A man who lived on the block told us of his experiences in the past year where he had nearly passed away because of unexpected complications from a medical condition. He said there were times when he was uncertain whether he would make it to the next day. During this time, a nurse or a doctor would come into the hospital room and tell him how good he looked or how he was progressing. He told us subsequently that he resented their attempts at providing these hopes for his recovery. He said he knew how he felt, and he knew the chart numbers were not in his favor. The efforts on the part of these medical personnel were certainly understandable and laudable given the circumstances. However, they were not genuine in the sense that they did not come from the patient himself. Only when he started to feel better in terms of his own sense of well-being, and in terms of his understanding of what health meant to him, did he allow himself to have hope. Only then could he integrate his own sense of hope with the standards of the medical community. This coming together of individual hopes and community hopes, and the potential for these to become widely dissociated, came to be a guiding point: a touchstone for my study on Italians, immigrants, and hope overall.

The genesis and development of this study, then, took place in a social context. The limitations of this study are mine alone, but whatever insights it produces are indeed a shared product. In a more specific sense, I owe an appreciation to a range of people both inside and outside the academic circle. Within the academy, North Central College has periodically provided funding for this project but always provided a collection of colleagues who represent the best that a small college environment can offer. From a supportive Provost, Abiodun Goke-Pariola, and College of Arts and Letters Dean, Stephen Caliendo, I have been able to pursue my research and teaching interests with an appropriate and meaningful balance. Other colleagues such as Karl Kelley and Tom Cavenagh have listened to my ravings on hope in a respectful but critical manner. Of course, Roger Waldinger at UCLA has always been a source of inspiration. He stayed in contact with me not because he had to but because he is intellectually curious, productive, but most of all a good person. Richard Juliani, Albert Melone, Jerome Krase are all-stars in the academy, Italian American studies in particular. I came upon their friendship later in my academic career but find them to be honest, intelligent, and persons of character. And Dominic Candeloro straddles the line separating the academy from those outside. He does this so well as a public intellectual that the division between the two appropriately becomes quite blurry. His ability to advocate for a rich, evocative history of Italians in America, and Chicago in particular, is unparalleled. His decency and willingness to help others is even greater. Plus, he also grew up in Chicago Heights. Along with Barbara Paul, who as head librarian in Chicago Heights for over forty years did more to preserve the vital history of the Heights than any other person, Candeloro provided the basic historical materials and images for this study.

I also need to acknowledge another former Chicago Heights ally. Michel Fisher came into my professional life in the middle of this study. He called me one day and explained that he knew a great deal about Italians in Chicago Heights. I was leery, but during several lunches and conversations I was impressed by his deep knowledge and commitment to the history of Italians in Chicago Heights. His stories and connections were invaluable to this study. He provided the detailed vignettes on Italian experiences in the Heights. One of the main, unanticipated benefits of engaging in this form of research involves the opportunity to make new friends such as Michael.

Somewhere toward the last stages of this project I was fortunate to receive a National Endowment for the Humanities (NEH) Summer Stipend for the completion of the final chapter. It is difficult to overestimate, the monetary stipend aside, the value of this award. On a practical level, it freed up valuable time to collect data, think, and write. On a personal level, it is always encouraging to know that the ideas ruminating in one's head are regarded as worthy and important by the distinguished NEH scholars. The NEH process is challenging but it forwards the intellectual debate and public dialogue across a range of institutions, social arenas, and communities. And of course I would not have been successful without the steady, secure guidance of Michelle "Shelly" Galasso, director of the Office of Sponsored Research at North Central College, and Bruce Janacek, North Central College history professor who commented on drafts of the proposal. The challenges, however, are well worth the effort, in no small part because the NEH staff does a wonderful job of providing information and support along the way.

There are countless others whose hard work and generosity went far beyond the rewards (if any) that they received. A number of students helped with the time-consuming but vital review of census manuscripts that produced the specific information and mobility tables on Italians in the Chicago Heights context. These include: Manuel Renteria, Raine Odum, Lauren Phegley, Kaya Goodwin, Keri Long, Steven Rotunno, Anita Herrera, Kaitlin Koncilja, Criscela Ceniceros, and Luis Tello. Luis, in particular, devoted hours upon hours to researching and codifying census information across decades. Others also willingly gave up their time to speak with me about life growing up Italian in Chicago Heights. While there were many to thank over the years, most recently Marie Iafollo, Angelo Ciambrone, Frank Melchiore, and Diane Melchiore represent what is best about being a part of the long history of Italians in Chicago Heights. They are equally inspiring in their own unique ways. And family members are always a source of encouragement—even if this encouragement is not always deserved. My sister, Jo O'Neal, and her husband Mike read chapters and made certain to correct me, as sisters and brothers-in-law tend to do. They are touchstones in a variety of ways. And my wife, Alison, made innumerable sacrifices to allow me to continue to work on this project and to supply the care and concern for our two daughters—Mia and Andie. I am a lucky man three times over.

Finally, the editors and the production staff at SUNY Press were great partners. Here they are far down on this list of acknowledgments but not in the debt and appreciation I owe them for their support and professional expertise. Fred Gardaphé, the editor of this series on Italian American studies, grew up in an Italian suburb outside Chicago in ways similar to my own. He is always a source of novel and challenging ideas, and his stewardship of this series on Italian American studies has been invaluable. I have also worked closely with James Peltz, editor-in-chief. He has been gracious in granting me deadline extensions but most importantly in providing a steady hand throughout this process—both intellectually and procedurally. I am fortunate to work with such a thorough professional and good person. Susan Geraghty, as production editor, provided such crisp and detailed information she makes the multifaceted production process appear seamless. Aimee Harrison, the cover coordinator, merged expertise with a sympathetic ear. Copy editor Michael Sandlin set new, higher standards for good writing. His work led me to a new understanding of what good writing could look like. Whatever shortcomings remain in terms of grammar, style, and clarity are mine.

Introduction

Hope in a Sociological and Community Context

In his travels throughout Europe, John Braithwaite speaks of the time he spent with his children and their playful attempts to guess the vices and virtues represented in the medieval sculptures and paintings encountered along the way.[1] Gluttony was the easiest to identify, to see objectified in the stone carvings and framed canvases. The most difficult was hope. As Braithwaite offers, this may be due to the modern temper that sees hope as passé, for the present-day world has given itself over to cynicism and skepticism. At the same time, these artisans may have faced an impossible task. The uncertain, dreamlike, and futuristic character of hope made it less amenable to a shared, outward manifestation.[2]

Along with this elusive objectification, hope has also escaped an easy characterization as a virtue or a vice. While acknowledging hope's benefits, classical scholars warned against the dangers in committing to hope to further the good life. They pejoratively categorized hope as "false dreams" or "false pleasures." Hope was thought to be intricately bound upon with fear, rifled with mistaken assumptions, and an exceedingly poor guide to a clear-headed adaptation to the present.[3]

Hope took a virtuous turn in the following centuries as both Christian writers and secular philosophers dissected its underlying assumptions and possibilities. From a Christian perspective, hope and faith were joined—with this alchemy leading to the creation of a theological path wherein one could achieve Grace in the face of earthly evidence to the contrary. John Milton's epic poem, *Paradise Lost*, speaks of this otherworldly mingling of faith and hope. Though Satan is defeated, the price is an expulsion from Paradise with the consolation that faith and hope, sent via the Archangel Michael, will bring salvation. "A Paradise within thee. Happier by far."[4]

The Enlightenment thinkers also embraced hope as a virtue. However, as an antidote to these religious dogmas, they perceived hope in secular terms. It was not premised upon an article of faith but upon reason. Rational thought was the liberating force that overcomes bias and immature ideas and frees humankind to pursue better lives. Robert Nisbet suggests that the rise of democracy, progress, and reason during the nineteenth century led many to speak of the "Century of Great Hope."[5] This Enlightenment conception freed hope from its otherworldly moorings and the shackles of tradition. Consequently, hope was welcomed into a host of earthly matters—medicine, politics, education, the economy. In the words of Richard Rorty, hope with its attendant mundane vocabularies became ubiquitous. These vocabularies became so many "stories about future outcomes which compensate for present sacrifices." They were stories tied to the temporal world with the counsel that "things might get better."[6]

A notable and recognizable manifestation of this worldly hope emerged in the social spaces of immigration, a connection that took root in the mid-nineteenth century. Previously, a broad and common response to the drudgery and misery in earthly matters involved a patient waiting for a religious salvation. Individuals were held captive and found this deliverance through dreams of a better life in heaven. This was countered by the development of a capitalist labor market, the rapid growth of cities, and increased means of transportation. Each set the stage for a secularization of hope. Individuals could improve their lot in life by struggling against and opposing oppressive forces in their home country. Less dramatically, they could transport themselves and their families to a better life and richer opportunities in other parts of the world.[7]

Most immigration narratives, accordingly, focus upon misery and then hope as the springboards to a geographic and consequential social mobility. As a presumed innate human universal, hope goes a long way toward explaining the massive movement of millions of people in the Western world over the last century. In the face of highly disparaging and life-threatening circumstances, individuals from vastly different cultures and historical situations leave their native lands because of hope and the prospects for social advancement. They leave with the expectation that a better life is possible, though by no means certain, in another country. In the American context, Ellis Island, the major immigration entry point in the United States for over half a century, was christened "the Island of Hope." Oscar Handlin's classic *The Uprooted* grounded the story of immigration to America in the psychological quests for "new worlds, new visions."[8] Stephan

Thernstrom explored the ideological assumptions underpinning the "promise of mobility." He argued that middle class opinion makers offered up one success story after another to minimize dissent and nurture "the hope that opportunity was just around the corner."[9] More recently, Richard Alba and Nancy Forner present the empirical observation that "most immigrants come to the rich societies of the West with the hope of dramatically improving their economic prospects."[10]

Thus hope, social mobility, and immigration are constitutionally joined. However, the central argument here is that these connections are messier and more complex than typically depicted. It is by no means clear that hope precedes the decision to migrate or that it is a motivating force thrusting the immigrant forward. This mechanistic conception is suspect because it assumes a purposive striving toward a steadfast, clearly defined goal or a push from within (or behind). Hope is a fixed element within some people and not others. On the contrary, and to paraphrase John Dewey's discussion of motive, hope may not exist prior to a set of decisions. "It is an act plus a judgement upon some element of it, the judgement being made in light of the consequences of the act."[11] At the same time, the painting of hope and mobility along a singular pathway, or at least common jumping-off point in vastly different local contexts, subordinates historical complexity to a general idealized casual model.[12] It reduces this complexity to one of a number of possible roads forward.

Further, even the assumption of social mobility as the steadfast goal orienting the actions of immigrants is also debatable. This one-dimensional focus upon social advancement may impose its own "alien conceptual framework" on a range of cultural aspirations and conceptions of success.[13] To be sure, hope may be a motivating force that guides action in search of economic or social mobility. However, a closer look may reveal that the association of hope and social mobility may also be a foremost example of what Lauren Berlant labeled as "cruel optimism" or a socially approved outcome that in reality few have the opportunity to achieve. That is, mobility is depicted in such hegemonic terms that it magnetizes "a cluster of promises" that are quite varied but that are recast, with the aid of others, as the socially sanctioned object of desire.[14]

Indeed, immigration may be prompted by a range of social forces that have little to do with hope and may be pursued (or not) at the expense of social mobility. James Henretta alerts us to the possibilities that "whatever their hopes for themselves, these migrants were not atomistic individuals, with an intense and over-riding goal of social advancement, but responsible participants in a trans-Atlantic kinship network with strong family ties and communal values."[15] Nancy Green and Roger Waldinger also stress the highly contingent and especially political character of migration such that the migrant's decision to depart one country for another "is not simply an individual, economic act but also ultimately a collective and political one."[16]

These questions regarding hope and social mobility arose out of *The Neighborhood Outfit: Organized Crime in Chicago Heights*. In that study, I offered an explanation of a long-standing, successful organized crime operation in this suburban city, a key component of the Chicago Outfit. The Chicago Heights crew consisted almost exclusively of Italian immigrants. Following upon and extending Daniel Bell's classic argument that characterized organized crime as a ladder of social mobility, I sought to distance Italian participation in these criminal affairs from the timeworn and self-referencing explanations based upon genetic predispositions, cultural affinities, or innate criminal motives.[17]

In the course of this study, I continually came up against the fact that the overwhelming majority of Italian immigrants did *not* attempt to climb that "crooked ladder." They failed to do so despite the dire circumstances they faced in America. Overcrowding, discrimination, substandard housing, dangerous workplaces, industrial pollution, low wages, high infant mortality, cultural affronts, and unsanitary living conditions were common. In such circumstances, questions as to whether this new life was better than the one left behind were never far from the surface.[18] Hope for a better life moving forward was existentially challenged and put into doubt. Yet, for many of these immigrants hope did not disappear. Giovanni Schiavo characterizes both the plight and the resilience of the Italian immigrant in the Chicago area. "He knew that his life in the new world would be one of sorrows, of sacrifices, of humiliations, of self-denials. But the desire to change his economic status was by far much stronger than any obstacle he was to overcome."[19]

I was faced, therefore, with a number of theoretical and practical questions. Why did hope persist? And why did it not succumb to the reality of the immediate circumstances? Why was hope and desire "far much stronger" than the here-and-now existence these immigrants experienced? As the trope of the "golden door" in America began to fade, how did immigrants maintain hope in this increasingly *terra amara* or bitter earth?[20] How and why did so many Italians maintain a sense of hope in an otherwise mundane world that objectively lacked promise for so many? Why did they continue to espouse hope in social mobility when "the climb up was often slow and gradual rather than a matter of giant leaps forward" and often punctuated with "painful setbacks and difficulties along the way."[21]

Simply stating that these Italians, or immigrants more generally, were in possession of a deep reservoir of hope is unsatisfying, if too convenient. As such, the standard narrative on hope as an explanatory variable in this immigration context—that is, hope as the "most human of all mental feelings," a form of mental energy, an innate attribute—became too strained.[22] These characterizations obscured and left unanswered a number of important questions. Most importantly, how is hope situated in the particular historical context? What are its social roots and functions? Whose aims and interests are furthered through the propagation of hope?

With these issues in mind, I approach hope and social mobility from a sociological perspective, as both a complement and challenge to the rich literature on hope from the more traditional sociological and psychological perspectives. In this analysis, I am guided by the sociohistorical field approach of Pierre Bourdieu. Bourdieu provides a most useful analytic framework with a conceptual scheme that highlights the tension between habitus and field (or social spaces), or more broadly the individual and society. Since hope may be at one and the same time an individual disposition and social fact, Bourdieu's analysis allows us to consider both and discover their contingent connections. In short, the aim is to reconstruct the social spaces of immigration for Italians in the Chicago Heights context and to show how hope and social mobility within these various social spaces were "produced, constructed, and perceived."[23]

Three orienting issues take center stage in light of this approach. First, following Bourdieu's general and innovative insight, hope is viewed as a cultural resource or a type of cultural capital.[24] It is a cultural asset or a practice that people learn to display and feel as they move through the processes of immigration. In the American context, immigrants realized with various degrees of intentionality that the framing of their experiences through the idioms of hope and social mobility worked best in advancing their acceptance in the society. Viewed from this perspective, hope and the attendant quest for mobility were elements of a language, parts of the cultural code, which allowed immigrants to distinguish themselves from the least favorable alien statuses and gain a cultural advantage in the social spaces of immigration. In Wittgenstein's terms, "the phenomena of hope are modes of this complicated form of life."[25] Their meaning and use begs the question as to a larger, expansive set of experiences and contexts they reference.

Second, hope was a contested ideological practice and, as such, a method of domination. Immigrants did not have exclusive control over their social relations or the strategic manipulation of hope. At various social locations along the immigration path, politicians, officials, concerned citizens, the press, and others molded and shaped the hopes and social mobility aspirations of the newcomers. Thus, the arrival in large numbers of culturally alien strangers posed challenges to the economic and social dominance of the native population. As such, social control mechanisms were in order. These mechanisms took various forms from legal remedies to cultural criticism and physical attacks. Yet, cultural assimilation was the most common and effective tool. And the most effective and intrusive assimilation practice was to reach inside individuals and structure their expectations, aspirations, and feelings in line with the dominant assumptions and values. In this sense the cultural encouragement of hope and social advancement took on disciplinary aspects. These were practices used to normalize and classify the alien newcomer. Borrowing and adapting Foucault's famous idiom regarding punishment, the institutionalization of hope was not to control less, but to control better.

Finally, hope is inherently fragile. Its dreamlike, voluntarist character makes it susceptible to doubts and uncertainties. Hope fades without worldly, tangible referents. As such, hope must be objectified in the social world both for the immigrant's own self-motivation and for the dominant groups' social control and assimilation interests. It must be made visible and accountable in some public capacity outside the mental images of the individual. The fulfillment of (or at least the path toward) hope needs to be codified and institutionalized in some predictable and recognizable fashion. This raises questions regarding what counts for success or the objectification of hope in particular historical contexts. Is it gainful employment, a recognizable occupational mobility, the purchase of a home, the acceptance into higher-level status groups, or the success of one's children? These raise further questions as to whether these paths were chosen by the immigrants themselves based upon their emerging cultural beliefs or formulated by more powerful interests as objective and ideologically marked criteria of success and control.

Hope and Classical Sociological Thought

The ability to ask these sociological questions requires first the extraction of hope from its individualistic assumptions. If hope resides only or primarily within the individual psyche or the "hard, unchangeable core of our anthropological specificity"[26] then the social world can only have a limited (if any) impact upon its genesis, strength, or development. Not too surprisingly, the classic social thinkers challenged these person-driven conceptions. Marx, Durkheim, and Weber all had something to say about hope, though rarely did they examine it directly.[27] In part, this inattention may have been brought about by the close relationship between hope and religion.[28] All three theorists sought to distinguish, if not radically critique, the theist conception of life on earth from their more empirical, secular explanations. From their perspectives, hope was too irrational, too individualistic, too faith-based to systematically include in their mature sociological theories.

All the same, in a world strongly imbued with religious beliefs, practices, and questions of salvation, Marx, Durkheim, and Weber were compelled to understand hope as an empirical fact. As one might expect, Marx was most dismissive of hope as an individualistic quest for a better life. The "privatization of hope" in the capitalist era undercut the necessary collectivist, class-based effort required to overcome the objective, socioeconomic conditions that imprisoned the working class. Still, Marx understood that the ideologies of hope found expression in a mundane world. Objectified in the form of religious doctrine and practices, hope or more properly religion was the "fantastic realization of the human essence . . . the sigh of the oppressed creature, the heart of a heartless world, and the soul of soulless conditions."[29] In this sense, Marx saw religion as a reflection of a distorted and alienating social order. In and of itself, it was an illusion that over time would succumb to the material conditions and contradictions in capitalist society. When this took place, a person would not need daydreams, wishes, or "fantastic" desires to realize species being, for then one would be able to "think and act and shape his reality like a man who has lost his hope and come to reason."[30]

Durkheim was primarily intent upon understanding hope in the context of his general discussion of happiness and the division of labor in society.[31] He argued that happiness was not a natural or inevitable consequence of the movement from a mechanical to organic society, with its increasing division of labor. Instead, happiness was a variable product of the social environment and the ability of people to turn their focus to the future. In particular, when misfortune surfaces, individuals will likely have learned that their present sufferings will reasonably give way to a better life. In other words, they will have developed a collective sense of hope as a social fact. As Durkheim said, hope "has not miraculously descended from heaven into our hearts, but it has to be formed, as all sentiments, within the action of the facts."[32] In this formulation, hope is not an illusion, not an empty promise, something Marx would have argued. And it is not a pure sentiment that arises solely for biological or psychological reasons. It is very much a social phenomenon produced by collective action and to be understood on these terms.

The most sophisticated and well-developed conception of hope belongs to Weber. In his analysis of status and social standing, Weber made a distinction between those who were "positively privileged" and those who were "negatively privileged."[33] The former derives their honor and respect from the world as it is, from their being or existence in this world. The latter must turn their gaze elsewhere, to lives that they do not now possess. They must generate the hope for a better life, a life of righteous status and respect in the Kingdom of God.

Weber took his sociological account of hope a step further, and in a somewhat different direction, in his classic work, *The Protestant Ethic and Spirit of Capitalism.* In this study, Weber concluded that capitalism and Protestantism were joined. They were joined not in a constitutional or endemic fashion but as a consequence of the "psychological sanctions" many Protestants (and Calvinists, in particular) adopted on their way toward discovering their state of grace. It was Weber's great insight to see that the spirit of capitalism—the productive investment of capital, the acquisitive activity, the moral righteousness of wealth—was motivated by the unknown distribution of salvation. That is, the Calvinist believed that one's salvation owned nothing to one's own achievements or cooperation but was "hidden in dark mysteries" of "His Majesty."[34] It was based four-square on hope and faith. As such, Weber surmised that the Calvinists experienced an "unprecedented inner loneliness" in their search to determine if they were one of the elect. Unable to change their destiny, Protestants took to the "market place of life" in an attempt to discover signs or evidence of their "certitude salutis."[35] They needed to objectify or ground hope. While this search took several forms, the most pronounced involved the acquisition of wealth. The rational, systematic pursuit of wealth, along with an avoidance of idleness and the sinful enjoyment of life, was assumed to be the most virtuous way to live in accordance with God's will. Most importantly, wealth was tangible proof of one's salvation status; it was an objective feature of the world, beyond individual desires and motivations, which would convince believers that they were among the chosen.

With these sociological perspectives in hand, the links between hope, social mobility, and immigration can be examined with fresh insights. Most immigrants are "negatively privileged" based upon their socioeconomic standing in their own country. And as they proceed along the immigration path and experience the context of reception in their new home, whatever status and honor they possessed beforehand is effectively nullified as they sink near the bottom of the immigration hierarchy. In one situation after another, they are at a personal, structural, and cultural disadvantage and are likely to adopt hope as a *stance* or a form of life to ameliorate their predicament. In this sense, hope is not random; it has not "miraculously descended from heaven" nor has it solely emerged from the "hard unchangeable core" of our psyche: it has social structural roots.

At the same time, there is a structural component not only to the sources of hope but also to its objectification. Immigrants may occupy variously disadvantaged positions in terms of their ability to witness their hope manifested in the "market place of life." Those toward the bottom of the immigration hierarchy may not have readily available and meaningful real-world references to sustain hope or confer on it the "accent of reality."[36] For example, if patterns of residential segregation create exceedingly high unemployment rates in a community, then it may be difficult for a person who lives in this community to hold out hope and secure a good job. This structural inability to ground hope in the here and now may cause it to dissipate. Conversely, if the immediate social environment provides objectified signs or representations that hope can move beyond a wish or desire and reach into the everyday world—for example, if the person down the block got a new job or a friend moved up to foreman in the factory—then hope will be emboldened.

Finally, as Marx said famously, "Men make their own history, but they do not make it as they please; they do not make it under self-selected circumstances, but under circumstances existing already, given and transmitted from the past."[37] In this sense, immigrants make their own history. They are not driven by the naturalistic or "animal spirits" of hope but shape their reality based upon what they perceive to be the demands of the situation.[38] Hope and the quest for social mobility, therefore, are practical and rational strategies immigrants adopt to further their wide-ranging goals and aspirations. But "under circumstances existing already" suggests that those in more powerful positions exert considerable influence upon these practices. They seize upon these practices in an ideological fashion and turn hope and the quest for social mobility "toward the maintenance of the existing order."[39] Taken all together, therefore, and following upon the singular insights of Durkheim, Weber, and Marx, hope has social structural origins, requires an objectification in the social world, and is susceptible to ideological manipulation by those in positions of power and influence.

The Community Context

This study will focus upon Italian immigrants in Chicago Heights, Illinois, during the first half of the twentieth century. It attempts to contribute to a rich tradition of scholarship in the field of Italian immigration. Since the emergence of a number of "Little Italys" across America, a store of detailed studies characterizing these settlements has emerged. Sociological and historical accounts provide a locally differentiated but common picture describing the communal satisfactions of living among fellow Italians but also the oftentimes miserable conditions associated with these enclaves.[40] Following this, most studies pay homage to the Italian immigrants for their grit, perseverance, and hope for a better life going forward. Stephen Puleo's study of Italians in Boston is representative. It draws a nearly linear connection between these impoverished conditions, social mobility, and hope when it states that Italian immigrants arrived in Boston "with little more than the clothes on their back and a flicker of hope in their hearts."[41]

In the Chicago region, Harvey Zorbaugh's *The Gold Coast and the Slum* was the starting point for a sociological analysis of these Italian areas. He suggested that the Italians were the dominant group that occupied the "slum" or "Little Sicily." He spoke of their presence through the imagery of the Chicago School's ecological perspective and talked of the near predatory character of Italians who engulfed, penetrated, or took possession of the area. There was little discussion of hope or social mobility per se because of the heavy weight Italians presumably placed upon their traditional and provincial culture.

This viewpoint was challenged by Humbert Nelli's *Italians in Chicago, 1880–1930: A Study in Ethnic Mobility*. Nelli saw these local, Italian communities as playing a critical role over time in the ethnic adjustment of the Italians to American life. Crediting Italians with an abundance of hope and extensive social networks fueled by religious and community ties, Nelli documents the upward movement of Italians who were "spurred on by economic success and a desire for better living conditions."[42]

This upward movement, however, was not uniform. This was a central point of Rudolph Vecoli's review of Italian settlements in Chicago. Vecoli argued that in the opening decades of the last century multiple Italian enclaves spread across Chicago and the surrounding communities—from Little Sicily, to Taylor Street, Grand Crossing, Twenty-Second and Oakley, Pullman, Cicero, Melrose Park, Chicago Heights, and so on. Each area had different patterns of mobility. Vecoli eschewed deterministic models that sought to explain mobility or its absence in terms of blind economic or ecological forces. At the same time, explanations that relied too heavily upon personal characteristics such as the differential distribution of ambition, hope, or desire were also suspect. Along these lines, Vecoli questioned Nelli's oversimplification of success in terms of the crude distinction between northern and southern Italians. Instead, Vecoli held that if we are to understand Italian immigration in all its complexity each of these settlements should be studied in ways that "allow for the play of contingency, cultural preferences, and human agency."[43] Indeed, Vecoli pointed to Chicago Heights as one of the settlements in need of further study in the service of offering a dense, multifaceted history of Italian immigration.

Several decades later, Thomas Gugliemo took up this challenge with a broad, historically driven examination across a range of Chicago's neighborhoods and suburbs, including excerpts from Chicago Heights.[44] Gugliemo reveals the differential treatment of northern and southern Italians across these different settings. He offers compelling evidence that this discrimination was blunted because Italian immigrants were largely viewed as "white on arrival." Specifically, being placed on this side of the color line allowed Italians to escape the cruelest forms of discrimination, most poignantly in comparison to nonwhite groups. Put differently, though Italians (mostly southern Italians) often found themselves at or near the bottom of the ethnic and nationality hierarchy, this hierarchy was essentially transformed following the restrictive immigrant legislation of the 1920s and the Great Migration of African Americans to Chicago in subsequent years. A new overlapping hierarchy, one that merged race *and* color, became a more ruthless basis for allocating the valued resources and positions in society.

Gugliemo provides rich, analytic insights that apply to the Chicago Heights context. Still, the broad, analytic focus adopted by Gugliemo did not allow for the "play of contingency" that characterized the Italian immigration experience in the Heights. To fill this space, newspaper articles have emerged periodically with journalistic accounts of these immigrant stories in the city.[45] These have been complemented by a recent spate of books focusing narrowly upon organized crime in Chicago Heights.[46] And most significantly, Dominic Candeloro has carried out detailed studies of Italians in the Heights in several pivotal articles and excerpts.[47] His work is invaluable, and I draw heavily upon these sources. The study here has a different focus. It attempts to place these descriptive histories of the city into the larger analytic frameworks and theoretical clues provided by Bourdieu and his analysis of social spaces, habitus, and cultural capital. It attempts to provide a more sociologically informed discussion of the dialectic between these Italian immigrants and the contingent, historical context of Chicago Heights.

Even so, why Chicago Heights? Perhaps a less than satisfactory answer is that it is my hometown and the hometown of Michael Fisher, who has provided trusted assistance in the collection of data and the substantive development of this study. Together, we have personal attachments, memories, experiences of the Heights—most of them good. Because of these personal ties, we also have an entrée into a set of connections and relationships that provide insight into the Italian immigrant experience. My paternal grandparents were Italian immigrants, my father a second-generation Italian American, and most of our friends and relatives were Italians. Michael's personal history is also steeped in the Italian culture of Chicago Heights. His descendants arrived in the United States from Sicily in 1917. Over the years the family grew such that Michael's relatives include people that stretch far beyond his immediate family—including, the Fushi, Concialdi, Sorrentino, Prospero, and Narcisi clans. Based upon these ties, we were able to talk with and informally interview over forty people regarding their family histories and immigration experiences in Chicago Heights. Apart from the distractions that come with the emotional ties connected to this personal history, these associations provided access to stories, a ready cooperation of many Italian residents, and a subtle feel for the Italian culture that characterized the Heights for decades. These experiences certainly create blind spots. And like all case studies issues of generalizability are present. Still, our experiences proved to be a firm starting place.

Hometown ties, no doubt, are not enough. Chicago Heights recommends itself because it was at the forefront of the leading historical processes that dominated the greater part of the early twentieth century (and at the back end of these processes in the latter part). First, it experienced a rapid urbanization and an early suburbanization. Thus, in 1890, the village of "Bloom" was not much more than a sleepy hamlet located some thirty miles south of downtown Chicago. The 1890 census listed just over fifteen hundred residents. By 1910 it had been pulled into the burgeoning Chicago metropolitan area and had a population of 14,525, nearly a tenfold increase. By 1920 it increased again to 19,653. These transformations made Chicago Heights one of the most populous cities in Illinois in the first decades of the last century.

Second, Chicago Heights was also an industrial town. This was due in large part to its ideal location near railroad transportation lines and the heavy industrial core of Gary, Indiana, and south Chicago. As Robert Lewis argues, the Heights, and generally the Lake Calumet region, was at the heart of the industrial push outward from the centrally located manufacturing plants in Chicago. Here, these open prairie regions provided new spaces and opportunities for networked, industrial growth free of the more fixed, constraining elements of the older factory districts in Chicago.[48] Specifically, spurred on by the Chicago Heights Land Association and led principally by Chicago developer Charles Wacker, Chicago Heights became home to some eighty active factories producing everything from pony wagons, to pianos, bricks, chemicals, automobiles, railroad cars, steel, and zeppelins. At its peak, the city could boast that it was "the best manufacturing city of its size in America."[49]

Closely related to these population and industrial developments, the Heights was socially, culturally, and demographically transformed by the ongoing processes of immigration. During the latter half of the 1800s, the city was dominated by native whites of Scotch-Irish and German ancestry. However, by 1910 foreign-born whites constituted 42 percent of the city's population, the vast majority of these second-wave immigrants coming from eastern and southern Europe. Among these new immigrants, Italians were by far the most numerous and had the most prominent cultural presence. Again by 1910, over 22 percent (or 3,244 people) of Chicago Heights' population was made up of Italian immigrants and their children. In Illinois, the Heights ranked only behind Chicago, though obviously far behind, in terms of the *absolute* number of residents with Italian ancestry. And in terms of percentages, Chicago Heights was clearly the most Italian city in Illinois and one of the most Italian cities in the country.[51] Dominic Candeloro estimates that by 1970, roughly 40 to 50 percent of the Chicago Heights population had Italian lineage.[51]

These Italians migrated to Chicago Heights for a variety of reasons. Many women had little choice: they were placed aboard a ship sailing to America and found their way to the city as a part of an arranged marriage. Others came for the sense of adventure and roguishness that America offered. Many came to simply escape the abiding poverty of southern Italy. For example, when I asked Marie Iafollo, a lifelong resident in the Chicago Heights area, why her father would leave the picturesque small hill town of Italy, she said her father always responded, "*non puoi mangiare le montagne*" (You can not eat the mountains).[52] Dominic Pandolfi explained his father's migration to Chicago Heights almost as an afterthought. "He and his brother came across to the United States in 1890 or 1893. They came during the world's Columbian expedition. . . . They heard about a town on the outskirts of Chicago, Chicago Heights. They went there and discovered there were a couple of Italians there. They decided to stay."[53]

This influx of Italian newcomers into the region paralleled the geographic and social mobility of other ethnic and racial groups.[54] The Polish immigrants faced comparable opportunities and challenges. Thus, by 1930, 3.2 percent of the city's population consisted of "foreign born" Poles and another 6.1 percent were second generation Polish residents.[55] Similiar to their Italian neighbors, the vast majority of these Polish men and women emigrated based upon the promise that America would provide relief from the distressing circumstances in Europe. As Wonzy contends, many were ready to take on the challenges of life in America for "being poor or poorer was the same" and hoped to climb the same mobility ladder and compete in the same immigrant field as their Italian counterparts.[56]

For the majority of Black migrants from the rural south the reception in Chicago Heights overlapped with the experiences of the European immigrants. Early on, the presence of Blacks in the city was negligible. Thus, in 1910 Blacks consituted less than 1 percent of Chicago Heights residents, barely over one hundred people. However, by 1930 Blacks made up close to 10 percent of the city's population, a number that remained stable in the 1940 census.[57] In ways similar to the Italians and Poles, the Black exodus from the South was driven by discrimination and poverty. And labor agents lured these Southern workers with "fraudulent promises" regarding conditions in the Northern cities and work places.[58] Once in the city, Blacks took up residence among the Italians and Poles in the crowded, industrial East Side.

However, the experiences of these Black migrants was qualitatively distinct from the Italians and Polish immigrants. The poverty in the South was infused with violence and threats that were a continual assault upon the dignity and physical presence of the Black citizen. And the reception in the North, including Chicago Heights, was often only marginable better. Thus, in response to a Chicago Heights manufacturer who requested help from Clarke Howell, editor of the *Atlantic Constitution*, on how best to recruit

Blacks to his manufacturing plant, Howell replied that many Southerners would "hesitate long before advising them to go north for work at the present time . . . the ideas of the labor rights of negroes in that section are antagonistic and dangerous." "And remember also," said Howell, "thast there are many towns in Ohio, Indiana, and Illinois where a negro is not permitted to live, or even get off a train at their town railway station."[59]

Needless to say, Blacks experienced a systemic racism that was incomparable to other racial and ethnic groups. In the terminology of Emirbayer and Desmond, they were at the lower end of the racial order or field.[60] Chicago Heights Italians, especially the southern Italians, were also pulled into this field and suffered disadvantages given their "swarthy" and "in-between" status.[61] Still, as Gugliemo said previously, they were predominatly perceived as white and thus the beneficiary of this white "racial capital." Their whiteness gave them a modicum of power to move within the established social circles of the Heights and escape the most noxious charactertistics of the immigrant and racial hierarchy.

These opportunities and sources of power were not available to Black citizens. The Black-white binary was pernicious in Chicago Heights. With but few exceptions, the Black citizens were unable to objectify hope. As Emirbayer and Desmond argue, "Fear, anxiety, cruelty, hope, joy, and desire are central to racial domination and progresss."[62] Unable to cash in their hopes for success and gain recognition and value from other other racial groups and mainstream society, Blacks distanced themselves as a means of protection and survival. As one Chicago Heights observer noted, "There has been an accomodation on the part of the Negroes. They have isolated themselves more so than before, and in this manner have been instrumental in preventing the renewal of racial hostilities."[63]

Chicago Heights, then, was a meeting ground for the defining economic, social, and cultural movements of the last century. It developed and prospered amidst a tangled web of urbanization, suburbanization, industrialization, immigration, and racism. It was a small town in demographic terms but large enough to reveal the interplay between these larger forces and the life-world experiences of Italians bent upon finding a place in a new and challenging social order, guided by the "gleam of light for a better day." "They came," the *Chicago Heights Star* continued, "with the hope for the realization of their dreams and faith in their ability to make good."[64] It is not clear if the elements of "hope," "realization," or the "ability to make good" were strategically allinged as commonly thought, but the Chicago Heights context provides a singular setting for an investigation of these processes.

With this focus upon Chicago Heights, we explore these critical immigrant connections by combining several social scientific methods—historical research, qualitative interviews, and census data. Thus, the story of the Italian immigrants will be told on the basis of the informal interviews I have collected over a twenty-year span and the conversations Michael Fisher and I have had with various members of his extended family. At the same time, I have relied a great deal upon interviews conducted as a part of the Italians in Chicago Oral History project at the University of Illinois at Chicago between 1979 and 1980. Eleven of these oral histories were from residents of Chicago Heights. In addition, the Casa Italia Cultural Center in Stone Park, Illinois, has a trove of relevant material related to the immigrant experience in Chicago Heights—these include additional interviews, personal letters, newspaper articles, and other documents.

The chapters to follow will draw upon this data and present a sociology of hope as it relates to the Italian immigrants in Chicago Heights. Chapter 1 focuses upon Pierre Bourdieu's concepts of social spaces, cultural capital, and habitus. Bourdieu did not explicitly focus upon hope as a cultural resource. Nevertheless, his analysis of field and social spaces provides a useful analytic scheme for understanding how hope was a practice or strategy that immigrants used to navigate the hierarchies of immigration. Bourdieu's framework roots hope in a sociological context and allows us to distinguish this practice from the less sanctioned forms of resignation and dissent.

Chapter 2 begins to construct in substantive detail the field or social spaces for Italian immigrants in this Chicago Heights context. It provides a broad description of the sociohistorical conditions that prompted the decision to emigrate. It then demonstrates how a series of officials, migrant brokers, steamship agents, inspectors, padroni, employers, and reformers played a role in framing the aspirations of these Italian natives toward geographic and social mobility.

Chapter 3 turns to the immigration work experiences of Chicago Heights Italians. By relying upon census data, historical materials, and interviews, the chapter argues that the hopes of alien newcomers were steered toward the pursuit of occupational mobility. While hard work was a cultural resource demonstrating a commitment to the emerging ethos of the American Dream, the pursuit of further advancement or the steps taken in bettering one's position would cement one's status as an American, for it signified an underlying personal commitment to the cherished values of hope and optimistic striving.

Chapter 4 contends that homeownership, as opposed to the more transitory aspects of renting, became yet another objectified sign of the commitment to an American identity and the shedding of an ethnic affiliation. Though owing a home had significant use value in economic terms, it had significant cultural capital in that it established a permanence in the country and an alignment with the American ideals of independence, pride of ownership, and loyalty. It represented these socially approved hopes with an objectified presence beyond the clapboard or brick and mortar materials.

Chapter 5 contends that if the social affirmations of hope and mobility were not readably available, then immigrants resurrected these cultural values in the lives of their children. Specifically, hope was pushed forward by investing these aspirations in the status advances of their sons and daughters. Immigrants secured a more favorable position for themselves in the spaces of immigration by reconstituting their relationship to their children. Children provided a malleable, elastic canvas for demonstrating the proper cultural codes of hope and social advancement in American society.

Finally, the conclusion summarizes the main themes of this sociological look into hope, mobility, and immigration. While acknowledging the strides that Italian Americans have made in overcoming their most humble beginnings, what was the price for this assimilation? Given the communal legacies and traditions of Italians, would individualized hopes be more meaningful and fulfilling if they were contextualized in terms of the wider community or what Robert Bellah and others describe as the "communities of hopes."[65] Would the "good society" be pushed forward by a dialectic that nurtured not only personal dreams and aspirations but also an interchange with communal hopes?

Chapter 1

Hope, Cultural Capital, and Habitus within an Italian Community

Hope is not distributed equally in society. Some have a greater expectation that despite uncertainties, life will be better moving forward. In this sense, one can explain the varied achievements of immigrants in society. Even when social circumstances are stacked against them, certain individuals dig deep into their personal resolve and create lives that closely match their cherished dreams and expectations.

The story of Gaetano D'Amico is one such example. Gaetano came to America in 1887 at the age of thirty-five. He came from Castel di Sangro, a small town in the Abruzzo region of Italy where he worked on a farm and married a local villager. However, tragedy struck when his daughter died at an early age, and his wife passed away just several years later. Gaetano married again and decided that the prospects for success meant immigrating to America. He left his new wife, Giacinta, in Italy, boarded a ship to Ellis Island, and began the uncertain path to a better life. This path first took him to the dangerous but readily available jobs in the coal mines in Pennsylvania and then to the aboveground but no less arduous work of laying railroad tracks in Missouri. In 1892, he made his way to Chicago Heights when he heard that the industrial plants were hiring workers to operate the heavy machinery and molten steel ladles. He got a job with the Inland Steel plant and soon after sent for Giacinta who arrived in 1893. They set up a home in Hungry Hill, a largely Italian enclave in Chicago Heights, and sent for their son who was still in Italy.

Even so, Gaetano realized that the prospects for success remained uncertain if he were to accept the minimum salary, the dim prospects for promotion, and indignities that came with low-skilled factory workers. Therefore, Gaetano summoned up all the ambition and hope he could, and in 1899 he set up a small grocery store in the Italian section of the Heights, while continuing to work at Inland Steel. Over the years, the store proved a huge success based largely upon the homemade traditional Italian products and also upon the family labor of Gaetano, Giacinta, and the six children who now made up the D'Amico family.

Of all the traditional products, their authentic macaroni was the most profitable. As such, in 1914 Gaetano decided to gamble further and establish the G. D'Amico Macaroni Company. The macaroni and spaghetti business prospered, and by 1928 the Chicago Heights location proved too confining. So the company moved to the nearby town of Steger. Each year the business grew despite the extortion bombing of his storefront, break-ins and robberies, and the economic ravages of the Great Depression. The D'Amico Company eventually became a major distributor of macaroni products throughout the country. As the company's motto boasted, its products were "known from coast to coast." In this journey—from the small hill towns of Abruzzo, to the perilous series of decisions and work experiences, to his triumphant success—Gaetano became an honored and legendary citizen (a major street in the Heights is named D'Amico Drive). Personal hope and desire are evident throughout.

Gaetano's success was exceptional. Most Italian immigrants in Chicago Heights experienced far less improvement in their social standing. Only a relatively small number could point to such substantial gains in their lifetime and instead followed the trajectory described by Mangione and Morreale who concluded in general that "the great majority of the lives of the Italians were not success stories."[1] Accordingly, if we assume that hope and ambition are the primary ingredients of success, most Italians were deficient in these valued personal resources, these "most human of all mental feelings."[2] The majority of immigrants, unlike Gaetano, could not conjure up the appropriate state of mind, emotion, or hopeful disposition to overcome their disparaging conditions.

These uncomfortable conclusions emerge when hope is reduced to a personal attribute, an inalienable possession of the individual. With these assumptions in hand, immigrants who do not fare well run the risk of being seen as deficient in an essentialist way. They are thought to be lacking the internal drive, vision, or ambition of their more successful fellow immigrants and, in a more consequential comparison, the fortitude of the native born or "those who came, stayed, and succeeded."[3] It is then a short leap to bestow in a public and recognizable manner a qualitative difference on those who do not succeed and to confer a pathology of hopelessness upon the immigrant. Or in a more generous vein, immigrants are thought to be dominated by conditions beyond their control and as such there is little breathing room for these latent reserves of hope to be awakened. The immigrant is depicted as "a passive soul, reactive and compliant before impersonal social forces."[4]

These individualistic conceptions of hope run counter to a strict sociological explanation. From this perspective, hope emerges—as Marx, Durkheim, and Weber suggest from different starting points—because cultural expectations of success run up against a set of structural constraints. Hope is called forth in a systemic manner to bridge or mend the gap between these cultural proscriptions and the economic/social constraints—this over and above the unique mental state or personal attribute of the individual. In this sense, hope and the experiences of immigrants go hand in hand for "immigrants lived in crisis because they were uprooted."[5] Immigrants gravitate toward hope because the cultural promises of success are inevitably thwarted when the "wretched refuse" find themselves at the bottom of this hierarchical social space.

Nevertheless, this distinctive sociological explanation is not without limitations. It has difficulty separating out the different patterns of mobility among immigrants. If hope has social structural origins, why is it that Gaetano and an array of other Italian immigrants were able to succeed, while again the majority of immigrants in Chicago Heights experienced questionable mobility? It would be misleading, if again too convenient, to hold that social structure impacts some people and not others, or that it "miraculously descends" upon some immigrants and passes over others. A pure structural argument, just as a pure individualistic argument, explains too much and too little at the same time.

As such, the most useful explanation transcends the overly voluntarist and overly deterministic explanations of hope. It needs to show how hope neither resides solely within the individual nor exists solely in social arrangements.[6] Here, the critical insights of Pierre Bourdieu and his attempt to overcome the false dichotomy of the individual and social structure may advance this discussion of hope, especially as it applies to the immigrant's experience.

Social Spaces, Cultural Capital, and Habitus

Bourdieu begins with the concept of social space, also conceptualized in later writings as the "field." Social spaces consist of a set of stable and durable social relations that transcend the immediate social environment. For example, the networked relationships of immigration constitute a social space consisting of positions such as native-born, first-generation, naturalized, sojourner, undocumented, and alien. These positions are historically crisscrossed in the American context with more substantive positions based prominently upon one's whiteness, otherness, gender, and radicalness.

Within this space, individuals occupy a hierarchical position relative to other positions based upon their relationship to the forces (or field of forces) that "impose themselves on all who enter this field."[7] These forces consist of the distribution of economic, social, cultural, and symbolic capitals. Depending upon the overall volume, the unique composition, and the amount and type of capital at a person's disposal, one can achieve a higher or lower rank or position within this social space. In concrete terms, a person who owns a factory, has friends who own factories or similar businesses, exhibits native sentiments and behaviors, and has social standing or prestige within the community will possess significant capital resources to purchase a higher position (and be less beholden to hope). An immigrant who toils for a subsistence wage, lives in an ethnic enclave with other immigrants, clings to old-world habits, and arouses suspicion or fear from the dominant culture will have far less capital and will typically resort to and be encouraged to invest in hope.

The struggles to gain and exchange these different forms of capital impact one's own fate and the fate of others. For most immigrants, the lack of economic capital (or property) is paramount. It is immediate and drives the decisions and actions on a daily basis—that is, to work on a railroad gang, take up residence as a boarder, or eat *paste e patate* (pasta and potatoes, the "poor man's kitchen) nearly every night. However, the appropriation of cultural capital, and what that capital will look like and how it will be spent, is more of a long-term, strategic concern. By cultural capital, Bourdieu means the physical habits, verbal skills, aesthetic tastes, social mannerisms, and body of knowledge a person lays claim to and employs to gain advantage within social spaces. While these preferences have idiosyncratic dimensions, they also have preconscious societal roots and origins. They are a product of past social experiences, traditions, and habits—an ensemble of dispositions and schemes of interpretations one has acquired over a lifetime. As such, they reside neither within the individual nor society per se. They are basic parts, on the one hand, of a person's mental life, feelings, and behavioral tendencies. On the other hand, they are reflections of the social structures and cultural codes that encompass a person's life.

Bourdieu argues that this cultural capital exists in three different forms. The first is as an "embodied state." In this sense, cultural capital is "converted into an integral part of the person" through its appropriation in the mind and body.[8] It comes to make up a person's ways of physically moving through the world, the linguistic styles of talk and affectations, a quasi-bodily involvement that prompts one physically to respond to food, situations, and others in a preconscious but culturally appropriate and legitimate manner. In Bourdieu's words, cultural capital is not just a " 'state of the mind' . . . but rather a state of the body."[9]

A classic scene in the movie *GoodFellas* speaks to the role and challenges of embodied cultural capital. In this scene, Billy Bates engages Tommy DeVito in barroom banter. As Tommy goes over to Billy to say hello, Billy gives him a big, gregarious hug, which makes Tommy uncomfortable. "Watch the suit, watch the suit," Tommy says as he physically recoils from Billy's embrace. The banter continues and Billy moves on to "bust Tommy's balls" by telling everyone in the bar about Tommy's first job as a shoeshine boy (a position with low cultural capital). Tommy takes offense at the reference, for now his embodied mannerisms, dress, and affectations reveal him to be a "wiseguy" (a far more favored position in this social space). Tommy stiffens as Bates continues to remind everyone how Tommy was a great shoeshine boy (with all that implies in terms of supplicant body positioning and kneeling). "This kid was great. They use to call him 'spit-shine Tommy.'" Tommy responds indignantly by saying, "I don't shine shoes anymore." When Billy makes one last wisecrack, Tommy explodes: now as a wiseguy the "feel for the game" means that words no longer have currency, and Tommy lets out a string of "motherfucker, piece of shit" descriptions of Billy and in a rage has to be held back from physically attacking him. In one sense, this is a physical battle between Tommy and Billy. In Bourdieu's terms, it is the embodied cultural capital of a "goodfella" and the internalized, enduring dispositions of Tommy's past that are the main antagonists, for embodied capital "always remains marked by its earliest conditions of acquisition. . . ."[10] Tommy is battling, figuratively and literally, with the gap that Billy has revealed between the objective conditions of success and Tommy's expectations and hopes for a better life, albeit in wiseguy terms.

A second type of cultural capital exists in an "objectified state." Culturally valued ideas, knowledge, and ways of life are given material referents in the world beyond the individual. They find expression in physical forms such as buildings, statues, and clothes. The possession or use of these external, culturally recognizable forms conveys and promotes one's position in a social space. "Watch the suit, watch the suit," Tommy says. The suit itself is emblematic of Tommy's change in status from shoeshine boy to "wiseguy."[11] In their physical presence outside of the individual, these objects have their own history, autonomy, and legitimacy—making them all the more powerful. They add substance to the otherwise difficult to fathom mental images or cultural capital resources that people carry around in their heads or exhibit in their bodily states. It is one thing to hope to be a "wiseguy," but to dress the part adds an air of reality in one's own eyes and the eyes of others.

Cultural capital also has a presence in an "institutionalized" form. In ways similar to objectified capital, it resides outside the person. It subtly inhabits social rules, classification schemes, and organizational structures. For example, Tommy's anger toward Billy Bates had to be restrained by fellow "wiseguys," for Billy was a "made man." As such an attack on Billy would be a challenge to the institutionalized set of rules and the legitimacy of the cultural capital Billy claimed. "Tommy was going nuts, but he couldn't say anything. Billy was a 'made man.' If Tommy so much as took a slap at Billy, Tommy was dead." Made-men were by "goodfella" rules and codes untouchable and could not be harmed, for they were "royalty."

With respect to the immigration field, newcomers to America fought to acquire the more favorable forms of institutional recognition and escape the less favorable ones. Thus, the designations as naturalized, undocumented, or without papers were not neutral, equally valuable classifications harboring the same consequences for recognition. At the same time, the crisscrossing assertions of "whiteness," "in-between-ness," "Southern Italian," "dago," "women's work," "anarchists," "gangster," and "enemy alien" foretold access to cultural power and the ability to live in certain neighborhoods, hold particular jobs, and occupy specific positions in religious orders.[12] Thomas Guglielmo's discussion of the pre–World War II experiences of Italians was appropriately subtitled, "Italians, Race, Color, and Power in Chicago."[13] His nuanced history of these racial brandings and countervailing privileges demonstrated Bourdieu's more analytic observation that "one sees clearly the performative magic of the power of instituting, the power to show forth or secure belief, or, in a word, to impose recognition."[14]

These different states of cultural capital—embodied, objectified, and institutionalized—come together in Bourdieu's most innovative concept, something he terms *habitus*. This concept escapes easy definition but is central to understanding how hope can exist both inside and outside the individual and resist being reduced to either dimension. Specifically, as people struggle to achieve their varied self-interests, they move through different but overlapping social spaces—for example, an ethnic social space, religious space, work space, political space, and immigrant space. Each social grouping has a unique randomness but is also structured according to an objective distribution of power where some individuals have greater access to capital(s). Depending upon the relative amount and types of specific capital one can strategically draw upon, movement to a higher position within the social space is variously within reach. Further, because a segment of the population occupies objectively similar positions within this field—similar in terms of access to financial, cultural, and social capital—people in these situations arrive at relatively homogeneous strategies. Through time, these strategies become commonplace, part of the taken-for-granted and commonsensical world, as individuals create bodily enactments, stylized appearances, collective dispositions and actions adjusted to the limits and possibilities present in the immediate social environment. More generally, individuals create a generative, practical scheme of apprehending and expressing themselves within this field. They build "practical patterns of thinking, perception and action."[15] As these practical responses are put into play or enacted in a regular fashion, they render "objectified, visible, and even official" that which had existed "in the state of the individual or serial existence."[16] Hope or a hopeful countenance as a form of habitus is born without ever becoming a cultural ethos or psychological characteristic on its own.

The well-chronicled provincialism attributed to southern Italians serves as a more concrete example. This practical pattern of thinking, perceiving, and acting developed in response to a historical series of discouraging and oppressive economic and social structures—a distant and uncontrollable government, a disparaging view of southern Italians, and economic arrangements that consistently worked to others' advantage.[17] In this context, southern Italians developed an ensemble of practical strategies and ways of being that allowed for an engagement with these extant conditions. Specifically, they approached life by focusing on the local community, taking pride in traditional customs, devising original but highly specific solutions to the persisting challenges posed in their daily lives. As these cultural strategies were enacted in situation after situation, they were objectified and became socially accepted recipes Italians could draw upon in order to gain a practical mastery of their environment. Provincialism became the habitus or enduring disposition of southern Italians, forged as it was between the objective structures and the collection of practices devised to maximize economic and cultural capital.

Provincialism as Practice

Southern Italians have often been tarred with the ethos of provincialism: a code of conduct whereby as part of their attitudinal and personality structures they approached life in a narrow-minded, helpless, and amoral fashion. These attributes were conceived as nearly immutable character traits passed down from one generation to the next and stood in the way of success. In our formulation, however, provincialism is a practice or strategy that allows for a successful adaptation to an often harsh environment. It is an ingenious, though at times problematic, response to challenges posed by the economic, social, and physical environment. It is less a pathology and more an organized artful practice.

The Italians in Chicago Heights devised their own ensemble of practices to move through their daily round of activities. For example, during Prohibition they set up stills in their basement or allowed the Chicago Outfit to set up alky facilities in their garage: not because they possessed criminal tendencies or motives but as a calculated strategy to pay the rent or put food on the table. At the same time, most eschewed a deeper involvement in organized crime activities for this did not make practical sense.

Perhaps, the most immediate set of these provincial practices were organized around food. Securing, gathering, and cooking food in the often unforgiving environment in Chicago, as opposed to the climes of southern Italy, required innovation. As Michael Fisher points out, activities related to food were intensely communal, this in ways drawing upon but also distinct from the practices in southern Italy where the ideas of "community" and "friend" were more circumscribed. Thus, community gardens dotted the East Side in Chicago Heights, especially on the land away from the industrial plants. At the same time, families shared new techniques for preserving or cooking food. Sue Marconi, the wife of Guiseppe Marconi who owned the still thriving Marconi Baking Company, taught members of the Sorrentino, Prospero, and Concialdi families how to prepare both traditional and American dishes. Indeed, the Marconi Baking Company would often allow families in the neighborhood to use their ovens after the bread baking was done to roast any manner of fowl.

"Any manner of fowl" opens itself to a number of provincial practices. Again, Michael Fisher speaks of the communal "hunting clubs." Here, families on the East Side would buy large nets and drape them on the back of shrubs where sparrows sought protection from the weather. Someone would then scare the sparrows on the opposite site, and predictably the sparrows would fly into the net and be captured. My grandfather, Luigi, would take a more singular approach. He would prop open a wooden box with a stick, tie a string to the stick, place the box with a piece of crusted bread in his backyard garden and wait for the next day's protein to fall prey. Whichever method for cacciando was employed, subsequently, the sparrows would be cleaned, defeathered, and thrown into the spaghetti sauce. Blackbirds, squabs, pigeons, squirrels, and rabbits would also meet similar fates. Such practices might be viewed as provincial, unsophisticated, a piece of Old World culture. They may instead represent an innovative, exquisite strategy formed in response to the demands of the immigrant experience.

Habitus, Social Practices, and Italian Immigrants

Bourdieu clearly suggests that habitus does not govern all behavior in a determinative fashion. Highly ritualized situations, on the one hand, leave little room for practical strategies. Situations of crisis or transformation, on the other, are those most likely to require active strategizing, though most always within some normative, objective context. Along these lines, immigration taxes an ever-widening circle of social relations and positions. In Handlin's terminology, the immigrant is "uprooted" across a range of experiences. The immigrant's life develops according to a logic that can no longer be translated in terms of the incorporated habitus. This new life unfolds in ways that present "simultaneously incoherent narratives" wherein the traditions and practices of the past become increasingly obsolete.[18]

In this uncertain world, the interplay of these traditional habits or narratives with these unfamiliar personal and social challenges generates a new series of practices or generative schemes. These took shape along three overlapping themes—resignation, dissent, and hope. Each response had a "family resemblance" to one another but at the same time a distinct practical logic with different strategies, ways of seeing, and social recipes.[19] In short, each presages a different habitus and adjustment to the challenges posed by immigration or the way the "game" of assimilation was played.[20]

Resignation as Social Practice

Resignation was an uncomfortable option. Immigrants accepted the inevitability of their position in social space and with this logic in hand grudgingly believed that their traditional beliefs, emotions, and ways of acting were no longer relevant or they needed substantial revision. Immigrants, thus, surrendered a measure of their habitual cultural capital and in the process gained a modicum of power or were at least tolerated in the more established social circles. Bethany Santucci's analysis of her great-grandfather's autobiographical narrative captures the subtle, practical, and emotional tone of these resignation practices. Having to abandon his traditions and heritage, Giuseppe Rocconi cannot help but think that his newfound habits of eating, praying, and loving go "against my destiny."[21] Santucci likens Giuseppe's resignation to the fictional Italian immigrant bricklayer, Old Nick, in Pietro di Donato's saga *Christ in Concrete*. "The barrow he pushed, he did not love. The stones that brutalized his palms, he did not love. The great God Job, he did not love . . . the ever mounting weight of structures that he *had to! had to!* raise above his shoulders! . . . The language of worn oppression and the despair of realizing that his life had been left on brick piles."[22] This was a resignation at a cognitive, emotional, and corporeal level.

This resignation played itself out in the lives of many women and men in Chicago Heights. Out of economic necessity, they gave up their habitus in incremental fashion as the social price for purchasing a position in their new environment. Thus, the Italian immigrants surrendered the habitual control of their bodies and work life to the grueling factory or railroad track gang regimes, they relinquished their communal *piazza* or marketplace sociability to the more privatized suburbanized spaces, and they resigned themselves to the American version of their traditional tastes and preferences for food.[23] In surveying the cultural landscape of her new home, Chicago Heights resident Pasqua Sparvieri expressed her resignation fears. "I never know America was like this, no otherwise I don't come . . . But then everything I got used to."[24]

Not far from Chicago Heights, this resignation emerged in the coal-mining towns of Ladd, Coal City, and Spring Valley (my mother's hometown).[25] Along with the other non-English-speaking immigrants, the Italians were encouraged to rid themselves of their traditional patterns of speaking, socializing, and eating. In response, they began to limit their interactions with local merchants and community members. Even then, these immigrants realized that their habitual food preferences would need to be abandoned lest these "garlic eaters" bring forth resentment and disparaging comments. And of course the daily descent into the hazardous coal mines represented a stark retreat from the harsh but still aboveground life they experienced in "sunny Italy." Every foray into the mine involved a psychological resignation and gamble. "The majority of immigrants in Coal Town," wrote Herman Lantz in his classic study of the coal-mining communities in Illinois, "are now resigned people. They consider themselves at the mercy of forces beyond their control and hope that in some fortuitous way disaster can be minimized."[26]

Dissent as Social Practice

If resignation is characterized by the acceptance of the cultural beliefs and rituals of the dominant culture, dissent consisted of a series of practices opposed to this culture. Realizing that in American society they were the "other half," the Italian immigrants developed or built upon schemes and dispositions at variance with the culturally reinforced and socially proscribed ways of thinking and acting in their new home.

Dissent as a practical strategy took various individual and collective forms. In a more understated fashion, immigrants turned inward into their communities, if not their own families, and proceeded with their lives as best they could, based upon the habitus of their pre-immigration experiences. They continued to engage in practices of speaking, associating, and identifying with the incorporated and objectified patterns of the past. In analytic terms, these practices were "defensive strategies" set against a contemporary world that offered unfamiliar and untested solutions to everyday problems.[27] Thus, the limited English-speaking ability of my grandmother, her benedictions to ward off evil spirits, and her routine of preparing meals based upon the traditional methods of the past were not simply the passive folkways of a provincial Italian woman. These strategies, however unintended, were inventions that took on new meaning in the immigrant social structure. They acted to maintain or regain a semblance of cultural capital in a hierarchical field that promised very little, especially for immigrant women.[28]

These processes of dissent also took place in a collective manner. For some, the retreat into a hyper-Italian culture or enclave was the best option as Italians "withdrew to a narrow circle of compatriots."[29] Neither the ideology of success nor the painful rhetoric of the nativist would have an impact if one lived broadly among fellow Italians and steadfastly maintained past cultural practices. Thus, in the Chicago Heights context, the East Side and the Hill areas enjoyed an "institutional completeness" or a structural and cultural distance from the larger society.[30] As one study concluded, "Practically all social, religious, and economic pursuits were undertaken by the Hill area itself. This isolation merely helped to enforce the ethnic identification that was so strong in the neighborhood."[31]

At times, these collective forms of dissent took on a more pointed and transparent form. No doubt, the periodic regional parades, religious processions, and provincial festivals had a celebratory, ritualized flavor. Yet they also challenged the larger society and put forth a claim to the ethnic hegemony of the area. The blatant displays of Catholicism (if not paganism), the festive dress of the marchers, and the Italian-inspired food and entertainment amounted to a public declaration of a contrasting set of values and beliefs: in Orsi's words, they constituted a "victory over the street life."[32] These ethnic spectacles signaled a distance from the common culture and a collective effort at buying back lost cultural capital.

These festive Italian street events have a long history in Chicago Heights. As early as 1911, the United Italian-American societies of the city staged an elaborate Columbus Day parade and spectacle with "lively patriotic music . . . brilliant banners . . . and a wealth of color . . ." While the event garnered little attention from the larger community, the organizers were clear in their intent. "The people at large did not pay much attention to the day . . . but they are gradually waking up to the fact . . . that our fellow Italian citizens are taking the lead in celebrating what is particularly our own affair."[33] As Candeloro suggests, these religious fests continued through the century. Though they grew less shocking and less an affront to the more established elements of the city, they proclaimed a still vibrant Italian culture at variance with the dominant, mainstream society.[34]

A segment of the Italian population practiced a more radical form of dissent. Bourdieu predicts something along these lines when he argues that the most far-reaching and oppositional schemes of thought, expression, and disposition typically emerge from those who expect little recognition from the dominant groups.[35] Numerous examples exist of Italian immigrants and their efforts to protest working conditions in the factories, living conditions on the East Side, and cultural discrimination in social circles. Many Italian anarchists and socialists saw American culture as just another example, if not the foremost instance of a capitalist world order diametrically opposed to the interests of the proletariat.

There was a militant contingent of Chicago Heights Italians who favored this habitual form of dissent. These individuals challenged both the ideology of social mobility and the anti-Italian beliefs in the community. Rudolph Vecoli wrote that the socialists in Chicago Heights "were quite vociferous."[36] In their account of the Italian American experience, Jerre Mangione and Ben Morreale state that two of the leading socialist organizers in the country, Giuseppe Bertelli and Emilio Grandinetti, developed their labor organizing skills while working with Italian immigrants in Chicago Heights.[37] Umberto La Morticella took it a step further by suggesting that "Chicago Heights had a goodly number of socialists and anarchists."[38] Nick Zaranti, longtime Chicago Heights resident, recalls, "the Italians organized a lot of unions in those days, in the early days."[39] And a number of Chicago Heights Italians were also members of the *Co-operativa di consume di Chicago Heights*. A co-operative grocery store, social club, and union hall that had deep ties to the socialist agenda as it sought to provide services "firmly rooted in the spirit and practice of Cooperatism."[40]

In their attempts to organize this dissent, these more vociferous radicals battled against the priests and the legitimacy of the church, supported a string of industrial strikes and protests, and promoted a socialist agenda in local elections and public speaking tours. For example, in 1908 the enmity of the socialists was directed against the local parish, Saint Rocco Church. The parish priests were deemed lazy "blood suckers" who in conjunction with the local industries kept the hard-working Italians in a state of suffering and oppression."[41] In 1911, a group of construction workers, primarily Italian, struck the Illinois Central Railroad for higher wages and "caused considerable disturbance" among the other laborers.[42] Throughout the ensuing decades, socialist organizers, through a local chapter of the International Workers of the World (IWW), took over leadership positions in the Steel Workers Union, the Brick Tile and Terra Cotta Workers, the Hod Carriers and Building Labors Union, and the Barbers Union. Indeed, Chicago Heights resident Joseph Giganti parlayed his socialist activities in the local area to a national position as a labor organizer.[43]

The socialist effort to challenge the core values and institutions in the Chicago Heights context reached a turning point during World War I. At this time, these dissidents regularly put up candidates for local elections, though they never garnered enough votes to seriously challenge the election outcomes. The highlight of the socialist campaign to organize the Italian workers in the Heights came about in 1918. With the assistance of the IWW, the socialists arranged to have the revolutionary activist, Carlo Tresca, speak at an organizing rally at the Italian Co-Operative. In thought, appearance, and action, Tresca manifested dissent. As Jay Meadows said, "The thing about Carlo Tresca was that he looked exactly like what a crazy bomb-throwing radical foreigner was supposed to look like: wild-bearded, wild-eyed, always passionately shaking his fist and thundering away about the oppressed workers."[44]

In the patriotic times surrounding World War I, Tresca's presence invited strong condemnation on the part of city leaders. Fearing that Tresca would make clear the yawning gap between the visions of the "promised land" and the "brutalizing conditions" of the workplace, Chicago Heights officials stationed four policemen at the entrance of the union hall to note who attended. Their presence had a chilling effect on the meeting as "many people . . . cowered at the sight of the police."[45] The *Chicago Heights Star* condemned these socialist dissidents and instead praised the counter-organizing efforts on the part of the "loyal Italians."[46]

Along these lines, the experiences of Chicago Heights resident Dominick Mormile provide a contrast with Gaetano D'Amico. Mormile came to the United States from Naples, Italy, and settled in Chicago Heights in 1907. A tailor by trade, Mormile was a member of the Socialist Party. As a part of his political activities, Mormile helped organize Tresca's appearance in the Heights. When this presentation, as suggested above, was met with resistance by the local police force, Mormile, along with several other leaders, was arrested and charged with violating the Espionage Act.

Though this charge was later dismissed, this did not stop government officials from looking deeper into Mormile's activities. Thus in 1919 and 1920, the Bureau of Investigation (the forerunner to the Federal Bureau of Investigation) visited Mormile several times at his tailor shop, surveyed the "radical" pamphlets and pictures adorning the place, and conducted a formal interview. This interview ranged over a number of topics, but the focus was upon Mormile's identification as a socialist or, more importantly, as a communist—and most dangerously as an anarchist. At one point the agent asked, "I also find among your effects the Communist Manifesto by Carl [sic] Marx and Fred Engels. Is that yours?" Mormile said he did not know who it belonged to. The agent then pressed Mormile on his views of capitalism. "You do not believe," the agent asked, "in our so-called imperialistic capitalistic form of Government in the United States?" Mormile refused to answer.[47] At this point, the agent's question turned sharply to Mormile's immigration status. After several questions regarding Mormile's "first papers," it was determined that he was not a US citizen. Even more damning, Mormile was thought to be a special risk because his propaganda efforts were aimed at "inciting the Italians in his neighborhood to the IWW cause."[48] Particularly disturbing from the agent's point of view was Mormile's distribution of several song booklets from the IWW to high school boys in Chicago Heights. Because of these organizing activities and because Mormile's place of business was deemed a "distribution place for radical literature," the agents labeled him an "alien" and recommended deportation.[49]

Mormile's case was unique. Though there was a socialist thread running through the Italian population in Chicago Heights, few followed Mormile's lead and engaged in such concerted activities. Still, the federal government's incursion into the Italian neighborhood and the attempts to assess Mormile's patriotism through interviews with Mormile's neighbors sent clear messages that this form of dissent was extremely risky. In the swirling and highly charged atmosphere of the times and in the Chicago area in particular—an atmosphere that included anarchist bombings, the Palmer raids, harsh new immigration quotas, Prohibition statutes and federal raids, labor strikes, and violence—dissent was met with strong cultural and disciplinary resistance. Under these circumstances, most Italian immigrants saw the impractical and unprofitable character of organized public dissent as they maneuvered in the immigrant hierarchy.[50]

Hope as Social Practice

Resignation and dissent, therefore, could not outweigh the strong, ideologically sanctioned strategies of hope. Hope was a practical logic that allowed for a movement up the immigrant hierarchy but at the same time the flexibility to exert a sense of agency or personal control. Neither resignation nor dissent could promise both. Hope, on the other hand, would allow these Italian immigrants to remain different and stay Italian but do so "in just the right way" or according to the standards of the dominant culture.[51] As such, many Italian immigrants made an emotional, cognitive, and behavioral investment in hope, because it was a practice best suited to fulfill their own aspirations "within the limits of the available means."[52]

This emotional investment in hope was uplifting because it promised a liberation from both the habitus (and stigmatization) of the past in Italy and the disadvantages that were coming into focus in the American context. It signified a break from the "bitter train of. . . . Misfortunes" that seemed to intrinsically characterize the lives of immigrants.[53] To be sure, this emotional response was mixed. Some immigrants had difficulty separating themselves from family, friends, and lives in Italy. They "pined for the old country and longed to be back in familiar surroundings."[54] Michael Fisher spoke of his great-grandmother, Nicisia Fushi. Though aware and grateful that America presented more opportunities for success than her beloved Sicily, Nicisia was adamant in her belief that "America was no good." She yearned to go back to Italy to be near the ocean and beach and to discard her necklace of garlic that she wore because "America was evil." Here, dissent and hope, and the emotional sensibilities of both, were mingled together.

These conflicting sensibilities notwithstanding, hope became the dominant practice for moving up and through the social order because in the broad context of early twentieth-century America it was a most valued cultural capital currency. Thus, for much of the 1800s and stretching into the early 1900s, there was considerable agreement that the expanding American economy positioned all Americans, native or foreign born, on the road to social mobility. American ideology held that this new country was the home of the "New Man" where a variety of strains and a different mixture of cultures nurtured a land of opportunity.[55] Freed from their conditions of birth, immigrants were expected to grasp these new freedoms and make a new world for themselves. There was a general sense, Wiebe argued, that "almost anyone with incentive, it seemed, could acquire the skills of a profession."⁵⁶ America was a place in which "one's personal condition could be improved through choice, work, and increased opportunities."⁵⁷

In this sense, the individual pursuit of success and social mobility became a key component of what it meant to be an American. Irrespective of actual accomplishments, to not at least have the hope for these successes, to not exhibit what Robert Foerster identified as "the practical and opportunist spirit," would typically bring forth charges of laziness or an insufficient progressivism.⁵⁸ In this manner, individualized hope was socially sanctioned. It gained cultural prominence in the American context as one of the "deeply rooted drives born in man" and, along with the innate drive to pursue economic gain, was the foundation on which to build this new social and economic order. Hope became an "ineffaceable fact of the individual."⁵⁹ The immigrant who exhibited this "joyful striving" was that much closer to acceptance by the economically and culturally dominant groups in society.⁶⁰

Hope, therefore, insinuated itself with the American ethos.⁶¹ Under these circumstances, immigrants were encouraged, and they came to see it within their interests, to practice hope across a range of corporal, objectified, and institutional levels. This was especially the case as these newcomers arrived with languages, religious practices, and political ideologies different from those of the preceding waves of immigrants—in other words, from places where the traditions could not be mapped directly upon the existing American cultural landscape.

Hope and the Incorporated Body

Immigrants were persuaded to adapt their bodies—in terms of shape, posture, gestures, speech, cleanliness, and manners—to the requirements of hope. This was a message that made its way to Italy before the actual journey across the Atlantic. Thus, coming upon several men in Italy who were renouncing their homeland and immigrating to America, an observer asked why they would undertake such a drastic transition. Perhaps in a metaphorical sense, but aware that hope had a corporal component, one man offered a pithy characterization of American culture. "In Italy, replied the migrant, the poor had to 'stoop,' to crawl. In the United States, even the humble walked with dignity."⁶²

Successful mobility, therefore, was enhanced with the habituation of the body. As Hana Brown argues, the body of immigrants often undergoes a retraining process, for the bodies that are "socialized to thrive in a rural, agrarian society" may not seem natural or coincide in a "wholly different institutional context."[63] In the developing urban and middle-class context of Chicago Heights, embodied hope had a sober and reserved presence. Gaetano D'Amico was what success looked like in the evolving culture. He was austere and resolute, far removed from the smell and dirt associated with a working-class culture where he began and where so many immigrants still remained. Gaetano and Giacinta's celebration of their fiftieth wedding anniversary depicts these more formal, middle-class comportments and mannerisms. Hope was expansive and culturally ordered.

This comportment and posture were in contrast to the slovenly girth required in the spaghetti-eating contests or the animalistic dexterity necessary in the greased flagpole competitions common in Italian festivals. Here, hope was ungainly and limited by the practices of the body. One Chicago Heights resident recalled how he had "learned to be agile" and how this helped him at the San Rocco Church picnic where he climbed the flagpole because "there were all kinds of things tied to the top of the pole, salami and lots of other stuff."[64]

This ability of the dominant groups to set the embodiment standards for hope went beyond posture. In the ongoing and often benevolent activities of these groups, cultural assimilation and the deemphasis on "gestural behavior" went hand in hand, so to speak. David Efron's classic study of the head, hand, and truck movements of southern Italians (and also eastern Jews) in early twentieth-century America, suggests that as acculturation proceeds, gesturing becomes more restrained. A comparison of "traditional Italians" and "assimilated Italians" found that the broad expansiveness of the Italian immigrant "appear[s] to be out of place to the Americanized Italian." Indeed, the Americanized Italian seemed to be "more embarrassed by the gestural voluminousness of his forebears."[65]

Figure 1.1. Hope produced a physical presence that was orderly, measured, and dignified. Pictured: Giacinta and Gaetano D'Amico's fiftieth wedding anniversary. *Source:* Courtesy: Casa Italia, Italian Cultural Center; Stone Park, Illinois.

In Bourdieu's terms, the traditional gestures, while culturally appropriate within the Italian community, carried little cultural capital outside this community. They signaled a mentality turned toward the past instead of an embodiment of hope focused upon the future. Chris Devatenos's firsthand observations in Chicago Heights capture these processes when he suggests that "the foreigner, striving to become Americanized, always imitates actions which he considers American."[66] And to ensure that foreign children were made aware of the close ties between body movements and the proper aspirations, a "modern system" of education was installed in the Chicago Heights schools. Specifically, students would be graded, at least in part, "according to cleanliness, attentiveness, appearance, deportment, initiative."[67] Body comportment, appearance, initiative were seen as different stands of the same cloth.

Hope and the Objectified Environment

Beyond corporeal movements and gestures, immigrants could lay claim to the status-enhancing values of hope and social mobility through the appropriation of material objects. Manner of dress, the character and style of buildings, and the physical adornments within the home are assets that can be cashed in to demonstrate an alignment with the socially approved beliefs and aspirations. For sure, these objectified goods are prized based upon their economic and aesthetic value. But they are also treasured in cultural capital terms. Following Bourdieu, they are signs of distinction that distinguish one position in the immigrant hierarchy from another. In an objectified and public manner, they reveal character, the type of person one makes claim to being.[68]

For Chicago Heights Italians, hope was materialized in cultural capital terms from the prosaic to the heavenly—from how to dress to where to pray. In particular, when immigrants first arrived, whether to wear the traditional Italian clothes (as distinct from the new American attire) had cultural consequences. Clothes communicate one's position in a social order. And because clothes are literally attached to the individual, they serve as an objective symbol of inner thoughts and dispositions. Thus, to dress in the traditional garb as pictured in figure 1.2 would open one up to cultural insults and assaults regarding one's personal drives and ambitions. As Casey and Clemente suggest, older immigrants who failed to adopt American standards of dress were found wanting not just in matters of style but also in terms of inner motivations. They "were criticized for their lack of effort."[69]

Figure 1.2. Formal, traditional dress of Italian culture. Manner of dress is often viewed as an indication of inner thoughts and dispositions. *Source:* Author's own material/Public domain.

Architecture and buildings can also evince hope.[70] This was most evident with the construction of religious buildings on the East Side and Hill neighborhoods in the Heights. In the early twentieth century, three Catholic churches were built on this side of town—Saint Casimir, Saint Joseph, and San Rocco. As mentioned previously, San Rocco was the predominantly Italian parish and was built in 1916. At the dedication ceremony, the *New World,* the newspaper of the Archdiocese of Chicago, characterized the physical structure of the church as harmonious and cheerful.[71] As such, and despite the exotic religious processions and occasional mystical practices, the Italian immigrants could point to these buildings in "glowing terms" as proof of their industriousness, ambitions, and hopes for themselves and their children. Described as "some of the most beautiful ecclesiastical property in the city," the church objectified the active and progressive activities taking place in the Italian community.[72] As Angelo "Sammy" Ciambrone said, "San Rocco has always been a beacon of hope for the Italian immigrants."[73] In sacred terms, it brought one closer to heaven; in secular terms it radiated a commitment to the practices of hope in the "here and now."

Yet, a number of Italian immigrants found the Italian character of San Rocco counter-productive to their hopes for assimilation and advancement in the larger society. As a national, Italian parish, the church injected an element of practical dissent. It allowed Italian immigrants to remain in their enclave and shun the more dominant Anglo and ethnic (primarily, Irish) staffed churches in other parts of the town. For some, San Rocco represented a set of beliefs and attachments not clearly in line with the American spirit of hope, freedom, and choice. It was a return to the provincialism of the past. One observer lamented how Italians had not fully embraced American culture. "Even though they have come to a country where they may enjoy complete religious liberty, the Italians have clung to the Catholic church. Aside from a few exceptions, they retain their religious faith and practices."[74] As Richard Juliani argued, these "nationality" parishes ran the risk of communicating a "self-segregation and cultural preservation" at variance with the values of the dominant culture.[75]

As such, an estimated 10 percent of the Italian immigrant population joined the Church of Our Savior, a First Presbyterian Church. Though always limited in their recruitment efforts, the Church of Our Savior stood more directly, more objectively, as an avenue for Americanization and the promise of mobility. As Candeloro commented, the "Protestant Italians in Chicago Heights seemed to Americanize at a faster rate and to move into business positions and the professions at a slightly faster rate than did Catholic Italians."[76] The construction and dedication of the Italian Presbyterian Church of Our Savior in 1912 stood not only, therefore, as a way to address the spiritual needs of its parishioners but also symbolized in concrete form the path forward for those Italians who had hopes for a rapid ascent up the American ladder of success. Shorn of a Catholic heritage, it was a more pronounced step in the direction of assimilation.

Hope and the Institutionalized World

Finally, hope was an institutionalized practice. It was embedded in the existing rules and social categories of the society and as such had a "relative autonomy vis-à-vis its bearer."[77] Beyond bodily adaptations, beyond objective materializations, hope manifested itself when immigrants positioned themselves on the respectable side of the values, rules and preferences of the society: hence the displeasure of so many Italians with the presence of organized crime in the community. The nefarious activities of these criminals devalued the currency of being Italian. Being associated stereotypically with the immoral activities of these underworld figures made it more difficult for Italians to lay claim to the proper pursuit of hope and a legitimate movement forward.

Even more directly, these institutionalized practices of hope were embedded in the differentiating categories of naturalization and citizenship. As Dorothee Schneider suggests, these naturalization processes (the declarations of intent, the specific forms, the hearings and adjudication procedures) allowed immigrants a welcoming and clear path to citizenship. They provided legal protections. Yet, at the same time, they aimed to create "better citizens" by managing the quality of these immigrant classes.[78] They served "to shape the citizenry in active ways."[79] Thus, the requirement to denounce fidelity to one's homeland, anarchy, and, for good measure, polygamy signaled an official rejection of the old world culture with its more provincial and, at times, dissent motives and desires. Yet at the same time, they were mechanisms for shaping the "good moral character" of these newcomers for they sought evidence of hard work, industriousness, and hope.

On a practical level, "a homeless, jobless worker could not be naturalized" for these social statuses conveyed something deeper and more sinister. They communicated an image of a wandering, reckless, and ignorant immigrant.[80] They signaled an immigrant who "arouses no enthusiasm" and who does not manifest hope sufficiently.[81] The immigrant, on the other hand, who made it through these legal and cultural gauntlets gained an institutional recognition and a supply of cultural capital. These naturalization processes conferred an official "certificate of cultural competence" and instituted "on its holder a conventional, constant, legally guaranteed value with respect to culture."[82]

Conclusion

As Italian immigrants came face to face with the socioeconomic realities of early twentieth-century America, three broad practical strategies for engagement emerged: resignation, dissent, and hope. Of these, hope was the most favored, the most rewarded. Exhibiting at least a "flicker" of hope for a hard-won social mobility would put one among the more desirable immigrants and on a path toward Americanization. Hope was a critical component of the cultural code, a presumed inner drive and set of beliefs that distinguished those immigrants who succeeded from those who did not.

This chapter offers an alternative, more sociological conception of hope and the connection to social mobility. Following the work of Bourdieu, it suggests that hope is a cultural resource, a form of cultural capital that immigrants used, though not always consciously, to purchase an acceptance in American society. As immigrants came in contact with the dominant American culture, some resigned themselves to their disadvantaged position; some dissented and escaped into an ethnic enclave or stridently challenged their lowly position in the social spaces of immigration; however, most ingested and practiced hope at a corporeal, objectified, and institutionalized level. They learned that a good American, in the words of twentieth-century sociologist Franklin Giddens, knew how to "play the game."[83]

Chapter 2

Drawn into the Social Spaces of Hope
The Italian Social Journey from Italy to America

The story of Italian immigration to America has been well told. The most widely accepted narrative suggests that in the face of a daunting and discouraging social environment, the *contadini* conjured up a reservoir of hope for a better life, which led to a decision to leave one's own country, and, if all went well, produced a social advance for these immigrants or their children. Hope was the springboard to social mobility, the catalyst that transformed the life circumstances of the Italian peasant. Robert Foerster's classic study of Italian immigration presented such an explanation. "Hope, passion, and calculation, colored for each individual among the millions who have departed Italy, have been the immediate precursors of the decision to emigrate."[1] Jerre Mangione and Ben Morreale's comprehensive social history of the Italian American experience argues that this quest "began with a revival of hope and ended with a mass exodus."[2] More broadly, Alan Kraut describes the decision to emigrate as "a gamble chosen deliberately and often chosen with hope and enthusiasm"[3] While acknowledging the wide-ranging motivations of the Italian emigres, Humbert Nelli concludes that "the majority were attracted by the hope of bettering their income."[4] Maddalena Tirabassi writes that the choice to emigrate was "a hopeful venture aimed at seeking a better life, especially for the next generation."[5]

Though both reasonable and persuasive, these accounts are suspect on several grounds. In the case of southern Italians, there is little to suggest that hope was the beginning point for this immigrant journey. One study after another has pointed to the dearth of hope on a personal and cultural level within the *mezzogiorno*. Edward Banfield suggested that a "grim melancholia" had settled over the region.[6] Frank Cancian characterized the long-standing historical processes where "all of the examples indicate denial of the hope of progress."[7] And F. G. Friedmann's classic study of *la miseria* identified the nuanced personal stance of southern Italians for "even when pointing to the hopelessness of their position, there is little tendency toward self-pity."[8]

Even more challenging is the link between immigration and social mobility. These processes may not have been as direct and immediate as often described. The assumption that the "act of emigration begins as a renunciation of country, a preference for another land's social ladder" might be more peculiar than commonplace.[9] James Henretta holds that "there is a significant amount of evidence which suggests that economic or social mobility was not the most important value."[10] His analysis of preindustrial American society concluded that these early settlers were not primarily motivated by the "spirit" or "propensities" of social mobility. For these early men and women, and especially for women, "the 'calculus of advantage' . . . was not mere pecuniary gain, but encompassed a much wider range of social and cultural goals."[11] As Henretta suggests, these "acquisitive hopes" yielded to a more complex set of desires and preferences.[12]

David Montgomery takes this reinterpretation further. He chastises historians and sociologists who assume a country of "self-made men" aspiring in their very being toward an upward social mobility. Such a self-confirming bias, Montgomery argues, often reduces the immigrants' more complex cultural values "to the level of social pathology."[13] More generally, these critiques provide historical substance to Max Weber's general observation that social mobility and the quest for a better life are historically contingent and not innate. "A man does not 'by nature' wish to earn more money," Weber theorized, "but simply to live as he is accustomed to live and to earn as much as is necessary for that purpose."[14]

This is not to argue that social mobility was unimportant or not on the minds of many immigrants. It is to challenge the conventional belief that hope was pushing from behind (or within) and that social mobility was pulling from the front (or outside). Instead, hope and mobility might best be understood by situating them within the field of immigration as forms of cultural capital. Thus, from the perspective of the dominant groups in society, these processes were effective social control mechanisms for shaping and forming immigrants according to the standards and interests of the established order. From the perspective of immigrants, these forms were coded resources that could be used to gain favorable positions in this immigrant hierarchy. In a new world that "favored individualism, self-reliance, and initiative" Italian immigrants adopted a pragmatic, practical stance in line with these dominant cultural values.[15] Being vilified as among the "least desirable immigrants,"[16] described as "short, sober, musical rapists,"[17] and patronized as "untrained children,"[18] Italians sought to thwart these distinctions by strategically and publicly embracing, if not fully committing to, the pathways held out for them——that is, hope and material gain. Though they were institutionally encouraged to "catch the American spirit of 'getting ahead,'"[19] they engaged in an ever-evolving sense of how best to play the game of immigration, how to "to improvise actions effectively," and all the while maintain a "commitment to the stakes of the game."[20]

Entering the Social Spaces of Immigration

The Italian revolutionary and patriot Giuseppe Garibaldi once famously said that the exodus of Italians from southern Italy was a "significant evil." The conditions in the south were so deplorable that emigration was forced upon many peasants. While these conditions had roots in centuries of foreign conquest and occupation, the onerous times encountered at the turn of the last century had the most consequential impact.[21] Specifically, the phylloerxa blight destroyed a sizeable number of grape vineyards and put many of the Italian peasants out of work. At the same time, citrus farmers were dealt another economic blow as the American market for these goods was effectively closed when California and Florida joined the global economy. More perniciously, the historic animosities between the northern, industrial regions and the southern, agricultural economy perpetuated a tax system and land-use policies that effectively turned many southern Italians into sharecroppers and tenant farmers. And when excessive debt made even these tenuous attachments to the land more vulnerable, many Italian farmers were forced to become day laborers and farmhands. These dire circumstances were exacerbated when a series of natural disasters—including earthquakes, tidal waves, and volcanic eruptions—rocked the southern provinces and killed thousands of people. Despite these exceedingly bleak realities, the majority of southern Italians remained in Italy with the expectation that they could once again survive and continue to live their accustomed lives.[22]

Many men and women did choose to emigrate, although it was not the poorest or the least skilled who made such decisions.[23] For those who did leave, family decisions were fraught with uncertainties and misgivings. The Italian literature on emigration documents these troubled times through personal narratives, community studies, and statistical accounts.[24] Across a range of approaches and levels of analysis, these studies reveal the complex decision-making processes and the external pressures that mitigated or enhanced the prospects of hope for a better life. For example, Pino Arlacchi's study of two towns in Calabria separated by only a few miles but with significantly different emigration patterns points to the relative importance of local culture, familial obligations, and versions of poverty.[25]

One of the few recurring themes across this literature is not the absence of hope but what Betty Boyd Caroli called the "politics of emigration" or the processes whereby "emigrants were manipulated for others' gain."[26] As individuals and families struggled with the decision to emigrate, powerful forces were working to take these personal experiences of anxiety and render them coherent along ideological lines. A series of social actors, with both benign interests and self-serving ones, translated these uncertainties into commonsense expressions of hope and a movement toward a better life. Precisely, as immigrants were drawn into the social spaces populated by officials, shipping agents, padroni, and profiteers, immigration became a favored, sanctioned path through which these individual anxieties were socially recognized or named. As Berlant suggests, hope or optimism "is ambitious, at any moment it might feel like anything." In troubling circumstances, it is a "place where appetites find a shape in the predictable comforts of the good life."[27]

Early on, the Italian government supported immigration from the *mezzogiorno* under the assumption that this exodus would ameliorate the "southern problem." Political leaders feared that the dramatic population growth in the southern provinces during the latter half of the nineteenth century had exacerbated the limited ability of the peasants to live off the land.[28] There, leaders were also pressed by the propertied: landowners in the south who feared that these poverty conditions would foment an already growing peasant movement. With socialism as the new specter haunting these elites, "now the formerly feared emigration was considered by many as a downright 'savior.' "[29] Under these conditions, the depiction of America as a country teeming with "golden" opportunities was presented as a way to mitigate the burdens of these demographic and poverty misfortunes. As Alexander DeConde concluded, the Italian government passed legislation and promoted immigration under the assumption that "Italians often helped themselves and the country by relieving the economic pressure at home."[30] And to the extent that the Italians who made it to America sent remittances or who themselves returned in better economic standing, political officials were more successful at balancing the Italian economy. There were strong sentiments among government officials, Caroli argued, that "the *americani* brought certain advantages to Italy and that official action should both encourage emigration and invite returnees."[31]

These official actions, though often unorganized and uncertain, paved the path toward immigration in a number of ways. Parliamentary decrees and administrative actions established the legal right to emigrate, regulated the recruitment of would-be immigrants, eased the process and dropped the fee for obtaining a passport, and encouraged shipowners to establish regular routes to the Americas. In a most practical manner, the *Commissarito dell' Emigrazione* backfilled the more fantastical hopes of peasants in a wide-ranging series of hands-on pamphlets entitled *Bollettinmo dell' Emigrazione*. These bulletins provided detailed guides on how to obtain passports, arrange sleeping and eating arrangements, and find jobs in the different industrial centers and mining regions in America.

Having been prompted to leave Italy, if only on a temporary basis, the immigrants then had to commit to the physically and emotionally challenging process of moving themselves, and at times their family, from their remote villages to the far-off and poorly sensed destination abroad. At each step along the way, an array of brokers and agents, with the continued assistance of domestic and foreign officials, made themselves available as they processed hope and mobility. These brokers emerged from numerous positions, as they were the more literate people in the village—religious leaders, mayors or town officials, teachers, pharmacists, bar owners, steamship agents, and previous emigres. At the beginning of the twentieth century, an estimated ten thousand agents were at work in the Italian towns and villages.[32] And while their motives may have varied, most all engaged in the singular effort to "convince fellow countrymen to migrate," for there was considerable profit to be made at every step along this path.[33]

The most scrupulous agents sought to present a balanced picture of what lay ahead: the "half-bitter, half-sweet" character of American life. But most all extolled the appropriate cultural values of hope and progress and promoted the ideological and emotional sentiments necessary for successful assimilation in America, the *"terra promessa."* Along these lines, travel literature "suggested the prospect of a rapid improvement in the moral and material standards of living in comparison with the mother country."[34] At the same time, a common procedure was to translate American newspaper

Figure 2.1. As one of the leading shipping companies in Italy, Navigazione Generale Italiana had a particular interest in encouraging emigration on the part of Italian citizens. *Source:* Courtesy: Paolo Cresci Foundation for the history of Italian Emigration, Museo Dell' Emigrazione Italiana Online, From Italy to the World, Emigration Agents.

articles and editorials in a manner that emphasized American prosperity, a practice forbidden but rarely enforced by Italian law. In a more direct manner, brokers sought to lure peasants as they entered churches by reciting and presenting hymns and prayers extolling the chances for a better life in the United States. And it was not beyond the pale of some agents to infuse hope with sacred religious symbols. Grazia Dore reports that many immigrants were often recruited "with the promise of being led to the land where Jesus Christ had been born and died," only to find later, as these peasants discovered, that "these places were Hell."[35]

Drawn into the Social Spaces of Hope | 47

More broadly, agents and government officials took advantage of the emerging medium of print advertising to produce popular circulars, posters, and guidebooks extolling the virtues of immigration. Posters, produced both in Italy and in foreign countries, flooded the southern regions, finding their way into the smallest villages and farmsteads. Throughout the markets and piazzas, persons were surrounded by graphic posters meant to "convince them of the fortunes of America."[36] The underlying theme and tone of these guides tilted heavily toward hope, happiness, and an idyllic setting. They "showed images of paradise on earth: boundless plains with exuberant vegetation, tidy houses, tidy city districts."[37]

Figure 2.2. This emigrant guidebook presents a flowery, pastoral picture of life in South America. *Source:* Courtesy: Paolo Cresci Foundation for the History of Italian Emigration, Museo Dell' Emigrazione Italiana Online, From Italy to the World, Guide for Emigrants.

These propaganda techniques were also evident in the more subtle but evocative advertisements of the steamship companies. Many of these companies were only able to stay financially afloat because of the large flow of emigres to the Americas and the periodic returns to Italy. These advertisements, as Max Gallo points out, presented images of the New World that not only appealed to the adventuresome traveler but also to the desolate poor. They depicted the new attitude that exodus should be preferred over misery. As the most suggestive media of the day, these posters expressed hopes for a better life through dramatic images of the open seas, the advance of technology, clear blue skies. "The poorest travelers, the steerage passengers to America, were not particularly moved by the romance of travel," Gallo argues. "Yet their hopes too were attached to the curls of smoke issuing from the stacks of locomotives and steamers."[38]

Figure 2.3. The riches and hopes of different worlds and travel were often displayed in colorful, dramatic posters that brought together blue skies, the open seas, and modern technology. *Source:* WorldPhotos/Alamy Stock Collection.

Clearly, not all agents, brokers, and officials were disingenuous. Most viewed immigration as favorable to the long-term interests of the Italian citizen. And not all these citizens were naively pulled into this immigration field against their better wishes. Most chose to enter this pathway after careful calculation. Still, it is difficult to ignore the powerful cultural forces that were swirling around these individuals and families as they dealt with the difficult decisions to leave their homeland. As Chicago Heights resident Elizabeth Damiani said, "They told us the streets were paved with gold and we expected that."[39] Overall, as Feys suggests, these migrant brokers engaged in a continuous campaign to spread the "propaganda on opportunities in America."[40]

The activities and propaganda techniques of these migrant brokers often overlapped with the padrone system. This system played a significant role in bridging the cultural, economic, and geographic distance between Italy and America. As Gunter Peck suggested, "The padrone system simplified a bevy of troubling doubts."[41] These Italian "bosses" "excite(d) the imagination of potential immigrants" once again by means of circulars and advertisements in Italian newspapers.[42] More often, the padrone himself, or "traveling agents" hired for these purposes, would migrate between the United States and the local village and in a personal manner persuade the local peasants with "golden tales" regarding life in America. Through "vague, uncertain, or indefinite promises" they sought to mold and objectify the aspirations of these peasants in line with the culturally acceptable and profitable views on hope and mobility. Specifically, the more dreamlike vision of life in America—a vision in which padroni "promised heaven and earth . . . where farm tools—spades, hoes, and plows—were made of solid gold, instead of iron"—were offered as an antidote to the impoverished conditions in Italy.[43]

With the assistance then of both these travel agents and local padroni, the Italian peasants next had to confront the demanding tasks of traveling from their small towns to the major seaports of Napoli, Genoa, or Palermo or other departure points. Early on, this journey may have been by horseback, wagon, or simply on foot. Typically, it would take days. As such, these sojourners often had to sleep wherever they could find a safe place away from thieves and brigands. Later on, the rail lines provided more efficient and marginally safer transportation options. Once at one of these departure ports, peddlers and hucksters could make life miserable. Solitude and loneliness also added to the already heightened sense of anxiety and fear. The time to get permission to board a ship could take anywhere from a few days to months.[44]

Once on board, the immigrant, upon confronting the degraded conditions, was forced to rely upon hope more directly. Consigned in most cases to the steerage section of the ship (below deck, windowless cargo holds that once housed the steering components but now served as a makeshift holding pen), the migrant passengers were forced to tackle the immediacy of the overcrowded conditions, the lack of fresh air, and the highly unsanitary conditions. These led many to look for comfort and hope with their fellow travelers. As Paolo Cresci and Luciano De Crescenzo detail, close friendships were formed, especially with those who spoke the same dialect, based upon their shared sense of pain, humiliation, and misery.[45]

Even so, the passengers struggled mightily. They picked worms and other unknown objects out of their small rations of food, endured limited access to toilet facilities, and found relief only by escaping to the top deck that was typically overcrowded and covered with food, vomit, and the remains of animals slaughtered on deck.[46] Olivia Kowalski (née Messacci), Chicago Heights resident, recounts, "I often remember my mother speaking about the trip on the boat and how horrible it was and how long."[47] My father, Andy Corsino, said it took thirty days for his mother to cross over and forty days for his father. "They were treated like cattle. They would put them down in a hole and treat them like animals."[48] These abhorrent conditions led various government agencies and benevolent organizations to advocate for more humane treatment.[49]

Despite these degrading experiences, hope was not extinguished. Indeed, though not the intent of these steamship companies, these physical, mental, and moral challenges drew the connection to hope all the more closely. "The spirit of the steerage!" as one immigrant declared. "It would be well if every phase of the life of America were as full of hope and promise."[50] Unmoored from family and friends and with little to show for their heart-wrenching decision to emigrate, most immigrants had little more to rely upon than hope. There was an increasing awareness that whatever their status in Italy, they now found themselves in an immigrant hierarchy where the "spirit of the steerage" had become a critical cultural resource. One Italian immigrant offered the following comment: "Passage across the Atlantic seemed to have been so calculated as to inflict upon us the last, full measure of suffering and indignity, and to impress upon us for the last time that we were the 'wretched refuse' of the earth; to exact from us a final price for the privileges we hoped to enjoy in America."[51]

At least temporarily, this "full measure of suffering and indignity" was allayed when immigrants set eyes upon their new home. Though Italians arrived at various ports, Ellis Island in New York was the gateway for most. The first glimpses of the Statue of Liberty were tangible signs that the demanding seafaring voyage was about to end. Typically, the weary passengers would rush to one side of the ship to catch their first sighting of America, in the process ignoring the admonitions of the captain who feared that the ship would capsize. But it was also a symbolic step toward cementing hope as a valuable cultural resource. Though Liberty's torch was to symbolize the light to freedom, it was also an instance of objectified cultural capital.[52] Seeing the statue for the first time, immigrants could invest their feelings and expectations in its material form and moor hope to a physical object. One immigrant's words capture this cultural exuberance. "Before the monument the emigrant forgets the distant patria and with it the sorrows experienced; He opens his heart to the sweetest hopes and he is impatient to touch and kiss the Promised Land."[53]

The relief of having survived this most unpleasant journey was soon countered by the formal admission processes at Ellis Island. The bureaucratic procedures and the intrusive physical examinations—the iron bars that directed immigrants to the appropriate inspection officers, the wire enclosures separating the detainees from those allowed to proceed, the calculating questions regarding future employment status, the painful eyelid probes and examinations of hair and scalp—were foreign experiences at multiple levels. Though these processes were weighted *toward* accepting immigrants, fear and confusion were always present. This was especially the case for southern Italians who came under more scrutiny than other newcomers.[54] For example, Hap Bruno, longtime Chicago Heights resident, said he was separated from his mother for unknown reasons at Ellis Island and it took eight days before he was reunited with her.[55] Elizabeth Damiani reported that her family did not have the forty dollars necessary for admission into the country and as such her family "had to sleep in a locked room" until the money arrived.[56] Ellen Paros, a Chicago Heights resident, invoked a similar criminal analogy. "Ellis Island was like a prison to me."[57]

These administrative processes left many immigrants unsure of themselves and their first introduction to their new homeland. These doubts were magnified as these newcomers went through the medical sifting and sorting processes. These examinations were ostensibly concerned with the spread of contagious disease—tuberculosis, trachoma, favus, and venereal infections. But as much as these procedures may have been medically justified, they were also mechanisms that transformed and allocated the immigrant's body and spirit into the appropriate social spaces—that is, in line with the expected normative standards of hope and mobility.

Public health officers administering these examinations typically interpreted their mission broadly. Beyond these health concerns, they were intent on classifying immigrants according to the likelihood that they would eventually become a public charge. And in a more intrusive manner, these medical exams served an initiation function. They alerted the unsuspecting immigrant to life and expectations beyond these narrow public health functions, to the rapidly changing demands of the industrial working-class system in American society. As Fairchild suggests, these immigrant medical inspections led the way in "disciplining and managing the work force . . . in a more far-reaching social effort."[58]

Whatever their necessary medical rationales, these physical inspections served initiation and normative functions. Specifically, they were instances of "normalizing power" wherein "each individual, wherever he may find himself, subjects to it his body, his gestures, his behaviour, his aptitudes, his achievements."[59] The stereotypical languid and docile bodies, the disparaged culture, the near-atavistic mental capacities assigned to southern Italians required a reconfiguration if immigrants were to achieve success in the society. The stream of peasants who proceeded to the inspection stations "stolidly, steadily, submissively, like so many cattle" needed to be transformed.[60] As Amy Bernardy, an Italian journalist and ethnographer, documented, "the faces of the immigrants wore signs of 'poverty and ignorance.' "[61] Alan Kraut argued that the facial expressions, the manner of walking, the tendency to slouch were often associated with temperaments, habits, and a "moral obliquity" that many feared would tear away at the fabric of American society.[62] As such, the "golden door opened wide" for those deemed physically able but also morally prepared to exhibit the American ethos of success, for those who demonstrated "fitness of body as well as of soul."[63]

This message of enacting the right bodily manifestations and attitudinal expressions of hope and success was not lost on the majority of Italians. Most immigrants anticipated these inspection processes. By relying upon stories from prior travelers and the admonitions of migrant brokers, they rehearsed scripts for answering questions, developed strategies for demonstrating economic sufficiency, and adopted a range of physical disguises to cover up bodily mannerisms and maladies that might be taken as grounds to disqualify one from entering the country. Avoiding the diagnosis that one had a "poor physique" and thus would have little hope of finding a job was an immediate concern for immigrants.[64] Though the number of applicants rejected for physical reasons was small, these very inspection processes and standards conveyed to immigrants that the look and appearance of self-reliance and hope were important. And just in case these messages were too indirect, a more hands-on, right-minded rearrangement of the body was in order. As Irene Zambelli suggests when she passed through the processing lines with her cousin, "The inspector put one hand on the back and one in front of my cousin's chest and tried to straighten him out. He had a bad habit to stoop over."[65]

These procedural obstacles behind them, most immigrants then faced the challenges of traveling by train to their new place of work and residence. Some of these newcomers were met in New York by sponsors and relatives. Or in some cases, an immigrant who had spent a few years in America would go back to Italy and escort family members through the entire journey. Nick Zaranti, Chicago Heights resident, said, "My dad came here in 1900. He came to Chicago Heights in 1900. . . . He was 17 years old when he came here from Cacamo. Came here with his older brother and grandfather. My grandfather was here five years before that. . . . They pooled their money and went back to get the rest of the family."[66] Yet the majority of immigrants were on their own, especially if their destination was beyond New York City. Immigration officials would escort these travelers to the appropriate railroad terminals in New York, in large part to shield them from the agents and hawkers who would attempt to exploit the bewildered newcomers. Beyond that point, the immigrants relied upon fellow travelers or padroni.

This was especially the case for those Italian immigrants who were on their way to Chicago and eventually Chicago Heights. Chicago Heights resident, Cosmo Ciarrocchi, told the story of his anxiety-filled experiences at Ellis Island. After becoming separated from a couple he was traveling with, Ciarrocchi met up with his uncle who was there to meet him. But as they moved through the crowd, Ciarrocchi was again separated from the only person he knew. As he was wandering around the area, Ciarrocchi met an Italian man who bought him a ticket from New York to Chicago. As he boarded the train, Ciarrocchi had the address for his final destination pinned "in every pocket."[67]

As these immigrants left the challenging but highly structured spaces aboard steamship liners and Ellis Island, they now faced the more open-ended decisions regarding travel, places to live, and employment. Even here, subagents and "sharpers" hired by railway lines sought to capture the immigrant trade with promises of cheap fares and connections once they arrived in Chicago. Cheap fares often meant railroad travel by way of "immigrant trains." Such trains segregated immigrants from native-born passengers based on the belief that this would be to the benefit of these newly arriving peasants. Perhaps, this was so, but this practice was also telling regarding the less than welcoming institutional responses to these foreign newcomers. On a practical level, it also meant that these travelers would most likely ride in converted box cars with only wooden benches, few if any windows, limited toilet facilities, and no spring suspension system to cushion the ride. And immigrant trains, though extremely profitable for railroad companies, were the slowest trains, often giving the right-of-way to freight, mail, and other passenger trains.[68] In a common refrain, and a not exactly subtle indication of the underlying attitude toward immigrants, one observer bemoaned the fact that "immigrants are . . . huddled like cattle in the uncomfortable and foul smelling cars of this unlawful pool."[69]

Upon arriving in Chicago at the Grand Central, Polk Street, or later the Chicago & Northwestern stations, immigrants were once again challenged to find their bearings within the available physical and social spaces. Typically, relatives or friends were there to meet the weary and disheveled travelers, though the unpredictable schedules of the immigrant trains often meant long delays; sometimes the immigrants were left to find their own way. These newcomers were often immediately confronted by a barrage of circulars, pamphlets, and agents extolling the virtues of settling into one of the nearby Midwestern states. For the most part, these recruitment efforts were directed at northern Europeans of German, Norwegian, and Swedish descent, though some Italians made their way north to Racine, Wisconsin, and the iron range of Minnesota. These efforts frequently extolled hope as they "overdrew the picture, describing a veritable El Dorado for the benefit of prospective settlers who in responding to the lure of America were perhaps naturally too sanguine."[70]

For many Italian immigrants, the first halting steps into Chicago often took them into the nearby city blocks populated by boarding houses, saloons, and employment agencies. Since the vast majority of immigrants were single men or others who had left their families behind in Italy, especially in the early years, these employment agencies (or padroni) provided a critical service in immediately connecting these newcomers to available jobs and places to live. However, the term "padrone" in America covers a wide range of practices and forms of aid. At one end of the spectrum it is used to describe a form of "white slavery" in which workers were de facto obligated to work for the gang boss for a series of years until their debt to him was paid off. Along the way, these immigrants were financially and physically exploited in ways they did not suspect.[71] At the other end, the padrone was providing a necessary service as a man of respect for a fellow countryman. He profited from this service, no doubt, but the norms and culture of the Italian community served to limit and control the exploitative nature of this system.

As the Italian immigrants made their way from Chicago to Chicago Heights, it was this latter version of the padrone system that was most prevalent. A number of men assumed this role. For example, Tom Cellini was born in Italy but managed to achieve a favorable position as a "section foreman" for the Chicago and Eastern Illinois Railroad (C&EI), which had a station in Chicago Heights. Candeloro reports that Cellini was remembered as "a railroad 'boss' who hired numerous workers for his crew from among his neighbors."[72] Even today, there is an honorary street named after him in Chicago Heights. Antonio Sanfilippo was another Chicago Heights businessman and drugstore owner who was elected to the city council for a short two-year period. After failing to be reelected, Sanfilippo continued to provide immigration services for fellow Italians, most importantly helping them navigate the naturalization processes of citizenship. Many tavern owners such as Pete Cassaza, Pasquale Luongo, and Tony Longo also appeared a number of times as "witnesses" on the naturalization petitions of immigrants and served as agents helping to secure work, room, and board for each wave of immigrants. John Montella came from Italy, settled in Chicago Heights, and "used to support people coming from all over Italy. He used to get people jobs on the railroad . . . and he knew an Italian foreman at the scrap yard—Hicks Car Works. He got a lot of people jobs there. He also helped them find a place to stay."[73]

Perhaps Dominic Pandolfi was most representative of the padrone style in Chicago Heights. Pandolfi came from San Benedetto, Italy, to the United States in 1889. He settled in Chicago Heights with his family and opened up a saloon with the assistance of a local brewery that built his tavern and upstairs residence. As was common with other padroni, Pandolfi sold steamship tickets, directed immigrants to places of residence, and helped them find jobs at the nearby steel plant a few blocks away. However, since Illinois law made it illegal to conduct labor contracting in places where liquor was sold, the upstairs residence provided a convenient "office" for Pandolfi's activities.[74] Even so, in the ensuing years, Pandolfi moved out of the tavern business and offered financial services more directly where "he would arrange to exchange them (money) by going to the bank."[75] Eventually, Pandolfi was so successful in these agent practices that he became a director in one of the local community banks; then he retired and returned to Italy in 1926.

Settling into the Social Spaces of Immigration

The need for a padrone-like figure was essential in Chicago Heights, for the city's relatively small size limited residential and work opportunities. The Italian community was insular, and many of the city blocks on the East Side and Hill Area (the sections of the city where most immigrants lived) were further differentiated by *campanilismo* ties. Specifically, people from Calabria and Sicily (in particular, from Nicastro and Caccamo, respectively) lived on Fifth, Wentworth, and Portland Avenues; the people from the Lazio province (primarily from Amaseno) lived on Twenty-Second and Twenty-Third Streets; and the people from the Marche region (primarily San Benedetto) were scattered in enclaves throughout the city. So, even as the immigrants were lured to the Heights with promises of employment at one of the many industrial plants, access to these jobs was often dependent upon these regional connections to tavern owners, political leaders, and industry insiders.

Living Arrangements

This was also the case for finding a place to live. Slightly more than half of the Italian immigrants in Chicago Heights in 1910 were "boarders" or "roomers."[76] A number of these newcomers may have known or had some connection with relatives to secure a place to stay. Most had to rely upon padroni for a connection to room and board and, consequently, for their subsequent sojourn through the social spaces of the American immigration system. In a larger sense, as Jared Day concluded, the padroni became "the economic and social gatekeepers of the American Dream."[77]

The "dream-like" character of these arrangements varied dramatically. As with a number of other Italian families, my grandmother, Josephina, offered a bed to sleep in, laundry services, a lunch pail meal, and nightly dinner with the family for two dollars a month. Several of these boarders became fictive kin. Indeed one of these boarders, Vito Chimienti, became

Figure 2.4. Title: The Corsino family photo (with boarders as well) in the early 1950s with "Zizi Vito" (standing in the back row with white shirt and tie) and "Zizi Ralph" (seated at the table with white shirt and tie behind the multiple beer bottles). *Source:* Personal Collection of Louis Corsino.

my godfather. Another, Ralphael Marino, or Zizi Ralph as we called him, embedded himself in our family for over thirty years often showing up in family pictures in a Zelig-like fashion. Theresa Gianetti said her family had a different experience. There were a number of boarders who came and went. She said for the most part the boarders were "very cold. They kept to themselves. Very demanding, very demanding." This put a strain on her mother. And when the family grew too big, they stopped taking in boarders.[78]

This family living arrangement for boarders was in contrast to the "bunkhouses" that were often supported by the industrial firms and manufacturing companies themselves. Chicago Heights had a number of these rugged housing arrangements nestled within the factories and railroad switching yards. These types of accommodations housed a large rotating collection of immigrants. For example, in 1910, there were twenty-five boarders (an

58 | Hopelessly Alien

Angelo, Luigi, Federico, Antonio, Pietro, Tomaso, and on) listed as living at one boarding house on Twenty-Second Street in the Heights.[79] Just blocks away, another housed eighteen men, another seventeen. Rudolph Vecoli, who conducted research on Italians in Chicago Heights during this period, pointed to the "barracks-like boarding houses" that populated Chicago Heights.[80] And a study of the Hungry Hill area of the Heights suggests that it was not unusual for a large number of men to share accommodations on a round-the-clock basis such that while some were at work others slept in their beds.[81]

As an immigrant institution, the practice of "boarding" played a significant role in the distribution of hope and mobility. The immigrant's desire to stay in America and to conjure up the necessary complements of hope and advantage were more likely enhanced in the familial boarding experience. In such an environment, the immigrant became in many instances a part of the household and came to understand how the adoption of hope and "joyful striving" were critical. The immediacy of the family members and their struggles to gain a foothold were socializing experiences. However, for those individuals who found themselves in the barracks-like housing, hope and mobility carried little cultural value. As Michael Piore argues, temporary

Figure 2.5. Boarding houses in Chicago Heights were sometimes private homes, sometimes owned by industries, sometimes hotels. Pictured above is the Chicago Terminal Hotel, which served new immigrants and transitory workers. *Source:* Courtesy: Casa Italia, Italian Cultural Center; Stone Park, Illinois.

migrants were able to divorce themselves from the dominant social and cultural arrangements because these migrants still conceived of themselves as occupying a physical and social space far removed from that in American society.[82] Living together with other co-ethnics, these workers were far less focused upon staying in the country, less concerned with developing a path to occupational mobility. Camaraderie, work, sleep, traditional ethnic meals, and creating a *gruzzolo di denari* (bundle of money) at the end of the season were more important. As Harney suggests, "institutions of acculturation or culture mattered little" for these types of boarders.[83]

By and large, these immigrants paid a price for this personal and institutional dissent. They were often associated with the criminal element and with the undisciplined rowdies who were viewed at the heart of what Chicago Heights leaders often termed "the Italian problem." They were vilified for their gambling, drinking, and frequenting houses of prostitution. They were depicted as being lured by the "slot-machine trust" in the city and thought to be largely incapable of making their own decisions moving forward or as "men who could ill afford to part with their money."[84] The failure of these men to exhibit the moral, attitudinal, and behavioral expectations of the dominant culture placed them near the bottom rung of the immigrant hierarchy.

WORKING ARRANGEMENTS

Beyond these living arrangements, the American Dream of a better life had to be tempered with the harsh realities of work during this era. Jobs in the hazardous industrial plants, in the hot sun laying railroad tracks, or in the frozen lakes cutting blocks of ice with hammers and chisels may have paid a daily wage, but they extracted a toll in ailments, lost limbs, and diminishing aspirations. Candeloro points to these dangers in Chicago Heights when he states that "industrial accidents were not uncommon. Oral history sources have no trouble recalling—and accounts in the *Star* confirm—frequent deaths of Italian workers in construction, at the brickyards, and on the railroad."[85] John Wozny speaks of the inherent dangers involving industrial accidents in Chicago Heights when so many new and untried innovations such as electricity, the combustible engine, the use of chemicals were all being formulated for increased production. "But danger lurked at every corner," Wolzy argued. Though the east side chemical plant was one of the "choice" places for employment, "overhead pipes carried phosphoric acid . . . occasionally one would spring a leak, worse yet, burst spewing hot acid over anyone in the area. The highly corrosive acid would eat away clothing and flesh in seconds."[86] Umberto La Morticella recounts the plight of the typical factory worker who "worked under brutalizing conditions. Chicago Heights had steel mills, chemical factories, foundries, dye factories, very dusty wood-working factories, etc. Every place was a place of heat, grime, dirt, dust, stench, harsh glares, overtime, piecework, pollution, no safety gadgets, sweat, etc. The workers were, as the Italians called them, 'Bestie Da Soma,' beasts of burden. Emphysema, stomach ailments, heart ailments were common."[87]

Nick Zaranti also spoke of the always insecure and personally challenging labor market for immigrant workers. He recounts how his father worked during the summer laying track for the Michigan Central railroad. Around October his father would be laid off and then typically head down to New Orleans to pick sugar cane, being hired to do this back-breaking job only after agreeing to give some 20 percent of his wages to the section boss or padrone. Zaranti recalls,

> I remember my dad telling me he worked on the Michigan Central railroad and he worked in Dyer, Indiana which is six, seven miles east of here . . . he and my uncle they would walk to work early in the morning on Monday, and then they would work through the week and stay in Dyer and not come home every night. They had to stay there and worked there and on Friday nights they would come home late at night. So, here you're only six or seven miles away from home. And you have to live in a box car by the railroad because you had no way of getting home.[88]

There were immigrants who expressed public dissent and called for a collective response to these workplace indignities and dangers. In the rough-and-tumble industrial environment of the era, these dissenting challenges were met with strong resistance from community and economic leaders who saw these protesters as beyond hope and beyond the disciplinary practices of Americanization.[89] Socialists and union organizers were often considered a new breed of "modern criminal" that required the formation of a state police organization to thwart the threats that "bore from within."[90] The attempt was to legally and symbolically exclude these dissidents from the immigrant social spaces altogether.

Giovanni Fusci (1871–1967)

Giovanni Fusci (Americanized as "Fushi" upon arrival through Ellis Island) came to America in 1902 and like many others returned to Italy a number of times to be with his family in Caccamo, Sicily (a small town outside of Palermo). Prior to this, Giovanni traveled throughout Europe in search of a job. Lured by the promises of employment in America, he settled in Chicago Heights, where his brother had migrated several years earlier. Giovanni quickly found a place to live in the East Side enclave in Chicago Heights—an enclave that put him among many fellow Sicilians, mainly from Caccamo, and among the Polish, Black, and Mexican families who also lived within walking distance from the nearby industrial plants.

Giovanni found work quickly but was unable to take advantage of the short commute to work through the winding streets, alleys, and passageways that barely separated these industrial factories from the residential homes. Instead, Giovanni found work as one of the original members of the blast team at Thornton Quarry, north of Chicago Heights. Giovanni was thrilled to find steady work and provide for his wife and six children, though the salary was well below a dollar a day. However, the quarry was more than five miles away. Thus, Giovanni had to walk nearly eleven miles a day, often during the brutal summer and winter days in Chicago. As his granddaughter, Celia Concialdi told us,

> He use to get up every day at 4:00 and walk five miles or so to the quarry. He did this year round—summer and winter. And think about this in winter. The further he went down in the pit, the colder it was. He then had to walk back each day and would not get home to 7:00 or so—about two hours. We had to hold him up because he had such a difficult time taking off all the layers of clothes he had on. We had to thaw out his clothes, get him dressed, ready for dinner, and then to bed.

A resilient man, Giovanni worked in the quarry for decades, though he experienced little advancement or promotion. Arguably, he may have been motivated by a hope for a better life and perhaps achieved it. Just as likely, however, he was driven by constant worry for the welfare of his family—a concern that compelled him to take those long treks back and forth to the quarry, beginning in the early morning and ending in the late evening.

Geographic Arrangements

As immigrants filtered into Chicago Heights, their place in the immigrant hierarchy was solidified further in terms of place. They soon learned that there were designated places where they would feel comfortable or uncomfortable and where it was permissible to be Italian and where it was not. Thus, many immigrants spoke of the dividing line in Chicago Heights as the C&EI railroad tracks, which split the city into the more prosperous scenic West Side and the more industrial immigrant enclaves on the East Side and Hill areas—a dividing line that geographically, economically, and culturally separated immigrants "from the mainstream of Chicago Heights life."[91] The West Side was characterized as the "better half" or the part of the town that represented forward thinking and hope. The East Side was characterized as a "slough," or the part of the city that represented backward thinking and hardship.[92]

With these geographic divisions in mind, immigrants were seen to possess "dangerous bodies" in need of special control. As Nick Zaranti, long-time Chicago Heights resident said, "The whole west part of town, starting from the railroad tracks, the CNI [sic] railroad tracks moving west. We hit the downtown area and then beyond that you couldn't even go. . . ."[93] Art Marks (previously, Marchegiana) another Italian resident, tells a similar story. "Being Italian wasn't easy in those days. You couldn't cross Chicago Road."[94] Celia Concialdi said bluntly, "We were colonized on the east side."[95] Instead, most Italians had to be content with the grind of metal on metal, the periodic white industrial ash or black grit falling from the sky, and the foul odors that often accompanied the steel mills and chemical plants.[96]

If physical settings can represent hope, they can also represent hopelessness.[97] This seems to have been the challenge for the immigrant groups in Chicago Heights. With few exceptions, they could not appropriate their geographic location in a manner that would signify a commitment to social mobility and achievement. In a nostalgic sense, the "Hill" area of the Heights is looked back upon fondly for the sense of community and happy memories it produced. Yet, in the early years, most homes were constructed out of discarded box-car lumber and were squeezed among the industrial plants and rail yards. The full nickname for the area was "Hungry Hill" because by most accounts people in the area were always hungry for food and work.[98] As such, living in the area, as culturally rich and meaningful as it may have been, did not easily align itself with the cultural goals of success and opportunity. This would require, as many immigrants would do years in the future, moving out of the area to the west side of Chicago Heights.[99]

Institutional Arrangements

As these newcomers settled into the community, several local institutions had entrée into the Italian family and in a largely benign fashion sought to reconfigure the moral and physical characteristics of the Italian immigrants and their children. Vecoli speaks of the difficult times Italian immigrants had not only in the Protestant churches but also in the Irish-dominated Catholic churches. The cultural capital most valued in these churches with their "coldly, rational atmosphere, the discipline, the attentive congregation were foreign to the Italians who were used to behaving in church as they would in their own house."[100] As a consequence, it was not unusual for Italians to be relegated to the basement of these churches for religious services. Richard Juliani speaks in general terms about the development of the "annex" church as the nativist population struggled to solve the "Italian problem." Before the advent of the "nationality parish," these basement chapels were awkward attempts at locating a provisional place for Italians in the immigrant hierarchy, especially with respect to other American Catholics. These assimilation accommodations offered Italians at best a "second-class citizenship" whereby Italians may have been "spiritually tolerated, but sometimes disdainfully at a distance by their co-religionists."[101]

Along with the churches, schools presented a problem. In the midst of many efforts on the part of teachers to respond genuinely to the needs of their students, the alien, un-American character of these immigrant children surfaced again and again. For example, Italian children were often assigned seats in the back of the classroom where the foreign smells and odors would be less offensive. Dominic Pandolfi speaks of the problems of being an Italian child in the Chicago Heights schools. "The teachers of course were quite concerned about these foreigners and we all wanted to be 100% American. . . . The school was rather tough. The teachers were very strict. They use to be difficult once in a while. But we never forgot we were Italians and foreigners."[102] Theresa Gianetti echoed these comments with respect to her school experiences when she said, "But there was always that—Italian from the Hill. I don't know if it was because I was Italian or came from the Hill. It was there."[103]

This elusive but palpable distinction was more clearly in evidence at the Harold Colbert Jones Memorial Community Center. The center was a limited settlement house run by the Presbyterian community in Chicago Heights. Many Italian children frequented the center in the early part of the century, for it provided shelter and a variety of recreational and educational programs. In their attempts to foster an abiding "self-sufficiency," the officials and staff began with the cleansing of the body but then proceeded to the more intractable dispositions and habits of these children. Thus, "hot showers" constituted the first steps in sanitizing these "dirty little urchins," but these efforts were quickly followed up with "clean sports" and "wholesome recreation" oriented toward the more invasive goal of "sow(ing) the seeds of a new self-respect and moral cleanness in these little fellows."[104] Cleanliness became a taste, a mark of distinction, an objectification of hope and success moving forward. If these immigrant children were to aspire to higher positions, they needed to incorporate these moral and accompanying bodily components. Hope needed to be infused at a fundamental level into "the most automatic gestures or the apparently most insignificant techniques of the body."[105]

Conclusion

This chapter described the evolution and cultural production of hope across a range of immigrant experiences. It suggested that a sizeable number of Italian natives who experienced disparaging situations were pulled into the social spaces of immigration through the efforts of government officials, travel and steamship brokers, and padroni. Though their motives and practices differed, the efforts of these agents coalesced around developing a taste for hope in the would-be immigrants. Through word of mouth, advertisements, and government actions, men and women were encouraged to suffer the rigors of overland travel, steamship indignities, and intrusive inspections buoyed by the promises and acceptance of hope at a corporeal, objectified, and institutional level. Once in America, some immigrants prospered and saw their commitment to hope ratified. However, many found that the process of settling into America was uneven at best and found themselves in vulnerable, unsavory positions in a new, emergent immigrant hierarchy.

Chapter 3

Purchasing an Acceptance in American Society
Occupational Mobility as Cultural Capital

As these Italian newcomers settled into American society, there was an increasing awareness that their movement within the immigrant field, as one among several fields, had to be purchased. This ability to purchase this acceptance varied as each individual brought different human, social, and cultural capital resources to this market. These assimilation transactions were negotiated with respect to the ability to speak English, a respectable religious orientation, the possession of formal school training or work skills, a favorable political ideology, and a collection of personal references. Moving to a preferred position in this immigrant hierarchy depended upon some combination of these attributes, and as such the need for hope was tempered by these individual resources.

Hope, therefore, was not a crucial ingredient for all who entered this field. Acceptance could be won through other means. Still, since most Italian immigrants did not possess these favored attributes, hope became a valuable resource, a form of cultural currency for demonstrating their belief in and commitment to the American ethos of opportunity, hard work, and success. And the most prominent, objectified investment one could make in hope entailed a recognizable quest for *occupational mobility*. That is, immigrants could climb the ladder of recognition and acceptance if they demonstrated that within their essentialist character there was to be found an invariable spirit of "exertion, striving, enterprise, individual achievement" in the workplace.[1]

Occupation Mobility as a Practical Investment

Steady employment was the foremost promise made to Italian peasants in their search for a better life. Abundant opportunities and prosperity awaited villagers in their new American home. These hopes were fueled (but also mystified) by the prospects for occupational mobility. Even if these immigrants started out as lowly industrial workers or "pick-and-shovel" laborers, hard work and ability would produce material rewards. The *Chicago Heights Signal*, the "Official Newspaper of the City of Chicago Heights," put a public, authoritative stamp on these hopes and dreams when it declared that "the industries provide work for all of the local population and many other towns in the vicinity." Further, the availability of jobs along with the town's other amenities would make possible the "moral and material advancement" of those who chose to live in the city.[2]

Occupational mobility or the incessant pursuit of a higher occupational status varied among the Italian immigrant population. Immigrants made different investment choices. As previously suggested, many men were sojourners who came to America to work hard, save their money, and return to Italy. They came at the bottom of this hierarchy and were content to stay there, for they envisioned their future back in Italy. "Moral and material advancement" in America was for others.

Others had intentions to carve out a life in America but were not guided by the "calculus of advantage." For example, Vito Chimienti, mentioned previously, came to America in 1920 from Bari, Italy. He traveled from Ellis Island to Chicago, where he eventually made his way to Chicago Heights in search of a job. He took a room in my grandparents' house in 1927 and outside of several short return trips to Italy and several years in the US Army during World War II, lived in their house until he died in 1998—this despite the fact that my grandparents both passed away before him. He was a kind, gentle man who worked in some not so kind and gentle work environments as a coal laborer, steel worker, ice cutter, bartender, and factory janitor. With this background and limited skills, it would be difficult to characterize his immigration experience as a quest driven by the pursuit of occupational advancement. Providing adequately for himself and being generous toward others (both to his relatives back in Bari and his new family in America) were his major concerns even at the expense of his own social mobility.

Still others like Giuseppe D'Amico responded to the immigration challenges by embracing an entrepreneurial spirit. Though starting out on the lower rungs on the immigration social ladder, they championed the ideals of hope and personal advancement. Thus, as early as 1910, Chicago Heights had nine Italian-run barbershops, four tailors, and fifty-five local merchants (the majority in the saloon, restaurant, or grocery business), as well as a variety of other ethnic businesses.[3] For the rather limited population in the Heights, the number of Italian-run operations was substantial. Most of these merchants developed their businesses as ethnic enterprises where they drew upon Italian loyalties for a supply of cheap labor and a built-in ethnic market. These merchants were exemplars of the American Dream. They came from lowly backgrounds, but through a mixture of hope, ambition, and favorable social relations became cultural and economic leaders in the Italian community.

Along these lines, we find the star-crossed story of Giuseppe Pressendo. Giuseppe was an Italian immigrant who settled in Chicago Heights in 1904. By 1910, he had exhibited the drive and ambition to open up a saloon on the east side of Chicago Heights. As the *Chicago Heights Star* put it, Pressendo was "typical of the many who came to America and Chicago Heights to seek the benefits of a free enterprise situation."[4] He founded his own company and turned his skills as a stone mason into a career as a general contractor. He built a successful and thriving business and acquired various properties in the Heights because he exemplified the enterprise and promise of the American ethos and was "generally known as a man of strong character and sterling integrity."[5] Yet, he died suddenly in 1917 when he was involved in an automobile accident as he attempted to navigate the now inadequate and treacherous Chicago Heights roads built years previously for horses and buggies. Still, in a short period, Giuseppe had fulfilled the promise of the American Dream. After sixteen years as an Italian immigrant to America, he was able to bequeath to Elvira, his widow, assorted properties and a substantial sum of money. Elvira was a heartbroken but rich woman, at least in immigrant terms.

Most Chicago Heights Italians can be identified somewhere along this particular continuum of hope, specifically this variable commitment to an occupational striving and mobility. That is, there were those who planned to return to Italy after a few years with little allegiance to America; others stayed but were never fully dedicated to the culture of success and occupational advancement; and there were those immigrants who exemplified the most cherished values and hopes of the American Dream. Perhaps it is safe to argue that most Italian immigrants made investments in these hopes and material advancements but not with the verve of some ethnic entrepreneurs. They congregated with fellow Italians in the East Side or Hill areas and lived according to the time-honored communal practices of producing their own food, visiting among themselves, and caring for their family.[6] Mobility was valued, as was a larger paycheck. But in the traditional Italian perspective, loyalty and commitment to communal values and activities were prized the most.

Even so, to advance materially even in a limited sense meant that immigrants had to step outside these ethnic social spaces. Beyond peddling fruit, running a local barbershop, or organizing other ethnic businesses, the newcomer's livelihood and that of the family depended upon finding work in the surrounding factories, industrial plants, quarries, construction sites, and onion fields. Many of these jobs offered little beyond a minimum salary and brutal working conditions. As difficult as these jobs were, they nevertheless differentiated those immigrants who were more acceptable members of society from those who were not. To trudge to the factory every day, endure the foul smells and incessant clanging of machines, and return home with blackened faces and clothes culturally identified those immigrants thought to possess an allegiance to the American spirit of hard work and hope. Certainly, jobs provided economic capital, a day's pay to maintain the material necessities. But these arduous work environments also furnished the cultural capital that immigrants could spend to buy entrée into mainstream American society. Anthony Scariano who grew up in Chicago but worked most of his adult years in Chicago Heights said as much when he advised that the Italian immigrants "were socially disadvantaged and culturally deprived."[7] A steady job, ironically one that was all the more punishing, was a public statement on the part of immigrants that they were committed to the work ethic and spirit of "getting ahead" in America. It carried symbolic value regarding the more difficult-to-decipher internal drive and grit. And as such it would cut into the cultural deficit presumed to accompany an Italian heritage.

In this sense, the large number of official and company-sponsored photographs showing bedraggled workers outside factories or inside industrial sites, and often including both management and laborers, gave witness in cultural capital terms to this American Dream. The photographs, which were quite common, offered cleaned-up versions of life inside and outside the factory. They provided tangible evidence of immigrants hewing to the economic and cultural demands of American society and in their public distribution objectified hope and the quest for mobility. They were down-to-earth, culturally recognizable displays that materialized the appropriate cultural capital at work.

Figure 3.1. Workers Outside the American Manganese Steel Company, circa 1920s. Pictures of workers gathered together, often interspersed with management, were common at the beginning of the century. They materialized the values of American culture—specifically, hard work, hope, and mobility. *Source:* From the Chicago Heights Public Library, Special Collection, Pamphlet File.

By contrast, to not work or to not demonstrate a desire for legitimate employment would solidify the status of the immigrant as a dangerous undesirable alien. As detailed beforehand, when Italian socialists, with the assistance of the International Workers of the World, sought to organize a meeting in Chicago Heights in 1918, local officials and "loyal Italians" denigrated them as opposed to both freedom and the American values of striving and achievement. The I.W.W.'s initials were pejoratively relabeled as "I Won't Work." Working, even more so working hard, was at the core the American ethos. To be charged with an insufficient drive or motivation to work was a biting critique. It carried with it not only a political and economic evaluation of one's intentions, but lent once again to a characterization as a "hopeless alien."[8]

In a similar fashion, those Italians who pursued success through the nefarious channels of illegal gambling and organized crime were castigated as members of the "slot-machine trust" and viewed as constitutionally distinct and separated from the dominant ideologies of American society. Members of this trust were placed at the bottom rungs of the immigrant hierarchy. They were shadowy figures characterized as "alien conspirators" or well-dressed, cigar-chomping men who brought their unique brand of criminality and unsavory ways over from the old country. Beyond their problematic motives and modes of operation, they were thought to possess illegitimate hopes and mobility aspirations as "organized practioners [sic] of immorality."[9]

An initial step, therefore, toward gaining an acceptance in America meant securing a legitimate job, many of which were available in the expanding industrial town of Chicago Heights. Even so, the aim went beyond jobs themselves. While hard work revealed something intimate and personal about the individual, to fully embrace the American ideal, one was expected to harbor an enduring commitment to "getting ahead." Occupational mobility—to advance, for example, from a laborer, to a foreman, to a supervisor—was a much sought-after career path. For the blue-collar worker, it was a cultural as well as economic mark of distinction that separated the immigrant from others who were content to reside at the lower levels of the

Figure 3.2. The Chicago Heights Octopus: At the beginning of the last century, the octopus was a common image for something alien, malevolent, and insidious. Here, it has reference to the alien, criminal character of the East Side neighborhoods in Chicago Heights. *Source:* Public domain.

immigrant hierarchy. It brought forth social acceptance by reaffirming the popular theme that America was the land of opportunity and that personal history was not destiny.

Along these lines, Alberto Spina's story is illustrative. Spina was one of the widely acknowledged Italian leaders in early twentieth-century Chicago Heights. Spina came to Chicago Heights from Acquaviva Picena in the Italian region of Marche in 1907. The twenty-year-old, largely unskilled immigrant went to work, like so many before him, as a common laborer in the steel mills in Chicago Heights. And like so many others before him, he lived with his wife and children in the immigrant enclave on the East Side of the Heights. Eventually, Spina found work at the American Manganese Steel Company (AMSCO), one of the largest manufacturing plants located in the Heights. Over the years, Spina ascended to a white-collar position as a superintendent. This occupational mobility provided Spina with a higher salary. But culturally it also provided a more wide-ranging access and acceptance in the higher-status circles in the Chicago Heights community. Spina not only parlayed his economic success into leadership positions in the Italian community, but these occupational mobility gains created prestige currency that Spina could spend in the more dominant culture. These led to memberships in local country clubs, recognition of family celebrations in the society pages, status-enhancing charitable work, and successful careers for his children. In other words, occupational mobility produced more than a higher wage and a less physically taxing job: it also objectified success along a widespread social dimension. It facilitated an ascendance in the immigrant hierarchy as it increased the overall cultural capital Spina could draw upon to show an affinity for the common tastes and aspirations of those at the higher reaches in the community. It revealed in a recognizable manner that his underlying dispositions were similar to or at least overlapped with those who held positions of power in society. It purchased a measure of acceptance.

In this sense, occupational mobility is one tangible, real-world proof of success in the "market place of life," to use Max Weber's phrase. The "moral righteousness of wealth," unavailable to so many, was communized in the form of a hope for social advancement such that the detailed changes associated with this mobility—for example, different occupational titles, new association patterns, increases in salary, white-collar work clothes—could objectify and spread hope out in a more realizable, prosaic, and managed fashion.[10] These changes reverberated in a small community such as Chicago Heights. The rise up the social ladder by select individuals spilled out into the wider circle of family and friends and the community at large. These stories of success lent credence to the otherwise difficult-to-pin-down inner thoughts, wishes, and desires. As Pessen suggests, these outside manifestations "give substance to a general belief in the prevalence of social mobility."[11] They ground hope in a personal and collective sense.

Beyond these individual stories, the question remains as to the more general patterns of occupational mobility in Chicago Heights. To assess these patterns, Stephan Thernstrom's scale for dividing occupations in a hierarchical manner, developed for an occupational world at the beginning of the last century, is most useful.[12] This scheme provides a measuring rod and a proxy for social mobility, though like all scales reveals general patterns rather than idiosyncratic detail. With these limitations in mind, we examine the occupational standing for adult (fourteen years old and above), male, Italians (foreign born and foreign stock) in Chicago Heights in 1910, 1920, and 1930.[13]

Table 3.1. Occupational Ranking of Italian, Adult Males, Chicago Heights, 1900–1930 (in Percent)

	1910	1920*	1930
High white collar	1	1	6
Low white collar	4	9	10
Skilled	8	20	13
Semiskilled	5	14	13
Unskilled	82	56	58
Total	100	100	100
Number	(1,420)	(787)	(1,613)

Sources: Department of Commerce and Labor, Bureau of the Census, Thirteenth Census of the United States: 1910 Population, Chicago Heights manuscripts; Department of Commerce and Labor, Bureau of the Census, Fourteenth Census of the United States: 1920 Population, Chicago Heights manuscripts;* Department of Commerce, Bureau of the Census, Fifteenth Census of the United States: 1930 Population, Chicago Heights manuscripts.

*The number of individuals identified with a particular occupation in this census is significantly smaller than in the 1910 and 1930 censuses. In part this is due to a temporary decrease in the overall Chicago Heights and Italian population brought about by the Spanish Flu epidemic, World War I, and the industrial depression immediately following the war. In addition, the census itself failed to record the occupations of over three hundred adult Italian males living in Chicago Heights at this time. Presumably, this was due not only to the normal difficulties encountered in recording census information but also to the fact that many of these men were without steady employment due to the factors above. Also, the 1920 census was beset by an array of political calculations and fears of reapportionment as well as a new starting date for census takers in the middle of the year rather than during the summer months. Presumably, a number of Italians immigrants may have escaped the harsh winters in Chicago and returned to Italy during these early months.

Several findings are most relevant. First, in an unmistakable manner, these Italian immigrants were concentrated in the lowest occupational rankings. Throughout the period from 1910 to 1930, nearly 60 percent worked as unskilled laborers, with percentages much higher in 1910. They held jobs where even becoming a semiskilled servant, cook, or deliveryman was a *step up* in the occupational hierarchy. And these unskilled laboring positions were far removed from the more culturally favored, skilled, blue-collar occupations such as mechanic, tailor, and engineer.

It is difficult to know precisely how these immigrants looked upon these jobs, how they compared them to their life back in Italy, and how they came to decide (or not) that their promised hopes and aspirations were being fulfilled. Marie Iafollo said that her father, Celestino Iafollo, always told her "it is better here, here you have opportunity."[14] Having a job and receiving a paycheck may have been tangible embodiments of success, juxtaposed against the harsh realities of life in southern Italy. Frank Corradetti's father told him "it's a lot better here, living in this country than over there, 'cause over there they don't have too much.'"[15] Others like Dominic Pandolphi achieved a measure of success but returned to Italy because the continued pursuit of mobility and opportunity was not sufficient to outweigh the Italian way of life and family.

For most, however, the daily grind of factory life, the numerous bruises and crippled appendages, the unsanitary and foul working conditions played a part in dampening aspirations. In describing the plight of these workers in Chicago Heights, John Wozny concluded that "the factory laborer was just a serf in the fiefdom of industrialists. The factory owners had the power of practically life and death over the workers."[16] In a similar fashion, Vecoli characterizes the plight of these Italian factory workers in the Chicago Heights area as "industrial feudalism."[17] Umberto La Morticella portrays the circumstances at Inland Steel, the largest employer of Italian workers in the Heights, in even more concrete, degrading terms.

> I started at 6:30 pm and quit work at 6:00 pm in the morning. I worked on the straightening machines. It was 11.5 hours of deafening noise . . . One could not hear his partner talk unless the partner, who was only six feet away, spoke at the top of his voice. We were five men on the machine. Four men worked as one rested. Each man worked two hours and rested a half-hour. When I saw the bathroom, I was horrified. It took me several years to get the courage to use it.[18]

Second, though table 3.1 shows a solid 70 percent of the Italian immigrants located in the unskilled or semiskilled sectors, it also suggests an uneven but upward movement of Italians into higher-ranking occupations. By 1930 the percentage of Italians working in the skilled trades and lower white-collar positions demonstrated moderate growth. This was significant because it likely meant an increase in salary and a basis for grounding hope in the future.[19] However, since the local labor unions were not formidable in the early years, it is unlikely that this advance, as limited as it was, resulted in a substantial increase in wages. Thus, in 1922, factory workers at Inland Steel were forced to stage a wildcat strike for just a six-cent-an-hour raise. A 1927 study commissioned by the Chicago Heights Chamber of Commerce found that the typical factory worker in the Heights was paid between forty and forty-five cents per hour, with Italians generally less than even these minimums.[20] Frank Corradetti, a mill mechanic at Calumet Steel in the city, reports only a thirty-four-and-a-half cent hourly wage in 1934.[21]

In terms of these overall mobility patterns, then, Italians experienced moderate gains in occupational status through the beginning decades of the twentieth century.[22] The data suggests the development of a small, nascent white-collar, middle class among the Italian population, consisting primarily of professionals, building contractors, established merchants, lawyers, clerks, and salesmen. However, for most the occupational world was not a fertile ground for affirming and presenting a sense of hope. Most Italians remained at the lowest rung of the occupational ladder, and the jobs themselves were less than promising because the work conditions were demeaning and the pay barely above subsistence levels.

Yet, even these modest aggregate gains in mobility should be interpreted with caution. Though the changes in occupational status detailed in table 3.1 suggest a general improvement in the lives of the Italian immigrants, they may also mask significant demographic movements within this population. For example, the Italian immigrants who came subsequent to the initial influx of immigrants in 1910 may have been more skilled, better off in terms of socioeconomic backgrounds, and more entrepreneurial. If so, even the overall increases in occupational mobility detailed above may largely be a consequence of the increased human capital of these new immigrants over and above the occupational mobility of the Italian immigrants who had settled in Chicago Heights years earlier. As Samuel Baily suggests in his comparable study, we must be circumspect with this type of aggregate data, for "we have no way of knowing if the Italians at the beginning of the period were the same ones at the end."[23] In other words, were there just more D'Amicos, Pressendos, and Spinas in these second or third waves and therefore more Italians in higher-status jobs? The aggregate occupational mobility gains of Italians through the decades may not adequately reflect the actual individual movements of the Italians in Chicago Heights beginning in 1910.

At the same time, we are left with the question as to the extent of movement up, down, or not at all during the period from 1910 to 1930 and beyond. In most North American cities and for most immigrant groups, "climbers" outnumbered "skidders," or those who fell backward from non-manual to manual positions.[24] Still, the possibility for losing ground—for example, for the Italian grocer on the corner being replaced by the A&P market downtown and having to return to the low-skilled job at the factory—was ever present.[25] Such a decline or even the lack of any substantial occupational advancement would in all likelihood temper the motivations of the Italian immigrant to succeed.

To put this another way, most people do not make life-enhancing decisions or develop a sense of hope based upon the aggregate social facts or patterns. They do not typically decide, for example, a particular course of action because the sociological data indicate an objective regularity. As Bourdieu suggests in drawing upon Marx's analysis, this is to confuse "the things of logic from the logic of things."[26] Instead, people draw upon their practical sense of the situation, the available "sociological loci" for their life going forward.[27] Thus, with various degrees of clarity and "feel for the game," the Italian immigrants developed or discounted realistic pathways toward mobility based upon the more nuanced and idiosyncratic patterns characterizing their immediate environment. To be more exact, the perceived avenues for mobility and the accompanying hopes may develop quite differently, if there was no aggregate mobility because everyone stayed at the same occupational level through the decades—that is, a laborer stayed a laborer, a mechanic stayed a mechanic, and so on. In this case, hope would likely be diminished as the sociological loci would caution against expectations. On the other hand, an aggregate summary of no mobility may also result because the number of climbers equaled the number of skidders—that is, a laborer moved up to a superintendent, but a superintendent moved down to a laborer, and so on. In this case, hope may be cautiously embraced.

With these more subtle differences in mind, figure 3.3 begins to present this individual data and the conceivable "loci" for believing in hope. It begins with the occupational status for our sample of Italian immigrants in 1910 and follows each immigrant in a linked sample, the data permitting, in roughly ten-year increments—for 1920, 1930, and 1940.[28] It focuses on the unskilled and semiskilled workers because it was this population in a structural sense that had the greatest need for hope and potentially the greatest investment in occupational mobility. To provide a comparative context, we have included similar occupational trajectories for the adult, native-born males in Chicago Heights and the adult Polish male immigrants in the Heights—this last group, while significantly smaller, than the Italian population was nevertheless the second-largest immigrant class.

There are several relevant trends. First, the combined percentages of unskilled and semiskilled Italian workers in this linked sample, as one would expect, approximate those in table 3.1, which examined the total number

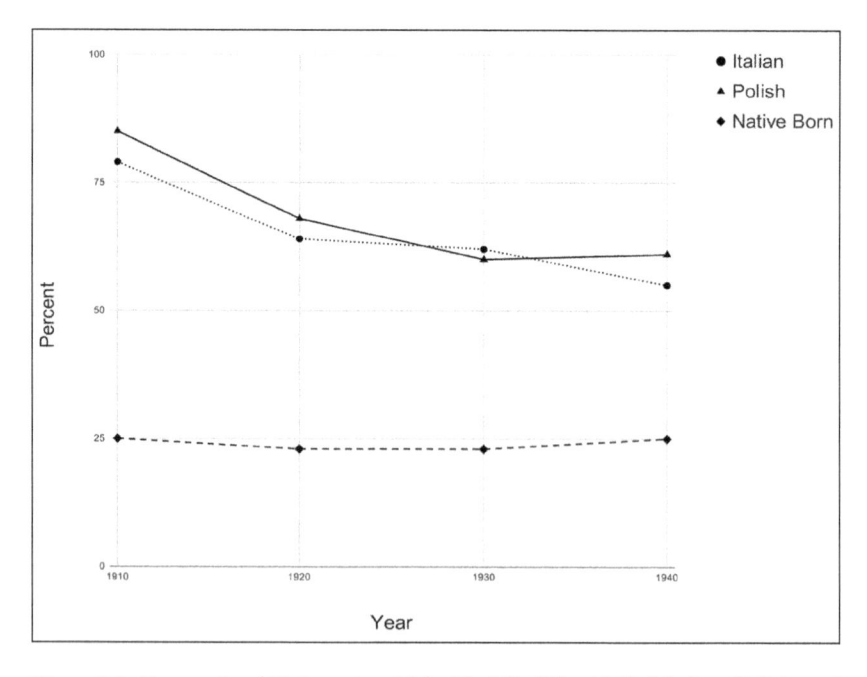

Figure 3.3. Occupational Trajectories, Male, Unskilled/Semiskilled Italian, Polish, and Native-Born Workers, 1910–1940. *Sources:* Department of Commerce and Labor, Bureau of the Census, Thirteenth Census of the United States: 1910 Population, Chicago Heights manuscripts; Department of Commerce and Labor, Bureau of the Census, Fourteenth Census of the United States: 1920 Population, Chicago Heights manuscripts; Department of Commerce, Bureau of the Census, Fifteenth Census of the United States: 1930 Population, Chicago Heights manuscripts; Department of Commerce, Bureau of the Census, Sixteenth Census of the United States: 1940 Population, Chicago Heights manuscripts.

of Italian immigrants. Second, the percentages of unskilled and semiskilled workers among the Italian population remained high through this thirty-year span. Though these numbers dropped in the immediate years after 1910, these movements plateaued or slowed precipitously in subsequent decades, exacerbated in part by the Great Depression. This suggests a continuous, structural need to invest in hope for many workers throughout this period. Third, the Italian and Polish residents had similar structural, if not always cultural, concerns as immigrants. By 1940, close to 60 percent of the original immigrants for both groups were at or near the bottom of the occupational structure. Finally, the gap between the native-born and Italian (and Polish) workers was substantial. Only 25 percent or so of the native born were in these low-ranking occupations through the decades. These native-born citizens certainly had hopes and aspirations. However, in a social-structural sense, the urgency and reliance upon hope were less pressing.[29]

These focused findings on unskilled and semiskilled laborers lead to a more direct examination of the overall mobility patterns for all types of workers (movements involving occupational changes at any level) in our linked sample. Table 3.2 summarizes these movements, as it again starts in 1910 and follows the individual mobility paths for Italians, Polish, and native-born residents of Chicago Heights.

These mobility patterns tell a slightly different story than table 3.1. No doubt, there is still a recognizable trend of upward occupational mobility for both the Italian and Polish immigrants. Close to or more than a third of each sample experienced an increase in occupational status (and presumably income and prestige) by 1920. These percentages of upward mobility were consistent through the next decade, and by 1940 nearly half the original 1910 immigrant population (respectively, 46 percent for Italians, 48 percent for Poles) had experienced what the *Chicago Heights Signal* had predicted previously—specifically, a "material advancement." These percentages compare favorably with the advances of the native-born sample, though as pointed out in figure 3.3 this population had fewer possibilities for climbing upward because in 1910 the percentage of native-born workers at the bottom of this occupational hierarchy was considerably less.

Taking a step back from this data, we could reasonably conclude that a sizeable number of Italian immigrants experienced an improvement in their occupational standing. Most, however, made relatively small jumps from one occupational category to the next. Since the vast majority of immigrants began as unskilled laborers, the movement upward generally consisted of advances into semiskilled occupations. For instance, a common laborer

Table 3.2a. Italian Occupational Mobility

	1910–1920	1910–1930	1910–1940
Upward	36	36	46
Stable	57	51	39
Downward	7	13	15
Total	100	100	100
Number	(559)	(476)	(310)

Table 3.2b. Polish Occupational Mobility

	1910–1920	1910–1930	1910–1940
Upward	32	37	48
Stable	58	51	42
Downward	10	12	10
Total	100	100	100
Number	(107)	(57)	(60)

Table 3.2c. Native-Born Occupational Mobility

	1910–1920	1910–1930	1910–1940
Upward	24	31	31
Stable	54	52	50
Downward	22	17	19
Total	100	100	100
Number	(702)	(450)	(341)

Sources: Department of Commerce and Labor, Bureau of the Census, Thirteenth Census of the United States: 1910 Population, Chicago Heights manuscripts; Department of Commerce and Labor, Bureau of the Census, Fourteenth Census of the United States: 1920 Population, Chicago Heights manuscripts; Department of Commerce, Bureau of the Census, Fifteenth Census of the United States: 1930 Population, Chicago Heights manuscripts; Department of Commerce, Bureau of the Census, Sixteenth Census of the United States: 1940 Population, Chicago Heights manuscripts. In addition, the identification of occupational status was aided and confirmed with a variety of other historical materials including marriage records, death notices, newspaper accounts, military records, and Social Security information.

was promoted to a roller or polisher in the factory. A few moved into the more skilled professions such as millwright or machinist. A very select few achieved lower white-collar positions such as foremen, clerks, or salesmen. And a handful followed the paths of D'Amico, Pressendo, Pandolfi, and others as manufacturers, bankers, and established merchants. In short, the hope for occupational mobility could be realized. Yet, for most, it needed to be sized down to more modest advances. Pete Monacelli, longtime resident of Chicago Heights, characterized this oftentimes uneasy relationship between the practical realities and lofty hopes of these Italian immigrants. He described them as men "who earned small wages" but nevertheless "nursed a big ambition."[30]

Though table 3.2 reveals the existence of "climbers" and several abbreviated paths to occupational mobility, it also indicates that a majority of Italian immigrants saw no appreciable change in occupational standing between 1910 and 1940, or that they were "skidders" and experienced a downward mobility. Time and again, a person who started out as a laborer in 1910 occupied that same ranking in 1920, 1930, and 1940. My grandfather, Luigi, may have been typical. His first job was as a coal miner in Ohio at the beginning of the century. Moving to Chicago Heights in 1906, he was recruited by a section boss and went to work on the railroad gangs out west in the Badlands, came back to the Heights and cut ice on Lake Michigan in the winter time, and then spent over twenty years in a railroad scrap yard breaking rails with a sledgehammer and blow torch. "Each day," Luigi used to say, "we would start with a mountain of rails so high you couldn't see the sun." Aside from working for the Chicago Outfit making moonshine in a nearby garage, at least until he was caught and sent to prison, Luigi's occupational career involved a steady stream of low-end jobs in which mobility was highly unlikely.

The lack of substantial mobility in the lives of so many workers could be attributed to a range of personal characteristics. Yet, it may well have been that occupational success was largely outside the immediate control of the immigrant. One could not simply create mobility by hard work or hope alone. Specifically, the structure of both the external and internal economic market had pronounced effects. With respect to the former, many Italian immigrants achieved a measure of success because of the processes of ethnic entrepreneurship—including corner stores, barber shops, taverns, restaurants, pool halls, and tailors. However, as Aldrich and Waldinger argue, "Business conditions in the ethnic market tend toward proliferation of small units, intense competition, and a high failure rate, with the surviving businesses generating scanty returns for their owners."[31] This seems to have been the case in Chicago Heights, for as the ethnic enclave developed the competition not only from fellow Italians but also from the Polish, Lithuanian, and Jewish entrepreneurs divided the market on nearly a street-by-street basis. And the plight of these entrepreneurs was exasperated further with the introduction of chain stores in the late 1920s and 1930s. This impacted the grocery business most dramatically, for in a short period the A&P, the National Tea Company, the Jewel Food Store, and a chain of Super-Service stores drove many of the Italian-run local markets (e.g., the East Side Grocery and Meat Market, Salvatore's, the A.D. Farina & Company) out of business and sent many of the proprietors back to work in the factory.

These external market challenges to occupational mobility were compounded by an unfavorable internal market structure. The majority of Italian workers were employed in large manufacturing firms such as Inland Steel, the National Brick Company, Calumet Steel, and the American Manganese Steel Company. As Catron's study of immigrant mobility in the nearby Pullman factory reveals, the internal labor market in such firms often worked against the employment and promotion aims for specific groups, especially the Italians. The hoarding of opportunities by different racial and ethnic groups, the differential access to job training, and the informal associations within these large firms kept many immigrants in "positions at the bottom of the occupational hierarchy."[32] As Umberto La Morticella commented, "The Inland Steel bosses were great practitioners of nepotism."[33] John Wozny reported that the hiring practices in the Heights were also stacked against the Italian and Polish workers. These workers entered the workforce decades after the first wave of German and Irish immigrants who were generally promoted to the more preferred jobs. "Factories always liked to hire people from the same family." In so doing, the factory could demand "company loyalty" because so many family members found work at the site."[34]

The hope for occupational mobility, therefore, was a realistic goal but hardly a universal achievement. Though the change in working conditions from a common laborer to a foreman was possible, objectified literally in terms of a transformation from a blue collar to a white collar, it was quite uncommon. Hap Bruno, Chicago Heights resident, said this ascent up in occupation was painfully slow. "It took a long time."[35] As Vincent Parrillo concluded more generally, "Upward mobility occurred more slowly for the Italians than for many other groups arriving in the United States at about the same time."[36] Most immigrants did not personally experience this movement.

Indeed, some fell backward, especially as the Great Depression caused many factories in the Heights to close or reduce the number of workers. All the same, hope and the quest for occupational mobility remained. Why was this so when most immigrants were confronted by a reality quite differently?

The Dialectics of Occupational Mobility and Hope

Hope is often described as the starting point for social mobility, for it supplies the positive mental state, energy, agency, and purpose. Economic historian Richard Sutch seems to suggest something along these lines when he posits that "immigration selects for the ambitious and hard working."[37] The core, organizing premise of the study here is that ceding this transformative power to hope, especially to immigrants, carries with it several uncertain ideological assumptions. Thus, it falsely divides the would-be immigrants from those who in fact leave their home country based upon this presumed surplus of mental energy or hope—the hopeful from the hopeless. And at a most basic level, it depicts these newcomers in passive terms. The complex and mature decisions immigrants and their families make on this harrowing journey are relegated to a mysterious, mechanistic process lying deep within the individual psyche.

On the contrary, the main point here is that hope is a practice, a common sense for logic for dealing with the inherent uncertainties posed by the ordinary challenges of the immigration process itself. In practical terms, this formulation of hope is a product not a precursor of immigration. That is, drawing upon their experiences as immigrants—the shipping agents, the challenging steamship voyage, Ellis Island processing, the general context of reception, and labor hiring processes—Italian newcomers developed a conception of hope and mobility aspirations as a cultural resource. Immigrants acquired a sense, unlike that found in the traditional systems in Italy, that mobility aspirations were a form of currency. Specifically, the hope for occupational advancement was a cultural signifier in the high-stakes game of social acceptance. The public commitment to these aspirations allowed immigrants to move up the immigrant hierarchy if not out of this social space altogether, and it differentiated the Italians from the rougher alien newcomers—the "foreign element," or lower ends of this hierarchy.[38] Indeed, even if this mobility was not forthcoming, as we have found broadly to be the case, this public quest demonstrated an allegiance to the practical faith of striving, betterment, and personal success. It gave evidence that one was willing to play the game and as such produced dividends in terms of recognition.

This was in contrast to many in the Black and Latino community. Because Italians were identified as white, they were accorded the benefit of the doubt regarding their intentions and dispositions. Blacks and Latinos were not afforded this privilege. In essence, they were not allowed, with few exceptions, to play the game and use hope as a cultural resource. As Dyer suggests, historical classifications of whiteness often carried a presumption of "spirit" or "enterprise" such that a "white spirit organizes white flesh" into an "exhilaratingly expansive relationship to the environment."[39] This capacity, or spirit for hope, therefore, further divided people along racial and ethnic lines—divided them more insidiously in an essentialist manner. Lacking this "white spirit" by definition, Blacks and Latinos, were historically in the Chicago Heights context deprived of this critical cultural resource for purchasing an acceptance in the society.

Hope and advancement, therefore, were persistent themes in the social spaces of immigration—cultural capital resources one could only ignore at a cost. These themes were driven by the fundamental and defining character of the American value system. There were also subsystems at work promoting this cultural link between hopes, occupational mobility, and an American identity. Thus, given the unfavorable working conditions and subsistence wages, workers were almost always on the verge of quitting or (in a more threatening manner) organizing. As suggested, the early years saw various socialist initiatives. Fears of a communist uprising and a growing "Red Scare" surfaced in a number of cities, especially in the postwar era.[40] In this context, a contingent of industrial and manufacturing leaders, primarily the Chicago Heights Manufacturing Association, were determined to produce workers who were motivated, compliant, and reticent to engage in union activities.[41] Indeed, these were major reasons that these industrialists moved to the far reaches of the Chicago suburbs, away from the more intense labor unrest in Chicago.[42]

These factory owners and managers pursued a number of strategies. When negotiations with workers broke down, some manufacturers were not averse to hiring strike breakers or calling for martial law to confront the protesting laborers.[43] Others refused to hire union workers. And when the "wobblies," a splinter organization of the IWW, formed in Chicago Heights, a group of some forty manufacturing firms joined together to subvert the union efforts, as this organization was deemed a "nemesis to the factory owners."[44] Besides this use of force and intimidation, these industrialists, with at times benevolent intentions, also sought to manage employees by refiguring hope along the lines of occupational advancement. An uncertain and potentially threatening workforce could be governed by promoting a transfer of hope from their moorings in the traditional but volatile ethnic associations to the more tractable occupational career paths put forth by these industrial concerns.

In broader terms, the management of these aspirations became a "control strategy."[45] Cohen argues that the 1920s saw a dramatic shift in the supervision of workers such that efforts to drive employees by means of the "iron fist" were gradually replaced by tactics focused upon supervision as a "psychological problem."[46] By providing pension plans, a wage incentive system, and most importantly, an opportunity for promotion, owners and managers not only changed the patterns of association of their workers but also changed the rules of the game by restructuring ambition and hope in a more dispositional but also corporate manner. Employers, Cohen suggested, endorsed the ideas of wage incentives and job ladders for a number of reasons, but chief among them was "they hoped that the opportunity to earn more money and enjoy job security would discipline workers."[47] Following this new human relations approach, the Chicago Heights Manufacturing Association called for the establishment of "pleasant relations" and "intelligent labor policies." These were policies aimed at co-opting the emotions of workers.[48] These new sentiment-based approaches sought to engage workers on a more personal level. As one national specialist in human relations stated bluntly, the creation of internal job ladders for promotion ensured that "the hope of better things tomorrow [will] take their minds off the difficulties today."[49]

For most immigrant families, the game of occupational mobility was largely unavoidable. The stakes of winning or losing were exceedingly high. Even in the face of sorrows, sacrifices, and few mobility gains, a public commitment to the ethos of getting ahead—as distinct from resignation or dissent—brought favorable evaluations and recognition. For some, personal hopes and societal expectations were nearly one and the same. For others, the game was more transparent. They were aware that the industrial leaders in large part set the rules for success in their favor. Thus, Hap Bruno, Chicago Heights resident, called them "economic royalists" and spoke of the "crooked" chances of mobility. These "are discussed pretty widely among our people. You have diverse opinions. Of course everyone feels that the guy that signed your pay check is making a hell of a lot of money." Still, Bruno held that striving for success, even when the larger structures are deceitful, is necessary. "I still feel that you don't have to be crooked, you don't have to be crooked, you never have to."[50]

Frank Corradetti, a longtime Chicago Heights resident, best captures the often ambiguous response to occupational mobility—a commitment but also distaste for a life devoted to these hopes. Corradetti worked at Calumet Steel in Chicago Heights for over forty-four years. Along the way, he progressed from a common laborer, to a shearer, to a mill mechanic. With each step, Corradetti boosted his position and salary. As Corradetti, suggests, "I worked there a long time, but starting from the time I got a job there, but I always went up the ladder. Up to the time I retired, I had, like I say, a top job."[51] Despite this success, Corradetti also expressed a sense of dissatisfaction and uneasiness about his choices—the "cruel optimism" in Berlant's terms. He speaks about how he had to adapt—physically, emotionally, and mentally—to the routines of factory work; how hopes had to be downsized in the face of the blast furnace, the daily grind of the monotonous schedule, and the acceptance of the bargain he had made with himself. In the service of achieving "an advancement . . . a better paying job," he "stuck it out." "There were times when I use to get so damned mad, I wanted to. . . . But then I'd stop and think. I'd say, well look, I have all these damned years in. Where the hell, where would I go?"

Corradetti pursued and even achieved an occupational mobility, but it was not the life he had hoped to live—a painful reckoning that his investment in hope had produced what Berlant described generally as an "incoherent mash."[52] In immigrant terms, he was indeed a success, but this success was unsettling. Following the approved pathways had brought acceptance and progression up the immigrant hierarchy but was *alienating* in a new, dispositional fashion.

Conclusion

The hopes for and journeys toward an occupational mobility colored the experience of the Italian immigrants in Chicago Heights. Climbing this ladder of success promoted a movement up and beyond the immigrant social hierarchy. In the American context, sustained laboring toward this betterment was a core feature and distinguishing element of what it meant to be an American.

The cultural significance of this hoped-for mobility was not lost on these Italian immigrants. Despite the hardships and, for many, the lack of any substantial occupational mobility in their lifetimes, immigrants espoused the virtues of these mobility aspirations. They were forms of cultural currency for buying an acceptance in the society. No doubt, there were transaction costs for these purchases. Immigrants were led to give up traditional ethnic values and cede a measure of control and hope to outside industrial and management interests. This was a compromise some embraced wholeheartedly, others cautiously and critically, and still others hesitatingly and regretfully.

Chapter 4

Purchasing an Acceptance in American Society
Homeownership as Cultural Capital

Many Italian immigrants placed their hopes for assimilation on a factory job and the prospects for advancement. It was a reasonable strategy because it provided a steady paycheck and mobility for a significant segment of the population. Nevertheless, it took its toll. Physical injuries and ailments together with a mental resignation or downsizing of the "big ambition(s)" seemed to be the lot of many who toiled for years in these uninviting work environments. At the same time, the ability to manufacture hope going forward was largely outside the control of the worker. Periods of unemployment, the uncertain and parochial paths to promotion, and the ongoing conflicts over wage increases undermined the belief that talent finds a "sure reward."

Under these circumstances, a more foundational and achievable path to acceptance was available. The purchase of a home, besides its more recognizable use value, had significant cultural exchange value. Others have argued with considerable insight that immigrant homeownership served as a "surrogate" for limited occupational gains.[1] It provided long-range financial security, protection against the rollercoaster economy, and social standing in the larger society. Building upon these insights, we argue that owning a house also served as a mark of distinction regarding the type of person the immigrant claimed to be. It was aimed, however unintentionally, at drawing nearer to and gaining acceptance from the dominant groups in society. But at the same time, and as a move to gain acceptance from these cultural gatekeepers, homeownership separated the owner from those who occupied the lower ranks of the immigrant hierarchy. It was a strategy that drew a distinction between the home-buying immigrant and those other newcomers whose personal ambitions and hopes were less valued because they were more alien, unrooted, or political. Homeownership was a game played at multiple levels and directions at once.

Within the immigrant field, therefore, the attempt to buy a home was a matter of taste—a process of differentiation and appreciation that in Bourdieu's understanding imposed a recognition. This taste for property differentiated the acceptable immigrant from the more stereotyped, more disparaged "bird of passage" who came to America first and foremost to make money and then return to Italy. As the Dillingham commission concluded, "The owning of a home does not necessarily indicate a high economic condition of a family . . . but the *intention* [emphasis added] on the part of the family of remaining permanently in their present location."[2] At the same time, owning property was a step up from being a renter and a step closer to being an American. The immigrant became a "better citizen" through homeownership, for homeowners were typically viewed as more resourceful, superior, and hopeful. As Edith Abbott suggested, ownership on the part of Chicago-area immigrants "was not synonymous with prosperity," but it signified "rather the effort [emphasis added] to secure property and future welfare at the cost of present health, comfort, and decent living."[3] And in an era of sociopolitical upheaval, growing anti-immigrant sentiment, and labor protests, homeownership sanctioned hopes of self-sufficiency, independence, and individualism against the more feared "pull of collective obligations" and social movements.[4] Though homeownership and an unshakable commitment to the social order did not always coincide, still, as Thernstrom argued, "possession of property is an important determinant of . . . social position and social allegiances," and it served to separate the immigrant class based upon "the rational pursuit" of success versus "*helpless* drifting [emphasis added]."[5]

Homeownership as "The Will to Possess"

As the *Chicago Heights Star* stated, "Chicago Heights didn't get to be an industrial city by accident."[6] It was helped along in this process by the entrepreneurial activities of a group of investors, real estate brokers, and manufacturers. These men formed the Chicago Heights Land Association in 1891 and with the assistance of local officials began the highly speculative task of land acquisition and town development, primarily on the eastern

Homeownership as Cultural Capital | 89

edge of what was then called Bloom Village. These investors spent a considerable amount of time attracting industrial facilities to the area through a series of promotions and inducements such as free water, free bricks, and favorable railroad transfer rates.[7]

FREE EXCURSION,

Sunday, May 7,

—— TO ——

CHICAGO HEIGHTS

TRAINS LEAVE

Polk-st. Depot

AT 1 P. M.,

STOPPING AT

Archer-av., 55th-st., 63d-st., 68th-st., and Kensington.

Call at our office for free tickets.

CHICAGO HEIGHTS LAND ASSOCIATION,

MAIN FLOOR
CHAMBER OF COMMERCE BUILDING.

Figure 4.1. The Chicago Heights Land Association promoted the benefits of living in and establishing industrial plants in the city as early as 1893. The sales pitch was anything but subtle, "Chicago Heights: The Men, The Land, The Money." *Source:* Advertisement Chicago Daily Tribune, May 7, 1893, 30. Public domain.

These efforts were so successful that one industry after another either moved their operations to the city or selected the city for their initial start-up location. As early as 1892, the *Chicago Daily Tribune* could report that "Chicago Heights will soon occupy a prominent place among the leading manufacturing cities in America."[8]

Perhaps most appealing was that the Land Association created a developmental plan whereby the area east of the Chicago and Eastern Illinois railroad tracks (the "East Side") would be divided into a mixed-use land pattern of industrial sites and some four thousand residential lots. In one week alone, 113 properties were purchased by prospective industries and home buyers.[9] The West Side was spared these industrial facilities, as the more prosperous citizens preferred not to be inundated with the "objectionable features" that accompanied the chemical plants, railroad switching yards, steel mills, and other heavy industries. Perhaps more telling, they also wished to separate themselves from the "slothfulness in the poorer half of town."[10] As Goodspeed and Healy's *History of Cook County* states, "The policy of the land association has been to keep the factory district segregated from the residential part of the town . . . the wooded and picturesque ravines and natural, beautiful scenery."[11]

Goodspeed and Healy's observations notwithstanding, the "residential part of town" also included the lots and houses designed for the East Side and Hill industrial workers. Thus, intermingled among the factories and railroad tracks, a variety of wood-framed, front-street-facing, narrow-side gangway, one- and two-story houses (often with an unfinished attic to accommodate borders) were erected. The combination of being within walking distance from most factory sites, a strong preference to live alongside coethnics, and the desire of West Side residents not to have immigrants move into their neighborhoods made this area the primary residential location for the Italian but also Polish, Hungarian, Lithuanian, Slovakian, Mexican, and Black newcomers. As such, we witnessed the creation of immigrant-rich, ethnic enclaves—for example, Twenty-Second Street in the Hill section of the Heights was dubbed "Macaroni Boulevard" because Italians dominated the shops and residential blocks in the area. Figure 4.2 shows the character of the East Side neighborhood during the 1930s.

In the earliest years, few Italian immigrants were bent upon homeownership in these East Side districts. Many were single men who had left their families to first gain a foothold in America, or sojourners intent on returning to Italy in the immediate future. As such, the desire to own a home was neither a short- or long-term strategy. Table 4.1 suggests this as the

Figure 4.2. Chicago Heights East Side Street. *Source:* Courtesy: Casa Italia, Italian Cultural Center; Stone Park, Illinois.

Table 4.1. Homeownership among Italians: Chicago Heights, Chicago, Illinois, and the United States, 1900—1930 (in Percent)

	1900	1910	1920	1930
Chicago Heights Italian Households	20.8	42.2	55.4	63.2
Chicago Italian Households	5.3	—	—	39.5
Illinois Households	45.0	44.1	43.8	46.5
United States Households	46.5	45.9	45.6	47.8

Source: The data for Chicago Heights Italian Households come from an analysis of the Chicago Heights manuscripts in the Department of Commerce and Labor, Bureau of the Census, Twelfth Census of the United States: 1900 Population; Thirteenth Census of the United States: 1910 Population; Fourteenth Census of the United States, 1920 Population; Fifteenth Census of the United States: 1930 Population. The data for Chicago Italian Households, 1900, is derived from the Department of Commerce and Labor, Bureau of the Census, Twelfth Census of the United States: 1900, Volume II, Population. Table 115, White Persons Owning and Hiring Their Homes, Distributed according to Parentage, fFor Cities Having 100,000 Inhabitants or more: 1900. The data for Chicago Italian Households, 1930, come from the Department of Commerce, Fifteenth Census of the United States: 1930 Population, Table 20, Special Report on Foreign Born White Families by Country of Birth of Head, 1933. These percentages may underestimate the number of Italian homeowners to a limited extent for it focuses upon "foreign born" Italians and excludes those presumably younger Italians born in the United States. The data for Illinois Households and the United States Households come from the Historical Census of Housing Tables: Homeownership, Homeownership Rates, 2000, (accessed May 20, 2021), https://www.census.gov/data/tables/time-series/dec/coh-owner.html.

rates of homeownership in 1900 were predictably low, especially compared to those of the state and the nation. However, there was a substantial shift from renting to purchasing a home through the decades. For those Italian immigrants who stayed on in America, for many of their children, and for the new immigrants who arrived in subsequent decades, homeownership far surpassed the state and national rates.

This dive into owning a home, or as Doucet and Weaver put it "the will to possess," was a consequence of a competing set of interests.[12] Sutch's review of immigrant housing during this age of mass migration identifies at least four of these interests—a precautionary motive, a bequest motive, an entrepreneurial motive, and a life-cycle motive.[13] Thus, owning a home provided considerable flexibility as a hedge against irregular employment, illness, and death. At the same time, a home was an insurance policy for old age, a place where one could live after no longer earning an income, and it was a form of wealth that could be handed down to children. Homeownership was also a potential source of revenue, for a home provided the flexibility to take in boarders depending upon the need for additional income.[14] Finally, homes provided the opportunity to "double or triple up" with relatives and to save on rent as these relatives anticipated purchasing a home in the future.

Yet, these interests needed to be balanced out against the extreme risks and challenges of homeownership. The economic disadvantages of owning a home were substantial. Thus, the average hourly rate for workers in the skilled building trades (e.g., bricklayers, steamfitters, plumbers) in the 1920s and 1930s was upward of $1.75. As suggested, there were few Italian immigrants who held these positions, as most were common laborers in manufacturing. For those who found steady employment in these nearby factories, the hourly pay rate was between forty and fifty-five cents per hour. The gross yearly wage for all Chicago Heights wage-earners employed in industrial jobs in 1929 averaged $1,557.[15] The Italian immigrant was typically paid at a lower rate, and, as a result, those who worked on average fifty hours per week had a yearly wage of around $1,200. The price for purchasing a house on the East Side or Hill area of the Heights during this time ranged from $2,000 to $5,500, with most houses around $4,000. Housing affordability, especially given the irregular patterns of employment, was, thus, an ongoing concern.

To circumvent these challenges, banks and money lenders offered mortgages and monthly installments. During the 1920s, a segment of the Italian population took advantage of these economic opportunities. For example, Luigi and Josephina Corsino secured a loan from the Citizens Building and Loan Association of Chicago Heights and paid $25 a month on a monthly net income of around $70. This required considerable sacrifice on Luigi's part and an added burden to Josephina, who out of economic necessity took on additional boarders. Even then, the very concept of a mortgage and monthly payments on interest were new concepts that many immigrants found difficult to grasp. "I tried to explain it to my father a number of times," Nick Digiovanni said. "He would shake his head, but I was never certain that he understood what it meant."[16]

The Depression of the 1930s dealt a more systemic challenge to homeownership. Thus at the beginning of this decade, city officials and the Chicago Heights business community, including the two major banks, suspended most all transactions for a period of weeks. Except for essential services, the doors of these establishments were to remain closed "as a means of restoring business confidence in the community."[17] Again, the concept of a "bank holiday" and the realistic prospect that a bank could fail and people lose their homes were difficult ideas to comprehend or worse confirmed suspicions regarding the "crooked" or rapacious character of money lenders. Genevieve Ford Reed, one of the first Black residents in Chicago Heights, said "then the Depression came in 1929. All the banks closed. The factories closed. No one had anything."[18] Immigrants could turn to the ethnic building and loan associations in the area, but these were also problematic because they were generally undercapitalized and not always sympathetic to the financial situations of their clients. For example, Theresa Giannetti was quite critical of one Italian lender. "We called (him) the villain. He was the mortgage lender . . . a loan shark. He would foreclose on people."[19]

Along with these financial considerations, purchasing a new home was confounded by housing shortages and processes of residential segregation. Thus, as the Depression took hold, the *Chicago Heights Star* advocated for new home construction, as the available housing stock on the city's East Side was rapidly becoming "inadequate, improper, and unsanitary."[20] There was housing growth in the city; however, the majority of new construction took place on the west side of the Heights, specifically west of the CE&I railroad tracks. During this era, and for African Americans during much of the twentieth century, Italians were excluded from homeownership on this side of the city. In 1930, over 88 percent of the Italian residents were residentially located in the East Side and Hill areas. The index of residential dissimilarity (a measurement of residential segregation) was .775, with indices above .600 generally considered evidence of high segregation. These patterns may reflect the preferences of Italian immigrants—both in terms of the proximity to work in the factories and the communal desires to live with fellow Italians. But they also signal the financial and social challenges to homeownership. As Hap Bruno said, "If you moved somewhere, my God, they were afraid of you. They didn't know what the hell kind of person you were."[21]

Homeownership, or the "will to possess," therefore, was not a foregone decision. It was undertaken despite economic and social concerns. It required a leap of faith, a commitment of scant resources. In the period from 1910 to 1930, many immigrants made this leap. However, as industrial production declined dramatically in Chicago Heights, the wisdom of homeownership was put on hold. As Cohen points out, the dynamics of the economy during the Depression era were so volatile that "all the things that seemed wise in the twenties, like buying a home, keeping up fraternal insurance, and saving at the neighborhood bank and building and loan association, only caused trouble in the thirties."[22]

As these complex economic and social processes intruded upon the lives of the Italian immigrants, the strong desire for homeownership seems less likely a consequence of economic factors alone—that is, a bequest motive, an entrepreneurial motive, and the like. Nor does it seem reasonable to tie these home purchasing decisions to the "foggy realm of psychological drives,"[23] or the "wish of former peasants to possess."[24] These drives and wishes need to be contextualized more fully within the swirling social and cultural currents characterizing the immigration field. Specifically, the value of homeownership as a cultural currency and as a marker of "acquisitive hope" needs to be understood.

Homeownership as "The Center of Sunshine and Scenery"

We have pointed to the social and cultural struggles of the Italian peasants both in Italy and in America. However, the decades of the 1920s and 1930s were especially harsh. The mass migration of Italians to America and their supposed "slough-like" living conditions confirmed what many believed to be the inevitable outcomes of this inferior class of people—poverty, sinfulness, and criminality. There emerged an increasingly vitriolic and structured opposition to outsiders. As Handlin concluded in general terms, "The fear of everything alien instilled by the First World War brought to fullest flower the seeds of racist thinking."[25] Thus, it was during these times that the rise of nativism—which spawned the eugenic movement, the Ku Klux Klan, and restrictive quotas on immigration—became an entrenched social control approach in the spaces of immigration.

Under these circumstances, the suitability and loyalty of immigrants to the American culture and society were being questioned anew. As Vincent Cannato suggests, though most Americans did not commit themselves to this "jaundiced interpretive lens of nativististic sentiments," nevertheless a "heated, loud, and nasty" debate took place over who could become an American.[26] The *Chicago Tribune*, led by xenophobic owner Robert McCormick, editorialized that the gates of immigration should remain closed as a means to bar those populations "foreign in modes of thought and in standards to our own." The "future of the American Dream" should not be undermined by "cheap labor" but should rest upon the "economic superiority of intelligence and character."[27] Suspicions and doubts were increasingly directed toward Italian immigrants, especially in light of their association with the exotic tales of organized crime and their unique rituals of Catholicism. Sarah Churchwell contends this was a time when "the question of how to judge the 'worth' of immigrant communities and ethnic minorities continued to gain urgency."[28]

In Chicago Heights, the debate was more muted. Nevertheless, in 1924 charges were put forth, though denied, that the "Better Government" party was a "Ku Klux Klan affair."[29] There were other accounts of Ku Klux Klan meetings and local Klan chapters in the suburbs surrounding Chicago.[30] Specifically, the *Chicago Heights Star* reported on a Klan event just a few blocks from downtown Chicago Heights in 1924. According to the account, this three-day gathering was disrupted most likely by Italian immigrants who set fire to the "Klantauqua" tent.[31] The Klan also took out several ads in the *Chicago Heights Star* with mysterious warnings that followers should "Go to Church on Sundays."[32] Other editorials warned against "letting down the bars of immigration" and argued in favor of immigration quotas that "have seemed soundly American."[33] A front-page cartoon in the *Star* warned against making America a "Dumping Ground" for undesirables from other countries.[34] The undercurrents of an "American First" mentality and an undiluted American spirit of hope and progress were joined. In this context, Italian immigrants in search of cultural acceptance and personal standing sought firm ground for demonstrating both in a publicly recognizable manner.

Many immigrants found this terra firma by pursuing homeownership. Owning a home, indeed owning the right type of home, was a personal sign of independence and citizenship and as such carried with it a strong moralistic bent. Gwendolyn Wright's history of housing and cultural conflict in Chicago at the turn of the last century suggests it was "the *idea* (italics in original) of the America home, as well as the physical object of shelter" that was an essential part of the American Dream.[35] Indeed, to many middle-class reformers, the appeal of socialism and the critiques of capitalism expressed by ethnic immigrants could be assuaged with "a proper model for suburban housing."[36] Homeownership, along with advances in household technologies, fueled the hope for freedom and progress. Henry Demarest Lloyd, offering a sharp contrast to the more dark and depressing factory environments, celebrated the benefits of owning one's own home, "where every house will be the center of sunshine and scenery."[37]

Renters or hirers, on the other hand, were commonly thought of as shifty, a bit unrespectable, and at worst, allied with the more radical elements of society. Along these lines, the *National Real Estate Journal* could write, "It is safe to predict that 'the homeowner' will never be found in the socialist ranks."[38] In the eyes of many, multiple-family housing was closely associated with transience. As one critic argued, "The dangerous classes are nomadic."[39] Apartment houses with their shared spaces encouraged "promiscuous sexuality, female rebelliousness, communistic sentiments."[40] The ravages of communism in Europe, argued one Chicago Heights citizen, resulted from the inability of citizens to own their own property. In such countries, a renter is a "wanderer" without an abiding interest in the community. On the other hand, a person who owns a home sees "nothing is to be gained through violence on others in the possessor-class." Such an individual does not present himself as a "moral hazard."[41]

These concerns regarding "communistic sentiments" and "moral hazards" increasingly made their way into the public discussion involving immigrants. As the Bolshevik Revolution and the rise of the Soviet Union began to take shape, these faraway political upheavals reverberated back to the American Dream. The core ideas of individualism and social mobility, especially in light of the uncertainty regarding the immigrants' commitment to both, found more vociferous expression in public discourse. For instance, Gwendolyn Wright reports, the *Ladies Home Journal* warned against the Bolshevik influence such that women who lived in apartments were more likely to be swayed by these communist thoughts.[42]

In Chicago Heights, numerous articles, sermons, and discussions strongly advised against the "blind, elemental passion" of Bolshevism.[43] At the core of this critique was the "attack on property" and the concern to not "to let the serpent of socialism creep in."[44] Warning against this growing specter of communism, one speaker in the Chicago Heights area was warmly welcomed when he spoke on the merits of "true Americanism" and when he cautioned that the native-born citizen was being overtaken by aliens and consequently in "danger of losing his home and his government."[45] Other concerns regarding socialism surfaced—the antireligious stance, the problems of a planned economy, and the government incursion into schooling. The main critique, however, was reserved for the right to own one's own home or business. Hewing to a socialist or communist economy would be a strike against the ideology of Americanism. "When they have succeeded in destroying 'property rights,'" the *Star* warned, "they have destroyed the hope of the people . . . every vestige of the promise for a brighter future."[46] Stated in more direct terms, the *Star* editorialized, "The home-owner and home merchant are the hope of Chicago Heights."[47]

Reading these cultural scripts, many immigrants could not help but see the importance of homeownership in terms of the cultural capital it would confer in their twin pursuits of Americanism and social mobility. As Garb suggests in her analysis of Chicago at the turn of the last century, "Immigrant workers, of course, continued to seek home ownership both within the city's boundaries and in suburban areas. Seeing homeownership as a mark of autonomy in a labor system in which steady work was unreliable and factory labor was disconnected from pride in skill, many workers purchased housing as a means of asserting an American identity and acceptability."[48] Garb was correct to point to the importance of home ownership as both a "concrete object and an idea."[49] And she was also correct to assert that the idea of homeownership permeated both Chicago and the surrounding suburbs alike. But for Italian immigrants, this attachment to homeowning took hold more firmly in Chicago Heights than in Chicago as a whole. As table 4.1 suggests, homeownership rates among Italians in Chicago Heights outpaced those in Chicago well into the century. One Chicago Heights observer wrote, "The business of renting habituations to others, which has been largely developed in big cities, has happily not spread to communities the size of ours."[50] Again, economic considerations may have played an important role. High land prices and the presence of multistory tenement housing in Chicago made home ownership a less viable option. At the same time, landowners in Chicago had strong incentives to discourage homeownership: as renting, especially in large tenement-style buildings, was a very profitable business.[51]

The differences between Italians in Chicago and Chicago Heights may also have cultural roots. As a "concrete object" the houses available to Italians in Chicago would provide less objectified cultural capital. By and large, they were located in unattractive, congested neighborhoods. For example, one commentator described Little Italy in 1915 as "a region of unpaved streets and filthy alleys of flimsy wooden dwellings and dilapidated sheds."[52] Though conditions improved through the decades, the physical character of the neighborhood and the alley houses was generally deplorable. Chicago Heights was a different place. As a prime example of a suburban "satellite city," the Heights had newer housing stock with more modern amenities such as central heating, plumbing, and electricity and even decorative design. Though still jerry-built and maintained, these houses stood in contrast to "the brick and motor waste" that was often associated with the distressed industrial and residential areas of Chicago.[53] In Chicago, therefore, the image of tenement housing came to be inexplicably interwoven with the life of immigrants, with the negative stereotypes, and with the places that Josiah Strong labeled the "tainted spots in the body-politic."[54] By contrast, the image of the private, single-family home, more common in Chicago Heights, came to be "considered the primary symbol of American cultural values."[55] As such, these homes were more valuable forms of cultural capital, for they presented a less immigrant and more American look.

The incentive to purchase a home, and thus become more American, was certainly an "idea" actively encouraged by the community leaders in Chicago Heights. Along these lines, the city was a focus point for the national "Own Your Own Home" program. Through an extensive advertising campaign initiated by the American Association of Realtors, Chicago Heights residents were presented with myriad newspaper stories, movies, and radio broadcasts that extolled the virtues of homeownership as a wise economic, cultural, and moral decision.[56] For example, as a result of the efforts of the local Real Estate Board of Chicago Heights, the movie entitled *The Great Idea* was shown over a series of days at the preeminent movie house in the city: the Lincoln-Dixie Theatre. This film not only provided practical advice on how to own your own home, but in the storyline involving the main characters the audience was made aware that the "re-uniting of a broken family," an issue thought to be of special relevance to immigrants, would be accomplished "by the strongest of all appeals—the owning of a home."[57]

Local real estate firms also made special efforts to present both the moralistic and mobility arguments for homeownership. Thus, one advertisement spoke directly to the hopes of the immigrants in terms of the emotional and corporeal cultural capital to be gained through the purchase of a home. "Home is the sweetest word in human speech, and for the love and ownership of a home, men have stood, without *flinching* [emphasis added], the hardest toil and torture that time and chance would bring them."⁵⁸ Another newspaper display touted a direct line between corporal posture, social mobility, and ownership, when it stated that buying a home meant that citizens were "standing up to the full height of their opportunities."⁵⁹ Frank McEldowney, a leading real estate developer in Chicago Heights, not only argued for homeownership as an escape from the "heavy atmosphere of the more crowded (rental) structures" but expressed amazement as to "how many people tie themselves to the grindstone of paying rent."⁶⁰ Again, hope is configured in bodily terms.

Schilling Real Estate Co.

Real Estate, Renting, Loans
Insurance
82 Illinois St.   Phone 27

A BURDENSOME LOAD
Which never grows lighter is paying rent year after year. There is no expenditure in life so unsatisfactory or unprofitable.

Figure 4.3. In the Chicago Heights suburban environment, renting was increasingly disvalued for financial, political, and personal reasons. *Source:* A. J. Klyczek, & Co. Advertisement, Chicago Heights Star, March 27, 1924, 8. Public domain.

Other advertisements connected investment in homes to the idealized American values of honesty, independence, and family. In essence, these realtors were selling their own brand of cultural capital. "Ask a dozen men who own their own homes why they would not return to renting. Their reasons will convince you that dollars are a secondary consideration. These men prize their independence from landlords, the comfort of their family, and honest pride of possession."[61]

Chicago Heights Italians would certainly have been exposed to these economic and cultural messages. Cecilia Massetti, a longtime resident in Chicago Heights, suggested there was strong pressure to own a home and keep up appearances in the Italian neighborhoods. She said that people on her street took a great amount of pride in the property they owned and worked to keep it as nice as possible.[62] Diane Melchiore said her grandmother who lived in the Hill area was so intent upon owning a home she would religiously "go directly across the alley to Ursitti's Hardware Store to make their payment until it was finally paid off."[63] Aldo DeAngelis, who grew up in Chicago Heights and later became a state representative, said, "Every Italian at the time . . . most of them . . . all had a desire to own something because they were incapable of doing so in Italy. So, if they could buy anything, whatever it was, they would go ahead and buy it."[64] Maria Iafollo said owning a home was important because "it meant that you had taken a step up."[65] Nick Monacelli recalled that even though wages were around $1 a day, the "new arrivals" were anxious to put down roots, to build something, so "they bought property."[66]

Homeownership, therefore, was an economic decision but also a cultural strategy or practice. It was an acceptable and publicly recognized way that Italians could distinguish and differentiate themselves from the "dark mysteries" swirling through the social spaces of immigration. It was a hope that these immigrants appropriated to signal a commitment to the extant values, institutions, and assumptions of the emerging American society. It conveyed the independence and "get ahead" character associated with the dominant American culture. It fell in line with the boosterish credo that buying a home was an unmistakable sign of progress and commitment to hope going forward—a piece of evidence that immigrants could point to and demonstrate that they wanted to be counted as participants in the American Dream.[67]

Conclusion

Hope can take on many forms. In this chapter, we have identified hope as a cultural resource. In particular, homeownership was one of the more concrete, explicit, and socially approved objectifications of hope. Though the decision to own a home was often ringed with doubts, the majority of Chicago Heights Italians took on this financial challenge, as it promised a measure of economic security and, most importantly, differentiated these newcomers from those further down the immigrant hierarchy—specifically, sojourners with little intention to adopt an American cultural perspective, dissidents who sought to transform these American values, and the tenant and renter class. Owning a home gave witness to the American spirit of hope and prosperity and put one culturally on "the road to happiness.'"

Chapter 5

Purchasing an Acceptance in American Society
Children as Cultural Capital

For a considerable number of Italian newcomers, social affirmations of hope and mobility remained elusive. Occupational mobility and homeownership were difficult to navigate or control. Under such circumstances, immigrants were forced to look elsewhere to purchase an acceptance in American society. Oftentimes they turned toward the *lives of their children*. "A defining feature of the 'American Dream,'" Abramitzky and others suggest, "is the view that even immigrants who come to the United States with few resources and little skills have a real chance at improving their children's prospects."[1] Without question, most parents want their children to succeed and to shelter them from the most noxious environments and circumstances they themselves had to endure. They put their children first. But in a more subtle fashion, children can also serve as mediums or proxies for parents as they struggle to advance in the immigration hierarchy.

Along these lines, Andrew Greeley characterized the plight of many immigrants in the following way: "A few achieved their dreams in their lifetimes. Others lived to see their children and grandchildren enjoy success. Still others died, wondering if their dream had been replaced by a nightmare."[2] Under these circumstances, turning to their children (or grandchildren) may have been a favored response in order to "enjoy success." That is, the lives of children could reasonably be appropriated to project and capture the socially approved values, hopes, and dreams. Children, for all their other uses and identities, became viable sources of cultural capital to garner acceptance and esteem in society.

Appropriating the Hopes of Children

The oft-quoted and memorialized lament of the Italian immigrant held that the American streets were paved with gold, but upon entering America one soon realized this was not true: indeed, one was put to work paving these roads. Hope and a ready-made path to social mobility succumbed to the grimy, backbreaking, weather-taxing challenges of building roads and streets. While in large part apocryphal, this adage underscores the main theme of this study. For the majority of Italian immigrants in Chicago Heights, the promised success was not certain and not immediately forthcoming.

This is also a general conclusion of the path-breaking research by Ran Abramitzky and Leah Boustan in *Streets of Gold*.[3] Abramitzky and Boustan are intent on challenging several conventional myths regarding the American immigration process. And in ways parallel to this study, they marshal a longitudinal, linked sample by developing the rich sources of information provided by Ancestry.com. As they put it, they moved from family history to American history—a contemporary version of Oscar Handlin's discovery that immigrant history and American history are inseparable. To be sure, their study is far more comprehensive than my own. They have millions of data points, while I have thousands, sometimes hundreds. Their study offers sophisticated data analysis techniques and their scope is broader in terms of multiple immigrant groups and policy questions. Nevertheless, and beyond their research methodology, they confirm the general conclusion that "climbing the ladder" of success in the period from 1910 to 1940 was "dramatically slower than originally thought." And though new arrivals did experience a modicum of progress, "past European immigrants often struggled when they first arrived, and most of them did not succeed in reaching the American Dream within their lifetimes."[4]

Perhaps, Abramitzky and Boustan's most striking finding concerns the children of immigrants during this age of mass migration (and in the modern era). Specifically, the authors conclude that in a thirty-year span from 1910 to 1940 these children (more precisely sons) achieved on average a rank percentile income exceeding that of their parents in 1910. These findings pertain to children raised at all income levels but are most pronounced for children who grew up in poor homes or below the twenty-fifth percentile income distribution. Even more surprising was that the children of immigrants achieved more upward mobility than children of US-born parents during this same period. Further, of the sixteen European countries that sent the vast majority of immigrants to America, by 1940 the sons of Italian fathers were the most successful in terms of moving past their parents' lowly beginning. Specifically, in 1940, the average income rank for Italian children born to parents in the twenty-fifth percentile or below in 1910 well exceeded the fiftieth percentile.[5] For many, therefore, the promises of mobility, at least in the long run, were redeemed for the immigrants in their children, if not always directly for the immigrants themselves.

Despite these findings, the discussion of the Italian parents' attitudes toward their children in the literature has generally taken a critical tone. The assimilation of these second-generation children is thought to have been thwarted or at least delayed by the provincial attitudes of these Italian parents. As Perlmann suggests, these studies and conclusions center on the difficult choices parents had to make regarding the collective fortunes of their families.[6] Should children be sent to school to learn the skills that would promote the long-term success of the family as a whole? Or should the children be encouraged to enter the labor market as soon as possible, earn a paycheck, and provide for the family's immediate economic survival? The lament found in most studies is that Italian parents chose the latter course and thus inhibited the success of their children. Humbert Nelli's classic study of Italian mobility in Chicago echoes this theme: "'Southerns' were notorious for inducing their children to leave school and find jobs. Contemporaries saw a shocking and serious problem in the tendency of many immigrants to put their children to work at the first opportunity. The reason, noted *L'Italia* in 1902, lay in carry-over 'on the part of Italian parents, especially those of the south of Italy, of an old country attitude.'"[7] As these narratives unfold, therefore, Italian parents were presented with these two basic choices regarding what to do with their children. Both options, one more favored than another, were formulated on the basis of the parents' economic calculation—one promising more immediate rewards, the other more long-term success. Financial considerations, tempered by cultural legacies, dominated.

Yet, these decisions stretched well beyond these economic concerns. Namely, as these immigrants made their way through the immigrant field, children became forms of cultural capital. Children were not simply economic variables plugged into the workforce "at the first opportunity," nor were they long-term economic investments. In the quest to gain a foothold in society and a ladder to mobility, immigrants acquired valuable cultural resources by making claims upon the hopes of their children. The lives of sons and daughters could be appropriated in a manner that created sources of *cultural* revenue, which immigrants could use to improve their own standing in the evolving immigrant hierarchy.

This was not a strategy steeped in Italian tradition. The ritual world of the past was characterized by a patriarchal structure, a collective spirit, and the subjugation of children's lives to both. But on American soil, both this structure and spirit were increasingly sources of conflict. It became difficult to hold on to the belief that the personal hopes of children were to be muted in favor of this traditional "cooperative ideal" or that parents could easily collect and control the social interactions, paychecks, ambitions, and desires of their children.[8] As these children, increasingly native born, became adjusted to American culture, they withdrew from their parents' circle of influence in language skills, mannerisms, and styles of dress. Most importantly, the individualism of American society was creeping into the traditional family. Personal goals and inclinations became more relevant. Parents steadily lost ground to their children in decisions regarding school, work, and marriage. As children became Americanized and adopted the pervasive adage that they should "follow their own dreams," the cooperative spirit of the family was threatened. Indeed, many children moved ahead and began to compete with their parents for the most valuable economic, cultural, and social capital in the immigration field.

These changes brought systemic conflicts to the Italian immigrant family. As Robert Orsi concludes, "Dysfunction, pain, and alienation were as much, if not more, a part of the history of immigrant families as mutual support and cooperation."[9] Paul Campisi characterizes this transition stage as one of "considerable confusion, conflict, and disorganization."[10] To a considerable degree, clashes over hopes and social mobility became a source of tension. As Riesman suggests, tradition-directed families did not place a high priority on such mobility. Instead, "Parents train the child to succeed *them*, rather than to 'succeed' by rising in the social system."[11] The seemingly "simple and explicit" paths laid out for the good of the family as a collective grouping were undermined by the individualistic character of American culture.[12]

These conflicts surfaced in the Chicago Heights context. Umberto La Morticella spoke of the time he casually mentioned to his mother that he had five more years of schooling to go. Upon hearing this, his father jumped up from his chair screaming, "Five years yet . . . What the hell do you mean five years? You better go to work. What the hell do you think I am, Roccofalo (meaning Rockefeller)."[13] Theresa Gianetti had a similar encounter. "I went to high school against protest . . . my mother's ideas was anybody who went to school was no good."[14] Maria Iafollo told of her family's supportive efforts toward education but how they were also reluctant to pay the minimal school bus fees to allow her and her sister to attend high school.[15]

Italian parents were destined to lose these battles. Theresa Gianetti said, "I was determined to get an education. I fought tooth and nail and I went."[16] Larger economic, social, and cultural forces were at work. Compulsory school attendance laws, restrictions on child labor, and the moral enterprise of reformers, would make it extremely difficult for Italian parents to command the hopes of their children. As Campisi argues, there was "the increasing recognition by both parents and children that the Italian way of life in the American community means low status, social and economic discrimination, and prejudice."[17] Many of the Italian children growing up in the broader American culture of "rising in the social system" now harbored different hopes.

These Italian parents, challenged from above by their own struggles in "climbing the ladder" of success and from below by their children's independence and achievements, arrived at new strategies, new dispositions, a new habitus in line with these changing objective realities. In Orsi's words, they created new ways of being in the world, dispositions that allowed them opportunities for "consoling themselves" with respect to their own status ambitions but that also provided measures for "disciplining their children."[18] At times, these new practices took one-sided turns as bitter fights and arguments within the family became regular occurrences. Corporal punishment, while not common, was not out of the question. As Beeson's characterization of the Italians in Chicago Heights suggests, "The foreign element as a rule demand strict obedience from their children."[19] At other times, when children deviated from traditional pathways, parents would resort to exclusionary practices and distance themselves from their children. In Orsi's terms they would engage in a subtle form of ex-communication.[20]

Moreover, and more favorable, these new dispositions were organized around hope in a reconstructed manner. Specifically, children became the canvas for objectifying hope and served as "parental surrogates in the occupational world" such that the parents' own achievements were earned "by interacting with and reflecting upon children's achievements."[21] These reflections enhanced parents' status by reversing the flow of resources that now traveled culturally *from* children to parents. Italian parents increasingly interpreted their own lives and their own successes through the lives and hopes of their sons and daughters (and grandsons and granddaughters), a distinct change from the dispositions and feelings of previous times where the parents' hopes were in large measure the children's hopes. Immigrant parents appropriated these hopes and status gains and in so doing demonstrated that they themselves were in line with the sanctioned cultural beliefs of their adopted home. In the process, the assimilation conflicts between parents and children were mollified. The children's hopes and successes were the same as the parents' own hopes and successes.

This strategic use of children, or the appropriation of their Americanized hopes, was not done in a coldly calculated manner. As Bourdieu suggests, such strategies are neither unconscious, nor entirely rational choices. Instead, this involved a practical logic enacted in a largely tacit fashion, more so to the extent that these Italian immigrants themselves became invested in the dominant American culture and developed a new set of dispositions. These immigrants engaged in what Bourdieu labeled generally as a "double game."[22] They sought practical solutions to their own family disorganization but in a manner that would not bring forth cultural sanctions from the more dominant groups in society. That is, they sought to preserve the collective character of the Italian family culture, not by opposing the mobility aims of their children but by making their own claims upon these hopes. In so doing, they took liberties with what it meant to assimilate: that is, they changed the asking price without assimilating as such. They were able to preserve the character of the Italian family or "save the essential part of what the rule (or in this case the family) was meant to guarantee" while at the same time effectively playing the game of assimilation.[23]

This connection between hope, parents, and children is captured in a colloquial and admittedly stereotypical sense with the oft-cited Jewish phrase, "My son the doctor" (or lawyer, or scholar, or rabbi). A part of Jewish folklore, this "typical mother's day-dream" contained an implicit investment in hope on the part of Jewish mothers for their sons.[24] The son's success would affect the parental status and cultural acceptance. In an era where being Jewish (or Italian, Polish, or some other ethnic group) was most immediately associated with an immigrant status and where that status often resulted in highly unfavorable characterizations and opportunities, the investment in the occupational success of one's children would predictably confirm what Leo Rosten once called "a universe of *yiches*-aspiration." Such status-defining feelings and aspirations are revealed in Rosten's quip regarding the Jewish mother at the beach who screams out "Help! Help! My son the doctor is drowning."[25]

"My son the doctor" may have been a hope too ambitious, too far beyond the horizon for most Italian, immigrant parents. As Alba and Foner conclude, "My grandson the doctor" may have been a more appropriate hope, for substantial status and mobility achievements (and then only primarily for men) had to await the third- or fourth-generational Italian immigrant.[26] Most Italian parents had more modest hopes for their children—specifically, to have a job wherein a "white collar" meant a steady paycheck, an escape from the dangers of manual work, and a sign of respect and status in the community. "My son the priest" or "My daughter the nun" were more realistic possibilities.[27] The occupational world, including specifically religious professions, provided a rich source of cultural capital for realizing this hope.

To be sure, securing a good job was a most valuable economic resource. But the value was enhanced dramatically because of its cultural significance. As sons and daughters achieved measures of occupational advancement, these successes brought more status and capital to parents than the children's purchase of a home, moving to a better neighborhood, becoming a local sports hero, and the like. Specifically, as Herbert Gutman has argued so persuasively, the processes of industrialization that took place prior to and at the beginning of the last century radically altered the importance and differentiating dimensions of work in America. The character and type of occupation one held "dug deep" into claims of class and status, coming eventually to override the cultural currency of ethnic and community associations.[28] Under these conditions, borrowing upon children's aspirations and successes in the occupational world was strategically a wise decision, over against the symbolic capital of ethnicity.

This has particular relevance in contrast to the cultural capital one could have acquired through a child's educational achievements. As suggested above, the Italian immigrants' distaste for schooling has largely been associated with the heaviness of the old-world culture and the emphasis placed upon economic survival. As such, these explanations reduce these complex school-related decisions to an overworked traditional set of beliefs. In so doing, they create characterizations of the immigrant as passive, stubborn, and hopeless. They do not fully account for the fact that as a stranger in a foreign land, the newcomer must fundamentally express what everyone else takes for granted, that as a prerequisite to acceptance the immigrant must see and believe as others do. In particular, the individual must present oneself as "the good player" or one who "is continually doing what needs to be done, what the game demands and requires."[29]

With this in mind, the Italian immigrant strategically reasoned that a child's success in school, beyond learning skills in reading and math, would not bring as many cultural returns and permissions as the investments in the occupational world. This was not an unreasonable assumption. Thus, at the beginning of the century, schooling was not an especially valuable cultural resource or strongly held value except at the upper echelon of society and for moral reformers. This was a belief held not only by immigrants but by many people across the society. The time spent in school, after the development of rudimentary knowledge, was often seen as disruptive to family values and parental control. There were heated debates throughout the society regarding the wisdom of compulsory education, especially as parents would lose the income from their child's labor and secularization would undermine religious beliefs. Indeed, in some circles, compulsory education was viewed as un-American. As Steinberg concludes, "During the early 1900s American society did not place much value on a continuing education. The vast majority of Americans were employed in occupations that required few skills . . . The individual who graduated high school was the exception, not the rule."[30] In Illinois, school attendance beyond the mandatory age of sixteen, only stood at 45 percent in 1930 for those seventeen years old.[31] In Chicago Heights, just over 43 percent, considerably less than half of those at this age, attended school in 1930.[32] This suggests, at least, widespread reservations about the value of schooling, as opposed to work, as both an economic and cultural resource.

These educational and occupational strategies broke differently along gender lines. The occupational careers of daughters were not viewed profitably for objectifying hope.[33] This was the case because the occupational aspirations for daughters were circumscribed beforehand. Thus, when daughters worked outside the home it was generally as secretaries, cooks, maids, agricultural workers, and seamstresses. These restrictions dramatically narrowed the opportunities for parents to demonstrate and affirm their own commitment to hope and mobility; needless to say, these restrictions dramatically diminished the opportunities for these women. Since many believed that "the women's role . . . as one of wife and mother only," hope was shuffled off to having a good marriage partner and a large family.[34]

There were exceptions. Marie Iafollo, who grew up in the Chicago Heights area and went on to become a world traveler and highly recognized teacher, said her parents pooled their resources to allow her and her sister to attend high school and eventually college. "My parents took a lot of pride when we did well," Mary said. "They were loving parents who felt that if any of us did well that meant that the family was doing well."[35] Dominic Pancrazio, as mentioned above, owned a small grocery store on the East Side. Dominic had a difficult time providing for his family, especially during the Depression era. Nevertheless, in line with the changing sentiments he thought it important that his children finish high school and even encouraged them to attend college. Pasqualina Pancrazio, one of his daughters, did so and graduated with a degree in education. "I always felt," said Pasqualina, "that my father wanted me to go to college not just for my own sake, but for his too. It made him feel good because he could feel that he had made it too."[36]

Still, the opportunities for parents to invest hope in their son's career were more numerous and direct. While a son's high school graduation, and for a few attendance at college, provided useful cultural capital for parents, the ability of a son to secure steady employment and advancement was the most valued commodity.[37] We gain some indication of the role that hope played in this process by examining a community study undertaken jointly by the University of Chicago and the Boards of Education for the Chicago Heights community in 1940. As a part of this investigation, the researchers

Figure 5.1. Daughters had a more difficult time achieving success outside the home, but the Pancrazio family was one of the exceptions. *Source:* Courtesy: Personal collection of Carolyn Cosentino.

Table 5.1. Fathers' Life Work and Job Choices of Sons as Reported by 336 Eighth-, Tenth-, and Twelfth-Grade Students (in Percent)

	Professional	White Collar	Skilled Labor	Semi/Unskilled
Father's Work	5.7	27.9	35.5	30.9
Son's Job Choice	40.9	25.8	31.0	2.3

Source: Field Course and Survey Greater Chicago Heights Area, Committee on Field Services Department of Education, University of Chicago; Published by the Boards of Education, Districts 170 and 206, Chicago Heights, Illinois, 1942.

surveyed 336 eighth-, tenth-, and twelfth-grade boys with respect to their own future job choices and their father's life work.

This data, which does not fully distinguish between native-born and immigrant families, suggests in a structural sense that hope for occupational mobility was on the minds of these young boys. Thus, for those sons whose fathers were semi/unskilled workers just a little over 2 percent wanted to follow in their father's footsteps. The vast majority, therefore, hoped for greater occupational advancement; they conjured up the American spirit of getting ahead. For the sons of professional workers, over 40 percent have professional aspirations. But hope also entered in here since there were few of these professional positions available in the Chicago Heights context. The field study authors seem to acknowledge this fanciful way of thinking when they concluded that "this can only mean thwarted hopes and wasted time for many youth, for they do not have the competency and/or the financial resources to enter the professions."[38]

As pointed out, the data above does not systematically distinguish among native born and immigrants or between different immigrant groups. Further analysis, however, led the authors to conclude that the "great numbers of aspiring young people come from lower socio-economic groups."[39] For example, for the sons of "Negro" fathers, over two-thirds expressed a desire for professional status, though no Black man held such a position; conversely, 72 percent of the Black men in the sample were employed in semi/unskilled jobs, yet no son chose to follow this career path. And perhaps most significant for this study, close to 42 percent of the sons from immigrant families had hopes of become a professional, but less than 2 percent of immigrant fathers had achieved this status.

What is most suggestive about this study is not the simple fact that the aspirations of these young boys were often at variance with their father's work lives. More importantly, it is that these boys sought to rise above their father in the occupational hierarchy. The hopes for occupational mobility had filtered down into their ways of thinking. And given their young age, it is perhaps reasonable to assume that these hopes involved a merging of parents' status aims with the nascent aspirations of the children themselves—a process whereby parents also gained a cultural advantage in the immigrant field. As such, these "thwarted hopes" may not have been "wasted," for in cultural capital terms they forwarded the more fundamental goal of recognition. Hope, therefore, abounded in the community. It was a social fact. Still, the very nature of hope—its uncertainty and future orientation—make it susceptible to doubt and disillusionment. As suggested, it requires a perpetual grounding in earthly experiences to take it from the realm of fantasy and wish-fulfillment and toward use as an economic and cultural resource. With this in mind, the question then turns to what were the realistic opportunities available to parents with respect to investing hope in their sons? In particular, how did the sons of the Italian immigrants fair in Chicago Heights?

Table 5.2 provides clues to these opportunities. It is an inflow chart showing the occupational positions (in the period 1930 to 1940) of 320 sons of Italian immigrant fathers—fathers who were residing in Chicago Heights in 1910.[40] It begins with the occupations of these sons and asks where these sons came from in terms of their fathers' occupations. This provides a measure as to the reasonableness of the parents' investment of hope in the occupational careers of their sons. That is, in the extreme, if every son ended up in a high white-collar, professional, position no matter where they started from, then these investments produced high returns, for hope was objectified, certified, made real. If, on the contrary, the careers of sons were exclusively located in unskilled occupations, then the straightforward objectification of hope may have been mismanaged on the part of parents.

Several revealing aspects of the data emerge. First, 70 percent of the sons (from the Total column) came from households at the bottom of the occupational hierarchy or the semiskilled and unskilled jobs. This is consistent with the percentages in previous tables. In broad terms, these percentages suggest a structural need for parents to invest in hope. Both parents and sons found themselves in disadvantaged positions where aspirations to change, or at a minimum to maintain their life circumstances, certainly entered into their thought processes. Ironically, these immigrants had a

Table 5.2. Son's Occupation from Father's Occupation. Inflow Mobility, Chicago Heights Italian Immigrants, 1910 to 1930–1940 (in Percent)

		Son's Occupation				
		White Collar	Skilled	Semi/Unskilled	Other	Total
Father's Occupation	White Collar	29	11	15	12	20
	Skilled	6	14	11	12	10
	Semi/Unskilled	65	75	73	75	70
	Total	100	100	100	99	100
	Number	(116)	(81)	(115)	(8)	(320)

Source: Department of Commerce and Labor, Bureau of the Census, Thirteenth Census of the United States: 1910 Population, Chicago Heights manuscripts; Department of Commerce and Labor, Bureau of the Census, Fourteenth Census of the United States: 1920 Population, Chicago Heights manuscripts; Department of Commerce, Bureau of the Census, Fifteenth Census of the United States: 1930 Population, Chicago Heights manuscripts; Department of Commerce, Bureau of the Census, Sixteenth Census of the United States: 1940 Population, Chicago Heights manuscripts. In addition, the identification of son's occupation was aided and reconfirmed with a variety of other historical materials including marriage records, death notices, newspaper accounts, military records, social security information. The category "Other" consists of sons who were incapacitated in some manner and not in the labor force, because they were in a mental institution or prison or had a disability. The total does not equal 100 percent because of rounding.

number of pathways to dream about or mitigate the "sorrows," "sacrifices," and "self-denials" they experienced. With uneven work careers and jobs that were hardly fulfilling beyond the paycheck, immigrant hopes cut across a range of radical, illegal, and conventional options. Some of these dreams went the way of labor organizing, some toward a foray into organized crime, most into achieving an occupational mobility.

Second, there were indeed pathways for mobility, where a hope for a better job and occupational mobility could be realized. Thus, 65 percent of the sons in white-collar occupations came from semi/unskilled families, with another 6 percent moving up into these white-collar jobs from skilled positions. In addition, 75 percent of the sons progressed upward into skilled positions from unskilled and semiskilled backgrounds. These findings are in line with Abramitzky and Boustan's more comprehensive analysis that the children of immigrants did on average achieve a measure of social mobility.

With respect to these white-collar workers in particular, the majority only made their way into the less prestigious, lower white-collar occupations such as clerks, salesmen, and foremen—not the professional class. Still, this was tangible proof of "rising in the system." As C. Wright Mills argued more generally, this movement into the white-collar world enabled these workers to put strong claims on status and acceptance in American society. The salaries were higher. And beyond the financial and cultural significance of a larger paycheck, the work was more mental than physical, required "street" clothes rather than "work" clothes, and associated these workers primarily with native-born, non-Italian citizens who themselves idealized the fulfillment of the American Dream, the fulfillment of hopes in their generational struggles.[41]

Third, it is nevertheless difficult to ignore the considerable degree of occupational inheritance among sons who worked in semiskilled and unskilled jobs. Some 73 percent of these workers inherited these more dangerous, low-paying jobs from their fathers. Certainly, the investment that parents made in their sons' careers may have produced dividends in terms of hope and the commitment to the game of cultural acceptance. The sons had gained a foothold in the society, and parents could take pride that they paved the way for their sons to follow them on the shop floor or the construction site. Still, there was little evidence at this point of the widespread "economic affluence" Portes and Rumbaut argued was to come to the children of the European immigrants in the subsequent decades.[42] And as the turbulent economic times of the 1930s began to unfold, even the ability of these sons to replicate their fathers' lives and carry hope forward in these low-skilled jobs was by no means assured.

Setting Hope Adrift in the Prewar Years

The 1930s were not kind to the immigrant industrial workers in Chicago Heights. Cohen characterizes the experiences of these workers in Chicago with the less than hopeful epitaph of "adrift in the Great Depression."[43] Over 36 percent of the semiskilled workers in Chicago were unemployed in 1931, and over 57 percent of the unskilled workers also met the same fate.[44] The rates in Chicago Heights were most likely similar. The Italians in Heights, wrote Fred De Luca, "being mostly unskilled laborers were the first ones affected and thrown out of employment as a result of the depression, and with the exception of comparatively few, they have not returned to work since."[45] In response, union-backed and wildcat strikes in the Heights were numerous, with Italians often at the forefront of these efforts. Calumet Steel and Inland Steel both experienced strikes that lasted for weeks and were punctuated by threats of violence. The more radical strains of organized labor, including the Communist Party, attracted more followers throughout Chicago and the Cook County region. Calls for social programs to address the ongoing problems of evictions, lack of food, and unemployment were debated in the newspapers and union halls. Along these lines, the metal workers in the Heights "got involved" in the national campaign to establish unemployment insurance.[46] And despite their stated aversion to welfare, Italians had a greater percentage of people on relief in Chicago Heights than any other nationality.[47] Even the pension plans that had come to replace the Italian mutual aid societies, and upon which so many workers had based their hopes for retirement, were riddled with so many contingencies few workers received this benefit. "No, it's a sad thing," said Dominic Pandolfi, "how they were beaten out of their pensions."[48]

It is difficult to get inside the personal and cultural dynamics of each family during this era. Even as the Depression closed one factory after another, there were stories of hope and success. The movement of Gaetano D'Amico from laborer to white-collar entrepreneur and the success of Gaetano's sons as managers and co-owners of the spaghetti factory were clear, objectified signs of hope. Yet, for many immigrants their own work experiences and the difficulties their sons (and daughters) had in securing jobs even at the bottom of the occupational hierarchy threatened to make hope obsolete. Many residents spoke of the lean times they experienced during this era. Joe Rossi said, "I personally always felt when I was a child that my family would never suffer like we did."[49] Genevieve Ford Reed wrote "then the Depression came in 1929 . . . the factories closed, no one had anything. The East Side was hit hard. People had to go on relief . . . Most of the time in the winter, we didn't have water because the pipes would freeze. My mother melted snow for us to wash our bodies, and to wash our clothes . . . we even had to drink snow water."[50]

At the beginning of World War II, the ability of Italians to move within these social spaces was dealt another cultural blow with the branding of Italian Americans (along with Japanese Americans and German Americans) as "enemy aliens."[51] This sinister phrase layered a cultural opprobrium on Italian immigrants. In both an official and unofficial manner, this characterization put the status and loyalty of Italian immigrants once again into doubt. Thus, the Smith Act of 1940 required all Italian immigrants (those not naturalized) over fourteen years old to register as an alien and be fingerprinted. Children under the age of fourteen were to be registered by their parents or guardians.

As a result, over ten thousand Italian Americans were interned or scheduled to be so, another six hundred thousand were thought to arouse sufficient suspicions so as to have their movements restricted or monitored.[52]

In response to this directive, the *Chicago Heights Star* kept a near weekly count of the "alien census" and published a series of editorials or warnings regarding the presence of a "Trojan Horse" or the "fifth column" working within America to undermine the war effort abroad. These editorials were quick to point out that this alien registration would benefit the "law abiding alien" who had "nothing to 'cover up,' so to speak" . . . and that "there is no stigma in being finger-printed under the registration act."[53] But nearly within the same breath, the *Star* cautioned "the foreign element" not "to lose time in proving to your community that you are first of all Americans . . . anything short of complete and enthusiastic co-operation many bring down the wrath of fellow citizens."[54]

All the same, once designated as an enemy, an "enemy alien" at that, it was difficult to contain these designations within the official institutional guidelines. Because the German population of Chicago Heights was long established and most Germans had naturalized, and because there were so few Japanese citizens in the city, these broadsides against the disloyal foreigners were largely aimed at the Italian population. Any Italian, naturalized or not, who refused to speak English, made too many visits to Italy, or were leaders in Italian social organizations, were potentially stigmatized or negatively distinguished. To counter these enemy accusations, a number of Italian social clubs encouraged its members to buy war bonds and to go door to door soliciting pledges from their fellow Americans. The Italian American Dante club made a public commitment to their "real Americanism" by pledging thousands of dollars to the war effort.[55]

Despite these efforts, the *Star* expressed concern early on that these registration processes were going slowly. They attributed this to difficulties with the form and transcription problems. Engulfed by patriotic war sentiments, the more established elites in Chicago Heights exhibited little understanding that this alien census was a challenge to the Italian culture and marginalized Italians. In general terms, these classification schemes, in Foucault's way of thinking, constituted an exercise of power and attempts to control these "anomalies in the social body."[56] These objectifying and dividing practices were particularly effective, as they commanded not just the behavior but, in a more insidious way, the habitus or subjectivity of those involved. As such, they had the effect of normalizing power under the combined auspices of hope and the American war effort.

In personal terms, I can speak about my grandmother, Josephina, who spoke little English, could not read or write, and who lived her life in America content upon providing comfort for her family and neighbors. Yet, after close to thirty years of providing these comforts, she was thrust into a lower immigrant position, nay an "enemy alien" status, with these new registration requirements. Though she hardly posed a challenge to the war efforts, she dutifully complied with these requirements but not, however, without imagined fears of official action, rejection, or deportation. There was now an official *dossier* on Josephina. This represented a transition in self-understanding as Josephina's knowledge of and hopes were now mediated by an external authority. She was now held personally accountable to the authoritative hopes of the larger society. And Josephina was not alone in this transition as other immigrants could now be charted and judged as to their American hopes and commitments.

At the end of the four-month registration period, over sixteen hundred people had registered, the vast majority of whom were Italians.[57] Many critics questioned not only the legality but also the moral appropriateness of these official actions, even in wartime. And the practical effectiveness of such actions could certainly be raised. However, the cultural significance could not be ignored. Such designations and any delays or forms of resistance reaffirmed among segments of the American population the "deep and lingering prejudice against Italians . . . whose ability to assimilate into American life was questionable if not hopeless."[58]

Though the situation was not totally hopeless, as once again the children of these immigrants provided a steady stream of cultural capital. As the sons (and a few daughters) enlisted or were drafted into the armed services, as they signaled their intent to fight the Axis powers—the Germans, Japanese, *and* Italians—they purchased considerable goodwill for themselves and their families from mainstream society. Wozny describes the patriotic sentiment in Chicago Heights. Despite the horrors and the tears shed by the families whose sons fought in the war, the old adage still applied: "Lucky is the mother who had a priest for a son, but luckier still is the one whose son is a soldier."[59]

As one would expect, the local Chicago Heights community supported the war effort with a series of patriotic events, war bond drives, and memorial honors. As a part of these public displays, the sacrifices endured by the families of soldiers played a prominent role. These sacrifices were widely acknowledged but never more so than for the families whose sons were tragically wounded or killed in action. Over a hundred Chicago Heights residents suffered fatalities in the war—African Americans, Polish, German,

Mexican, Slavic, Irish, and Lithuanian. The sons of Italian immigrants had the most fatalities, close to 20 percent of the total.[60]

And this does not count the injuries and permanent disabilities of so many resident soldiers. Thus, Marie Iafollo tells the harrowing story of her brother who was "called in" to the Army in 1945. After basic training, he was sent to Belgium to relieve the troops who were still fighting the Battle of the Bulge. He was wounded by a nearby explosion and the shrapnel went into his fingers and up his arm. He would have died there, as so many of his fellow soldiers did, but the weather was so cold "the blood froze and saved his life." He was evacuated and spent more than a year in rehabilitation back in the United States. He had bone grafts and metal plates and screws in his arm for the rest of his life.[61] On a personal level, Marie's brother literally gave his right arm to defend America. On a societal level, such acts of heroism played a significant role in erasing some of the negative stereotypes associated with the previous generation of Italian immigrants. As Candeloro puts it succinctly, "The public image of Italian Americans was . . . enhanced by service in the military."[62]

Indeed, in the period after World War II, the majority of the second-generation Italians in Chicago Heights were finally brought into mainstream society. They began to more fully enjoy the riches that society offered. They were employed in mainly well-paying union jobs in the local steel mills, chemical plants, and auto industry. Eventually, they came to hold government positions in the city and elected a series of Italian mayors. The sons and daughters and grandsons and granddaughters of the first immigrants moved more steadily into white-collar positions. Of course, this was too late for many of the immigrants themselves. And it did take a World War and the expanding economy after the war to bring about these changes.

At the same time, this mainstream society, which Italians were increasingly a part of and would come to dominate politically and culturally in the Heights, did not open up in substantial ways for most of Black and Latino individuals who in greater numbers were moving into the city. Thus, the heroism of Black and Latino soldiers did not bring the same cultural capital advantages as the children of the white immigrant groups. The World War II induction ceremonies and subsequent memorials were generally segregated affairs, especially with respect to the Black population. Such heroism, while admired, did not easily cross over or produce upward movement in the ever-changing racial/immigrant field.

Personally, I grew up in Chicago Heights at the end of the period described in this chapter. In moving through the school system, I had friends and classmates who came from a range of racial and ethnic backgrounds.

None of us were particularly brighter or more motivated than the other. But along the way, we began to separate. We separated not only residentially but in a related and more subtle manner in terms of our occupational aspirations and life going forward. Our hopes for the future became a mark of distinction along gender, social class, and racial lines. Not only were Blacks and Latinos given fewer opportunities for success, but their hopes, or what Foucault characterized as their "soul" or "subjectivities," could not be cashed in as readily for acceptance.

Again, this is disturbing and sobering with respect to the insidious character of inequality. As a grandson of Italian (and Lithuanian) immigrants, I grew up in a blue-collar environment with decided disadvantages, though in an era in which the prejudice against Italians had diminished significantly. As a white male, the field was heavily tilted in my favor. I am buoyed, nevertheless, by the words of one of my former Latino classmates who has written that assimilation and success is "more than just achieving certain levels of living." He goes on to say "many have not chosen this path because they do not see much value or sense to it . . . the price for joining the so-called mainstream American society has been too high. It has meant renouncing one's language, culture, sense of dignity."[63] In Bourdieu's sense, he is arguing that beyond the necessity of satisfying economic needs, not everybody has to play the same game. The Italian immigrants were inhibited in this sense because they came to this realization late and "under circumstances existing already, given and transmitted from the past." The immigrants and other disadvantaged groups today are entertaining a different set of circumstances: where the circumstances are crisscrossing, overlapping, and dispersed but not as unified. This provides some hope that they will be able to achieve a level of individual achievement and success but at a cost less damaging to their language, culture, and dignity. The Italian immigration experience serves as both an exemplar and caution.

Conclusion

This chapter argues that the Italian immigrants in Chicago Heights reconstituted their relationship to their children in line with the socially sanctioned American values of hope and social mobility. If success in their own lives was never certain or certified, then immigrants could demonstrate their commitment to the American ethos by appropriating the hopes of their Americanized children. In a world where control over children's hopes through traditional practices was becoming increasingly problematic and less assured, parents could mend family assimilation conflicts and purchase an acceptance in American society by binding themselves to their children's hopes and successes. In particular, the hopes surrounding the occupational mobility of their children and the sacrifices of their children during times of war were forms of capital to be accumulated and spent in the service of claiming a more favorable social space in the society. Children became marks of differentiation and distinction.

Conclusion

Individualized Hope and Communal Hopes

As Durkheim said, hope is appealing. It has its "pleasures even when unreasonable."[1] However, we are asking a lot of hope if we expect it to be a prime motivating factor to push millions of Italians at the turn of the last century to emigrate to America. While such decisions may have been influenced by these personal desires, assigning analytic priority to these processes runs the risk of overlooking the pragmatic, experiential, and social processes leading these Italians to give up family and homeland for the exceedingly risky prospect of success in a foreign country. Even conceding that hope for a better life played a significant part in these decisions, we are left to unravel the social aspects of hope. Durkheim again put it succinctly: hope "does not explain itself."[2]

With this in mind, we suggest that once these peasants stepped into the social spaces of immigration, they came to realize that a reasonable, hopeful disposition—in its embodied, objectified, and institutionalized forms—was the sine qua non of acceptance. Hope (or more specifically, hopeful striving) was a critical feature of the American cultural code. Once on American soil, to practice resignation or dissent would demonstrate that one lacked the feel for the game or what it meant to be an American. Hope—and its objectification through the cultural resources of occupational mobility, housing, and children—became the socially sanctioned pathway through which immigrants bought acceptance in their new country. To not exhibit hope in some publicly recognized manner would make one a cultural agnostic. Hope became a sacred object or a "timeless, encompassing, vital, emotionally compelling" public ritual that signaled a communion with fellow Americans.[3]

These commitments to hope paid dividends. Most Italians or their children achieved measures of success. In the post–World War II era and by the 1970s, Italian Americans gained relative parity with other Americans in terms of income, educational achievements, and occupational attainment.[4] Structural factors weighed heavily in this socioeconomic uplift. As Alba explains, these advances were partly due to the fact that the more privileged members of society were themselves moving up. This created patterns of "non-zero-sum mobility" whereby the upward trajectory of the Italians (and select other ethnic groups) was perceived in a less threatening, competitive, and antagonistic manner.[5] Alba also holds that these patterns of mobility developed because Italians elevated their perceived moral worth; they destigmatized themselves in the eyes of the mainstream society. They fought their way into the more advanced social spaces because they embraced the American Dream, which signaled that they were "worthy of the opportunities that the established members of the mainstream society took for granted."[6]

The claim that they possessed this intrinsic moral value was centered upon the expressions and manifestations of "joyful striving." Far from being the passive and simple peasant often characterized in popular discussions, these newcomers exhibited guile and a sophistication in cluing themselves in on the unspoken rules for acceptance in their new home. In dialectic fashion, they responded to the demands of their position in the immigration field by turning hope into a way of organizing their ascent. Immigrants used hope as a practice for interpreting, developing, and transforming their relationship in the existing hierarchy. To not play the game, whatever the chances of success, left the Italian immigrant vulnerable to the charge of being a "hopeless alien."

The accomplishments of these Italian immigrants should be applauded. Many second-, third-, and fourth-generation Italians in the Heights and beyond have lived good lives because of these self-sacrifices and determined efforts. We have briefly recounted the success of the DiAmico, Pressendo, Spina, Ciambrone, Iafollo, Melchione, and Fusci families. There were of course others—the Marconi, Patrizi, Zaranti, Domiani, Longo, Gianetti, and other family clans. Among longtime Chicago Heights residents, these names are recognized as social and economic leaders in the community. They embodied the belief in hope and success.

In a less public manner, there are stories of others who exhibited hope and the quest for mobility in a more untold fashion. They went to work each day and put up with disparaging conditions: but they managed to provide material and cultural advancement for themselves and family members. Frank Corradetti was an example. He worked in an inhospitable factory environment but managed over the years to obtain a "top job." He was a success and achieved what he had hoped for, though expressed troubling doubts about the value of his efforts. The stakes of the game were so high, Corradetti could not afford to do or think otherwise.

The stories of many others, especially women, also reveal this more guarded commitment to hope. Thus, some women, with babies and children in tow, found their way to the nearby onion fields and spent ten hours a day sorting weeds from onion plants for a dollar. Others took in boarders and sacrificed their home environment for several dollars each month and for the chance to get ahead of the mortgage lender. Beyond so many of these personal stories, the efforts of these immigrants provided collective evidence that the larger American narrative of hope and mobility, if at times overly mythologized, was how the game was supposed to be played.

Hope therefore was the catalyst but in a more complex sense than typically depicted. And Italians made good use of it to purchase a more favorable position in American society. Yet, accepting the American version of hope, with its utilitarian and individualistic elements, came at a cost, an experience that Mangione and Morreale described as being "at home and uneasy in America."[7] It meant relinquishing folk customs, as well as a reordering of the long-held dispositions and "habits of the heart." Certainly, giving up certain traditions was necessary and beneficial. Having children marry not only fellow Italians but Italians from the "old country" province, or better yet from the same village, would be difficult even in the large ethnic enclaves in America. This was not a custom easily abandoned. There was no shortage of *agita* on the part of my grandparents when my father announced he was going to marry a Lithuanian woman.

Forgoing other traditions, however, seems more problematic in retrospect. Most consequential was the loss or discouragement of a collective or communal hope. For the better part of the 1800s and into the 1900s, an *associazionismo*[8] was a dominant feature in Italian society, especially the south. Though particular regions of Italy exhibited variability, the time-honored approach to life emphasized a communion of interests and aspirations. At times these shared interests extended only to the family, but in most cases they incorporated the larger village for the family in all its blood, affinity, and fictive ties spread throughout the community. In this fashion, the idea of *campanilismo* meant a common identity, a loyalty, and the merging of individual interests with the well-being of the village, although often opposing the well-being of other villages.

On a more basic level, hope in a communal sense was practiced in Italy through the creation of co-operatives seeking to manage economic markets and the extremes of inequality. For example, the production of cheese and wine was often a shared activity involving a number of families; associative grazing of livestock was carried out in a noncompetitive manner; large-scale forestry or agricultural projects such as digging irrigation canals were undertaken in a concerted fashion for the collective good of the village; co-operative credit funds and banks were a staple in many communes. And small-scale *mezzadria* or share farming (as distinct from sharecropping) was to be found at various levels throughout the provinces of Italy. Lacking strong commitments to a distant and oppressive government and feudal class system, these collectives became primary social forms adopted by the *contadini* to manage their economic lives and abate the "cruel yoke which hangs upon their necks."[9] These collectives provided an immediate sense of "integration of aspirations for material betterment."[10]

Yet once Italians encountered the hopeful, instrumental individualism of American society it became increasingly difficult to hang onto this collective integration. In the modern world, hope became atomized, privatized, and desocialized.[11] These processes were accelerated with the decline of the Little Italys. As Jerome Krase argues, "the fuller community life" of these Italian enclaves were primarily waystations whereby "newcomers prepared for eventual entrance into the dominant society" with its expectations and hopes for success on an individual level.[12] As Italians moved out of these enclaves, hope became less social fact and more personality attribute. In now personal terms, hope was a liberation from existing conditions and a basis for pursuit of success and social mobility on one's own terms. This was at the core of being an American, with its "sense of open horizons, an impatience with communal constraints."[13]

The loss of the more communal, integrated practices of hope has had consequences. As suggested, persons of Italian ancestry have achieved relative parity with other Americans in terms of income and occupational status.[14] Nevertheless, they have also been exposed to the pathologies associated with an intemperate individualism in the form of increasing inequality among Italians, a range of physical ailments, and feelings of social isolation and loneliness.[15]

There are multiple, underlying causes for these maladies. The loss or the decline of a collective hope is arguably critical. As Durkheim theorized, unlike physical needs, psychological needs do not have intrinsic boundaries. There is nothing inherent in individualized hopes to set the limits for satisfaction and fulfillment. Reality is inexhaustible. The American Dream ushered in a competitive spirit and self-interest that worked against a communal life. It substituted a more broad-ranging set of individualistic values and an endemic culture of separation at the expense of an integrated and collective sense of hope. In the process, it threatened the very essence of individualized hope, for in Durkheim's way of thinking without communal hopes there is no individualized hope, without society, there is no person. Indeed, it is the dialogue between these different versions of hope that contextualizes self-interest in a manner that makes the differences among us more meaningful and less threatening.

In a concentrated fashion, we catch a glimpse of these transitions in the well-chronicled history of Roseto, Pennsylvania—a small, somewhat isolated village of mainly Italian immigrants and their descendants. For the greater part of the last century, Roseto gained renown in medical circles for the surprisingly low incidence of heart attacks, hypertension, strokes, depression, and related mental illnesses.[16] These favorable outcomes happened despite a diet and level of physical activity not always associated with positive results. In a comparison study of a nearby town, and in a statistically significant review of medical records, the most common conclusion was that the low rates of medical pathologies involved the social solidarity of the community. This social solidarity surfaced in the form of community associations, neighborhood gatherings, street festivals, and intergenerational family living.

Yet, beneath these social structures there were collective sentiments of hope as Roseto "emerged as a buoyant, fun-loving community that was more enterprising, more self-sufficient, more optimistic, and more prosperous than its neighbors."[17] The shared aspirations and sense of optimism in the village was the "cohesive quality extended to neighbors and the community as a whole."[18] Caroline Giovannini, a lifetime resident of Roseto, speaks of these communal feelings. She said the local parochial school building was a "symbol of community hope . . . we were like family." Parents would travel together to school-related sporting events involving their children. "And if one of the kids got hurt, it was like one of your own."[19]

Though it is easy to overstate the case, stress was minimized because undifferentiated strivings were measured against the common good. As John Bruhn and Stewart Wolf contend, "Rosetan culture thus provided a set of checks and balances to ensure that neither success nor failure get out of hand."[20] Inequality, especially ostentatious displays of status and wealth, was viewed as disruptive. Those who spent their money on "frivolous pleasures" were demonstrating a lack of concern for community needs. "Proper behavior by those Rostans who have achieved material wealth or occupational prestige requires attention to the delicate balance between ostentation and reserve, ambition and restraint."[21] Chronic episodes of social isolation and loneliness were rare since there was always someone (e.g., a family member, a neighbor, a workmate, a friend) around. Even instances of dementia were below the rates in the neighboring towns.[22]

Best-selling author Adriana Trigiani is intimately familiar with Roseto. Her grandfather was once mayor of the town. Her novel *The Queen of the Big Time* is a saga of American history, a romance novel, and a personal look back at Roseto. The story is centered on Nella Castelluca and her struggles to merge her personal dreams of a life well lived with the affection and appreciation she has for the Roseto community. At critical points, these lines diverge, and it was Nella's lifetime quest for the proper balance. Though never sure and always troubled, Nella seems to settle on her sister Chettie's more "sensible" approach to life. "She sees order in the world, and she fits her dreams into that order. She doesn't have high hopes or expectations that can never be fulfilled. She's practical."[23] In this sense, being "practical" and giving up on "high hopes" is not conceding defeat but a virtue instead. It is an understanding that individual hopes are constrained by a social order or a communion of hope lest they lack a necessary grounding, recognition, and sanctification. As Trigiani commented, "Hope is a thing without feathers . . . You have to have a value system where it is a part of your life."[24]

Individual hopes and community hopes were joined therefore in an uneven but systematic balance. Roseto was by no means ideal. It was not free of strife, conflicts, or prejudices. And it lent itself to unacceptable processes of social control and exclusion. We would not want to replicate its *gemeinschaft*-like character on a number of levels and suppress individual desires. Yet, it offered a contrast to the contemporary world. In the American context, it provided a version of the traditional Italian culture of *campanilismo* and a different meeting point between individual and communal hopes and between personal dispositions and the larger social structures.

The Roseto described above no longer exists. Though symbolic elements of the traditional culture are still celebrated, the internal cohesion and solidarity have long since been modified by more individualistic values as community members "acquired a taste for the material rewards typical of the American Dream."[25] This is neither surprising nor unwarranted. The relatively closed community of Roseto could not offer the economic or cultural opportunities available in the larger society. As a consequence, Roseto has long since exhibited a more pronounced economic and cultural hierarchy, higher rates of heart- and stress-related diseases, and a less filtered constraint upon individual ambition and hope. As Caroline Giovannini recalls, "The hope and dreams were never diminished but the sense of loss was always there."[26]

Chicago Heights was not exactly Roseto. It did not have a similar geographic and cultural isolation from the surrounding communities and the impact of mass society. There were too many elements of the modern, industrialized world for the Italian residents to create a viable community that acted as a buffer against the individualized reconfiguration of hope. And as suggested, a number of Italian immigrants, their children, and grandchildren did well in terms of assimilating into early twentieth-century American society, which in turn fueled the practical and ideological investments in private hopes and social mobility.[27] All the same, compared to Roseto the Heights had similar structures in terms of neighborliness, a sense of institutional completeness, and a shared concern regarding extremes of wealth or poverty—extending not just to fellow Italians but a variety of other ethnic and racial groups. Sorting through the nostalgic tendencies, my own included, of Chicago Heights residents, we still saw evidence for this community in the collective spirit of building homes, putting on wedding receptions, becoming ethnic entrepreneurs, purchasing items on unsecured credit from local merchants, farming community gardens together, assisting neighbors in financial need, mourning the death of community members, and so on. Art Marks said, "It was a neighborhood where everybody respected each other, helped each other. There was a unity."[28]

During the period from 1960 to the end of the century, most Chicago Heights immigrants and their children moved out of the Italian neighborhoods to the more prosperous areas of the city and neighboring towns, although maintaining a cultural association with the old neighborhoods by frequenting the few remaining merchants and attending the local parish, Saint Rocco. These residential changes were prompted by a host of factors. In part, they were motivated by fears of racial integration. But they were also spurred on by the younger generation's quest to move up the social ladder. For all the benefits that communal hopes offered, they could not compete with the cultural capital and economic gains produced by the privatization of hope.

From a more theoretical perspective, there is no inherent advantage in either of these individualistic or collective versions of hope. Both come with profits and liabilities. Individual hopes extracted from the social context produce a form of life where achievements can be anomic and uncoupled from a "context of meaning."[29] Communities of hope can be suffocating and mechanically deterministic. To avoid either extreme, the temptation is to look for a point somewhere in the middle. That is, the ideal mixture would allow private dreams of success up and until they confront the more integrated hopes of the social community. Perhaps, there have been examples where this middling blend has been achieved. The rich and detailed histories of Italian (or any ethnic group's) enclaves in America may reveal such periods. Most do not. They point to the ongoing, internal struggles in these communities between the emerging, individual hopes of success and the more traditional social and communal values. William Foote Whyte's classic study of the "college boys" and the "corner boys" (outside of its gendered character) still serves as an apt metaphor for these community processes.[30] It is difficult to imagine what a middle ground would look like.

Instead of looking for this evasive equilibrium, it may be more profitable to value this tension in and of itself. Privatized dreams and communal hopes exert a dynamic, dialectical force upon each other. And in this process something new, responsive, and transformative may come out of this struggle. In this sense, hope as a *practice*, in Bourdieu's sense, emerged in the Chicago Heights context. Hope was not simply an inward-dwelling, essentialist character trait lying dormant within the immigrant; nor was it a distant, constraining cultural value laid upon the immigrant. Instead, it was a practical, active logic forged in the extant setting that allowed these strangers to construct their own sense of worth and ambition within the confines of the early twentieth-century American value system. It was an improvisation that allowed these Italian newcomers, unlike resignation or dissent, to fit themselves personally and more effectively into the existing cultural patterns but at the same time change these patterns. In arriving at this compromise, there was a tacit recognition of the common interests between an individual self-consciousness and a parochial collective self-consciousness.[31] In idealized terms, individual hopes were nurtured, and communal hopes were strengthened and redefined in a mutually beneficial manner.

With this in mind, there is cause to worry that this dialectic has been muted in the present era. This is on two fronts. First, the encroachment of a highly autonomous and demanding quest for personal achievement, what Anthony Giddens refers to as the "reflexive project of the self," threatens to leave the individual standing alone and no longer effectively embedded in a group context.[32] Immigrants are subtly and powerfully encouraged to shed their group affiliations in favor of more personal choice and advancement. Indeed, continued attachments to their immigrant roots, both for the Italians in the past and particular immigrant groups today, are likely to bring forth anti-immigrant ideologies involving foreign conspiracies, fears regarding the spread of disease, and warnings regarding the invasion of a "criminal element." In this sense, immigrants are persuaded to move up and outside the immigration hierarchy by discarding their cultural legacies and grounding their mobility in the self. As Bellah and others contend, "The language of the self-reliant individual is the first language of American moral life."[33]

Decades ago, Richard Alba noted this tendency among Italian Americans as they came under the influence of the "achievement syndrome," which prompted "an emphasis upon the needs of the individual over those of the group."[34] More recently, Alba suggested that the assimilation processes may be more nuanced but still held that the long-term consequences of these processes have drawn the individual away from communal ties such that the best many Italian Americans can do is "feel Italian at moments."[35]

Second, and in a related fashion, "communities of hope" have been discouraged, if not disparaged. The collective past, both the stories of success and the less virtuous histories, are viewed as excess baggage. This has special relevance for the Italian experience in America with its long history of sacrifice and sufferings, as well as its triumphant successes, but also the sufferings Italians may have imposed upon others and the nefarious presence of organized crime. Without these "communities of memory" with their specific traditions, rituals, and stories, the dialectic between personal and communal aspirations is compromised. Aspirations and hopes become self-referential, static, and more difficult to maintain. And concern for the common good is diminished.

Chicago Heights is no longer—if it ever was in an exclusive sense—an Italian community. Thoughts of resurrecting a new ethnic social order where individual hopes and communal hopes are joined in a dialectic fashion are fanciful. Though there remains a sizeable Italian presence in the Heights, only a third of the population is in fact white; Blacks constitute a little more than a third, and the same with the Latino population.[36] And as we have pointed out, the Heights is like so many other communities wherein success is nearly synonymous with personal dreams, riches, and hopes. Small pockets of community pride and communal hopes aside, those who have "made it" are those who stand out from others or whose dreams have produced accomplishments that set them apart—whether in sports, business, politics, the arts, and so forth. The boosterish spirit of the early years or the unity produced by the enclaves in the subsequent decades are difficult to find, as is evidence of a more overarching sense of communal hope or common good.

Though fanciful, this necessary dialectic between individual and communal hope can be found; it can be resurrected across a range of groups in society. This would not entail a simple return to the traditions and sense of unity of the past. These produce wonderful memories but gloss over the exclusionary, stifling, and stagnant properties often associated with these social forms. More so, the emphasis should be upon "re-appropriating tradition" in meaningful ways or as Bellah and others contend "finding sustenance in tradition and applying it actively and creatively to our present realities."[37] At the same time, the integrity of individual hopes and communal hopes should not be compromised. This would do away with the necessary tensions or struggles that create a ubiquitous series of innovations or practices that serve as the basis for meaning and adaptability in the society.

With these caveats, among many others, in mind, how might we think of this mutually influencing, opposing domains of individual and communal hopes? First, the practical and political problem is to redraw the lines of communal hope to include the common heritages, traditions, and disadvantages of a variety of similarly situated or previously situated ethnic and racial groupings. The challenge, said Max Weber years ago, is to move beyond the "horizontal unconnected coexistences of ethnically segregated groups" and transform these "ethnically divided communities into specific political and communal action."[38] Of course we are aware, as certainly Weber was also, that this is a daunting task. It is important, therefore, to develop shared "communities of memories" that encompass the lived experiences of these different ethnic groupings. At the same time, the creation of common rituals that produce a pan-ethnic solidarity and the establishment of intermediary or secondary organizations that bind different groups together would be steps toward collective action and make the differences between these groups less threatening.[39] These would provide the cultural and structural supports for broadening but also intertwining individual and communal hopes. Fanciful or not, the Italian community in America has, in a manner of speaking, accomplished this of sorts by creating a common identity, forms of association, and a sense of shared experiences out of the myriad provinces and hill towns that at one time constituted the diverse lives of their immigrant forebears. Indeed, the historic animosity between northern Italians and southern Italians is of little consequence in the American context.

Second, this juxtaposition of individual and communal hopes should permit a variety of meeting points. There is no systemic equilibrium that is optimal. Matters of cultural legacy, shifting demographics, and existing forms of political and economic discrimination should weigh heavily upon the mix of individual aspirations and community sentiments. The goal is not to arrive at a set point but to carry on a conversation wherein private aspirations are articulated with common meanings and desires. Thus, the Roseto of the past is different from the Roseto today. Roseto was different from Chicago Heights. Chicago Heights was different from Coal Town. Both Chicago Heights and Coal Town were different, for example, from Highwood, Illinois—an Italian enclave that developed at roughly the same time but in the "blue-blood gentry," northern suburbs of Chicago wherein Italian immigrants established their presence in "a working-class community of small but well-tended lawns and single family cottages."[40] In short, communities differ in terms of their reliance upon the mix of individual and shared aspirations.

Third, an emphasis should be placed upon what Josiah Royce termed "wise provincialism." By provincialism, Royce means a sense of community wherein individuals have a love and pride, and, most importantly, a loyalty to the totality of their customs and ideals. Specifically, a community in which its members cherish their own "traditions, beliefs, and aspirations."[41] This provincialism is premised upon the assertion, in ways similar to Bourdieu's dialectic between habitus and field, that the individual and community are inevitably intertwined with one another. That is, the community provides a sense of coherence to otherwise unintelligible and untethered thoughts and feelings, whereas individuals provide the practical actions and communications that solidifies the community. Most importantly, both the individual and community are enriched when "each of its members accepts as a part of his own individual life and self the same *past* events that each of his fellow-members accepts" or what Royce termed a "*community of memory*" and similarly when "each of its members accepts, as part of his own individual life and self, the same expected *future* events that each of his fellows accepts," or what Royce called "a *community of hope*."[42]

To this idea of provincialism Royce adds the critical component wisdom. If provincialism involves a genuine feeling of pride and loyalty to the community, it must also be wise. Here, Royce argues that the viability and richness of the community require in pragmatic and moral terms an openness toward other communities. To do otherwise, would shrink the opportunities for learning from and adapting to ongoing challenges and would betray the hard-fought successes and sacrifices which lay at the foundation of the community or province. Emphasizing the solidarity of one's own group without gratitude and appreciation for the values and traditions of others does a disservice to the attempts to achieve the group's ideals. Loyalty to loyalty itself provides a common ground for associating with other groups, though provincial attitudes and customs may differ in substance. In Weberian terms, this provides a basis for bridging "horizontal unconnected coexistences," in Durkheimian terms it brings these different horizontal communities into a common "collective conscience," in Marxian terms it establishes a rudimentary form of class consciousness.

This is not a blueprint for immigration, social mobility, or assimilation. Instead, it intends to put each of these vibrant social processes into doubt. It does this by challenging the connecting link between all three: the idea of hope. In the secular world, hope should not get a pass, so to speak, because it is viewed as an empowering human spirit deep within our internal psyche, or as Durkheim cautions because it is thought to have "miraculously descended from heaven into our hearts." Hope cannot escape its ideological roots. For both noble and ignoble reasons, hope is a practice, cultural capital resource, rationalization, ritual, motivation, presentation, lure, and exercise of power. As such, hope begs our ambivalence. Depending upon one's personal situation and social standing, it is something that we should embrace, run away from, or approach with a healthy skepticism. Perhaps the only consistency to hope across these various incantations is that it promises something different. As Kieran Setiya concludes, "To hope well is to be realistic about possibilities, not to succumb to wishful thinking or be cowered by fear; it is to hold possibilities open when you should."[43] Maybe this is what the Italian immigrants had in mind all along.

Notes

Preface

1. Giovanni Schiavo, *The Italians in Chicago: A Study in Americanization* (Chicago: Italian American Publishing Company, 1928), 22.

Introduction

1. John Braithwaite, "Emancipation and Hope," *The Annals of the American Academy of Political and Social Science* 592 (2004): 80.

2. As suggested, hope is a difficult concept to pin down. It often merges imperceptibly with notions of optimism, dreaming, and wishing. Patrick Sharp's characterization of hoping in terms of the uncertainties and practicalities in pursuing certain ends begins to distinguish hope from its cognates. "Hoping," says Sharp, "differs from other activities largely because of the special circumstances attending its ends. Particular hopes are remote blocked ends which we nevertheless consider both desirable and realizable enough to merit our time and commitment" *Habits of Hope: A Pragmatic Theory* (Nashville: Vanderbilt Press, 2001). 42. Also, see Ariel Meirav, "The Nature of Hope," *Ratio* 22 (2009): 216–33.

3. Claudia Bloeser and Titus Stahl, "Hope," *The Stanford Encyclopedia of Philosophy* (Spring 2017 edition), ed. Edward N. Zalta (accessed June 30, 2018), https://plato.stanford.edu/archives/spr2017/entries/hope/.

4. Max Weber speaks eloquently of these religious and psychological struggles in his classic work, *The Protestant Ethic and the Spirit of Capitalism* (New York: Charles Scribner's Sons, 1958), 86–89. Also, see George Blaustein, "Searching for Consolation in Max Weber's Work Ethic," *New Republic*, July 2020, https://newrepublic.com/article/158349/searching-consolation-max-webers-work-ethic.

5. Robert Nisbet, *The Quest for Community* (London: Oxford University Press, 1953), 187.

6. Richard Rorty, *Contingency, Irony, and Solidarity* (New York: Cambridge University Press, 1989), 86.

7. Dick Hoerder. "From Dreams to Possibilities: The Secularization of Hope and the Quest for Independence," in *Distant Magnets: Expectations and Realities in the Immigrant Experience, 1840–1930*, ed. Dirk Hoerder and Horst Rossler (New York: Holmes & Meier, 1993), 2.

8. Oscar Handlin, *The Uprooted: The Epic Story of the Great Migration that Made the American People* (Philadelphia: University of Pennsylvania Press, 1973), 85.

9. Stephan Thernstrom, *Poverty and Progress: Social Mobility in a Nineteenth Century City* (New York: Atheneum, 1970), 58.

10. Richard Alba and Nancy Foner, *Strangers No More: Immigration and the Challenges of Integration in North America and Western Europe* (Princeton, NJ: Princeton University Press, 2015), 47.

11. John Dewey, *Human Nature and Conduct* (New York: Holt, Rinehart and Winston, 1922), 120.

12. This is Rudolph Vecoli's classic critique of Oscar Handlin's *The Uprooted*. See Rudolph Vecoli, "Contadini in Chicago: A Critique of the Uprooted," *Journal of American History* 51 (1964): 417.

13. James Henretta, "The Study of Social Mobility: Ideological Assumptions and Conceptual Bias," *Labor History* 18 (1977): 170.

14. Lauren Berlant, *Cruel Optimism* (Durham, NC: Duke University Press, 2011): 16.

15. Henretta, "Study of Social Mobility," 175.

16. Nancy Green and Roger Waldinger, "Introduction," in *A Century of Transnationalism: Immigrants and Their Homeland Connections,* eds. Nancy Green and Roger Waldinger (Urbana: University of Illinois Press, 2016), 11.

17. Daniel Bell, "Crime as an American Way of Life: A Queer Ladder of Social Mobility," in *The End of Ideology* (Cambridge, MA: Harvard University Press, 2000), 127–50.

18. Along these lines, a recent publication on the Italian immigration experience in Chicago was entitled, "Italian Women in Chicago, Madonna Mia! Qui debbo vivere?" The subtitle translates "You mean I have to live here?" See *Italian Women in Chicago*, ed. Dominic Candeloro, Kathy Catrambone, and Gloria Nardini (Stone Park, IL: Casa Italia Italian Cultural Center, 2013).

19. Giovanni Schiavo, *The Italians in Chicago: A Study in Americanization* (Chicago: Italian American Publishing Company, 1928), 22.

20. See Emilio Cecchi, *America Amara* (Florence: Sansoni, 1940); Gianfausto Rosoli, "From 'Promised Land' to 'Bitter Land': Italian Migrants and the Transformation of a Myth," in *Distant Magnets: Expectations and Realities in the Immigrant Experience, 1840–1930*, ed. Dirk Hoerder and Horst Rossler (New York: Holmes & Meier, 1993), 222–41.

21. Nancy Foner and Richard Alba, "The Second Generation from the Last Great Wave of Immigration: Setting the Record Straight," Migration Information Source (October 2006) (accessed December 30, 2019), https://www.migrationpolicy.org/article/second-generation-last-great-wave-immigration-setting-record-straight.

22. Darren Webb, "Modes of Hoping," *History of the Human Sciences* 20 (2007): 80.

23. John B. Thompson, "Editor's Introduction," in *Language and Symbolic Power*, by Pierre Bourdieu, trans. Gino Raymond and Matthew Adamson (Cambridge, MA: Harvard University Press, 1991), 29.

24. Along these lines, Patrick Shade's *Habits of Hope* offers a more sociological conception of hope when he describes it as an *activity* and suggests it "functions as a complex mode of interaction" (14).

25. Ludwig Wittgenstein, *Philosophical Investigations*, trans. G.E.M. Anscombe (New York: Macmillan, 1953), 174.ᵉ

26. Earnest Mandel, "Anticipation and Hope as Categories of Historical Materialism," *Historical Materialism* 10 (2002): 247.

27. Richard Swedberg, "A Sociological Approach to Hope in the Economy," in *The Economy of Hope*, ed. Hirokazu Miyazaki and Richard Swedberg (Philadelphia; University of Pennsylvania Press, 2017), 37–50.

28. See Nicholas Smith, "Hope and Critical Theory," *Critical Horizons: A Journal of Philosophy and Social Theory* 6 (2005): 45–61.

29. Karl Marx, *Early Writings* (London: Penguin Press, 1975), 244.

30. Karl Marx and Friedrick Engels, *On Religion* (Mineola, NY: Dover, 2008), 42.

31. For example, see Gerhard Vowinckel, "Happiness in Durkheim's Sociological Policy of Morals," *Journal of Happiness Studies*, 1 (2000): 447–464; Carlos Neves, "Optimism, Pessimism, and Hope in Durkheim," *Journal of Happiness Studies*, 4 (2003): 169–183.

32. Emile Durkheim, *The Division of Labor in Society*, trans. George Simpson (New York: Free Press, 1933), 245.

33. Max Weber, *From Max Weber: Essays in Sociology*, trans. Hans Gerth and C. Wright Mills (New York: Oxford 1958), 190.

34. Max Weber, *The Protestant Ethic and the Spirit of Capitalism*, trans. Talcott Parsons (New York: Routledge, 2001), 60.

35. Weber, *The Protestant Ethic*, 66.

36. Alfred Schutz and Thomas Luckman, *The Structures of the Life-World*, trans. Richard Zaner and H. Tristam Engelhardt Jr. (Evanston, IL: Northwestern University Press, 1973), 22–25.

37. Karl Marx, *The Eighteenth Brumaire of Louis Bonaparte* (New York: International Publishers, 1963), 15.

38. For a general cultural history of "animal spirits" as a driving, psychic force animating popular culture, politics, economics, and social movements in American society, see Jackson Lears, *Animal Spirits: The American Pursuit of Vitality from Camp*

Meetings to Wall Street (New York: Farrar, Straus and Giroux, 2023). I am indebted to Richard Martin for alerting me to this reference and the underlying assumptions tying hope to issues of vitality and spirits.

39. Louis Wirth, "Preface," in Karl Mannheim, *Ideology and Utopia*, trans. Louis Wirth and Edward Shils (New York: Harvest, 1955), xxi.

40. As Jerome Krase observes, the story of the Italian enclave in America has been told a number of times, though a general summary and comparison of these different settlements has only just begun. See Jerome Krase's steps in this direction, "Whatever Happened to Little Italy?" in *The Routledge History of Italian Americans*, ed. William J. Connell and Stanislao G. Pugliese (New York: Routledge, 2018), 523–37. For an incomplete but east to west geographical list of some of the major studies, see William Foote Whyte, *Street Corner Society* (Chicago: University of Chicago Press, 1943); Steven Puleo, *The Boston Italians* (Boston: Beacon, 2008); Donna Gabaccia, *From Sicily to Elizabeth Street: Housing and Social Change Among Italian Immigrants* (Albany: State University of New York Press, 1984); Robert Orsi, *The Madonna of 115th Street: Faith and Community in Italian Harlem, 1880–1950* (New Haven, CT: Yale University Press, 2010); Virginia Yans-McLaughlin, *Family and Community: Italian Immigrants in Buffalo, 1880–1930* (Ithaca, NY: Cornell University Press, 1977); Anthony Riccio, *The Italian-American Experience in New Haven* (Albany: State University of New York Press, 2009); Stefano Luconi, *From Paesani to White Ethnics: The Italian American Experience in Philadelphia* (Albany: State University of New York Press, 2001); Richard Juliani, *Building Little Italy: Philadelphia's Italians Before Mass Migration* (University Park: Pennsylvania State University Press, 1998); John Zucchi, *Italians in Toronto: Development of a National Identity, 1875–1935* (Montreal: McGill-Queen's University Press, 1988); Gary Mormino, *Immigrants on the Hill: Italian-Americans in St. Louis, 1882–1982* (Urbana and Chicago: University of Illinois Press, 1986); Dino Cinel, *From Italy to San Francisco: The Immigrant Experience* (Stanford: Stanford University Press, 1982); Deanna Paoli Gumina, *The Italians of San Francisco, 1850–1930* (New York: Center for Migration Studies, 1985).

41. Stephen Puleo, *The Boston Italians: A Story of Pride, Perseverance, and Paesani, From the Years of the Great Migration to the Present Day* (Boston: Beacon, 2007), XI.

42. Humbert Nelli, *Italians in Chicago, 1880–1920; A Study in Ethnic Mobility* (New York: Oxford University Press, 1970), 210.

43. Rudolph Vecoli, "The Formation of Chicago's 'Little Italies,'" *Journal of American Ethnic History* 2 (1983): 16. Along these lines, also see Dominic Candeloro, *Chicago's Italians: Immigrants, Ethnics, Americans* (Charleston, SC: Arcadia Press, 2003).

44. Thomas Gugliemo, *White on Arrival* (New York: Oxford University Press, 2004).

45. For example, see Fred DeLucca, "Our Neighbors in Heights—The Italian-Americans," *Chicago Heights Star*, an eight part series, April 14, 1936; April 17,

1936; April 21, 1936; April 23, 1936; April 28, 1936; May 1, 1936; May 5, 1936; May 8, 1936. Colleen Newquist, "Abbondanza! Italians Revel in the Sumptuous Feast that is America," *Chicago Heights Star*, September 3, 1993.

46. See Matt Luzi, *The Boys in Chicago Heights* (Charleston, SC, History Press, 2012); Charles Hager and David Miller, *Chicago Heights: Little Joe College, The Outfit, and the Fall of Sam Giancana* (Carbondale: Southern Illinois University Press, 2018); Louis Corsino, *The Neighborhood Outfit: Organized Crime in Chicago Heights* (Champaign-Urbana: University of Illinois Press, 2014).

47. Dominic Candeloro, "Suburban Italians: Chicago Heights, 1890–1975," in *Ethnic Chicago*, eds. Melvin G. Holli and Peter d'A. Jones (Grand Rapids, MI: W. B. Eerdmans, 1981); 180–209; Dominic Candeloro, "Mostly Melted/Still Connected: The Marchigiani in Chicago Heights 1893–1997," Casa Italia Cultural Center, Chicago Italian Archives, https://docs.google.com/document/d/1VeaUFTIXEK v6k9SXcEkOe0cqaSw45fjMPTtWou-DF4w/edit; Dominic Candeloro and Barbara Paul, *Chicago Heights: At the Crossroads of the Nation* (Charleston, SC: Arcadia, 2004); Dominic Candeloro, "There Was Never Just ONE Little Italy in Chicago," in *Reconstructing Italians in Chicago*, ed. Dominic Candeloro and Fred Gardaphé (Stone Park, IL: Casa Italia Italian Cultural Center, 2001), 13–29.

48. Robert Lewis, *Chicago Made: Factory Networks in the Industrial Metropolis* (Chicago: University of Chicago Press, 2008).

49. Chris Devatenous (Gregory), "Chicago Heights History" (working paper, University of Chicago, 1924), 27.

50. Department of Commerce, Bureau of the Census, *Thirteenth Census of the United States 1910, Volume 2, Population: Reports by States, with Statistics for Counties, Cities, and other Civil Divisions, Illinois* (Washington, DC: United States Census Bureau, 1911).

51. Candeloro, *"Suburban Italians,"* 182.

52. Personal Interview, Marie Iafollo, November 8, 2017.

53. Interview with Dominic Pandolfi, box 36, folder 449. Italian American Collection Records (IACR), (1979–1980), Italians in Chicago, Department of History, University of Illinois-Chicago Circle Campus

54. Today, close to 40 percent of the residents in Chicago Heights are of Latino origin. The vast majority of these residents came to the city in the latter half of the last century. Thus, the 1940 census only identified sixty-one persons of Mexican heritage in Chicago Heights [Department of Commerce, Bureau of the Census, *Sixteenth Census of the United States 1940, Volume II, Characteristics of the Population, Illinois* (Washington DC: United States Census Bureau, 1943)]. There is good reason to suspect that the population was greater in these early years, as the passage of restricted immigrant legislation in the 1920s reduced the influx of European newcomers. This provided openings for Mexican laborers, especially in the railroad and farm industry, though census takers had difficulty in recording Mexican citizens, for these workers feared deportation and were housed in temporary wooden

barracks and railroad cars. Similar to their Italian, Polish, and African American neighbors, these Mexican residents were influenced by the same lures of hope and false promises. As Garcia reports, a number of Mexican immigrants "stated that labor agents had misled them in an effort to contract them by showing pictures of beautiful houses which the railroads were supposed to furnish if they signed on." Juan Ramon Garcia, *A History of the Mexican American People in the Chicago Heights Area* (Chicago Heights: Prairie State College, 1975), 27.

55. Department of Commerce, Bureau of the Census, *Fifteen Census of the United States 1930, Volume III, Reports by States, Showing the Composition and Characteristics of the Population for Counties, Cities, and Townships and Other Minor Civil Divisions, Illinois* (Washington DC: United States Census Bureau, 1932).

56. John Wozny, *Growing up Polish: A History of the Polish Pioneers in Chicago Heights, Volume 1, 1900–1930* (Steger, IL: Growing Up Polish: 1993), 137.

57. Department of Commerce, Bureau of the Census, *Thirteenth Census of the United States 1910, Volume 2*; Department of Commerce, Bureau of the Census, *Sixteenth Census of the United States 1940, Volume II, Population: Illinois* (Washington DC: United States Census Bureau, 1943).

58. James Grossman, *Land of Hope: Chicago, Black Southerners, and the Great Migration* (Chicago: University of Chicago Press, 1989), 26.

59. "Whites Called Race of Demons," *Chicago Daily Tribune*, June 29, 1903, 2.

60. Mustafa Emirbayer and Mathew Diamond, *The Racial Order* (Chicago: University of Chicago Press, 2015).

61. See Fred Gardaphé "We Weren't Always White: Race and Ethnicity in Italian American Literature," in *Leaving Little Italy: Essaying Italian American Culture* (Albany: State University of New York Press, 2004), 123–36. For a brief review of the problems associated with classifying a range of ethnic groups as benefitting from their "whiteness," see Ali Meghji, *The Racialized Social System: Critical Race Theory as Social Theory* (Medford, MA: Polity Press, 2022), 48–52; David Roediger, *The Wages of Whiteness* (New York: Verso, 2022).

62. Emirbayer and Diamond, *The Racial Order*, 117.

63. F. S. Beeson, "History of Chicago Heights, Illinois, 1833–1938," 1938 (Federal Writers' Project, Chicago Heights Public Library Pamphlet File), 15.

64. Selma Lentz Morrison, "Freedom's Corner," *Chicago Heights Star*, November 14, 1958, 4.

65. Robert N. Bellah, Richard Madsen, William M. Sullivan, Ann Swidler, and Steven M. Tipton, *Habits of the Heart: Individualism and Commitment in American Life* (Berkeley, University of California Press, 1985), 153.

Chapter 1

1. Jerre Mangione and Ben Morreale, *La Storia, Five Centuries of the Italian American Experience* (New York: Harper Perennial, 1992), 138.

2. Ernest Bloch, *The Principle of Hope, Volume One* (Cambridge, MA: MIT Press, 1995), 75.

3. Mark Wyman, *Round-Trip to America: The Immigrants Return to Europe, 1880–1930* (Ithaca, NY: Cornell University Press, 1993), 14.

4. Alan Kraut, *The Huddled Masses, The Immigrant in American Society, 1880–1921* (Arlington Heights, IL: Harlan Davidson, 1982), 4.

5. Oscar Handlin, *The Uprooted: The Epic Story of the Great Migration that Made the American People* (Philadelphia: University of Pennsylvania Press, 2002), 6.

6. At the risk of understating the horrors of the Holocaust, the struggle of Holocaust victims to "invent hope" in the most degrading and totalitarian conditions of the concentration camps demonstrates the capacity of individuals to confront their immediate environment in a sociological sense. As Elie Wiesel concludes, hope is not something that simply exists to various degrees in a person but is founded upon the practices of community. As Wiesel stated, "Hope is not something that I can have if I am alone . . . ," for it was based in the commonalities of the shared experiences of the Holocaust prisoners and survivors. Howard Reich, *The Art of Inventing Hope: Intimate Conversations with Elie Wiesel* (Chicago: Chicago Review Press, 2019), 113.

7. Pierre Bourdieu, "The Social Spaces and the Generation of Groups," *Theory and Society* 14 (1985): 724.

8. Pierre Bourdieu "The Forms of Capital" in *Handbook of Theory and Research for the Sociology of Education*, ed. John G. Richardson (New York, Greenwood, 1986), 244–45.

9. Pierre Bourdieu, *The Logic of Practice*, trans. Richard Nice (Stanford, CA: Stanford University Press, 1990), 68.

10. Pierre Bourdieu, *The Logic of Practice*, 245.

11. In general terms, the stylized look of gangsters' dress—from Capone to Frank Costello to John Gotti—objectified and gave real-world presence to a shadowy underworld and culture that was otherwise difficult to identify. Even today, "Italian Mafia clothing" can be purchased by those who desire to express a "wiseguy" attitude or want to look the part. This clothing was an objectified, cultural form that signaled "a gangster style in the first half of the twentieth century, when suity bravado was a part of the whole threatening package." Rachel Tashjian, "Joe Pesci's Pointy-Collared Shirts Are the Scariest Garments in Cinema History," *Gentlemen's Quarterly*, November 14, 2019, https://www.gq.com/story/joe-pesci-collars.

12. Jennifer Guglielmo and Salvatore Salerno, eds., *Are Italians White? How Race is Made in America* (New York: Routledge, 2003). Also see Leslie McCall, "Does Gender Fit? Bourdieu, Feminism, and Conceptions of Social Order," *Theory and Society*, 21 (1992): 837–67.

13. Thomas A. Guglielmo, *White on Arrival: Italians, Race, Color, and Power in Chicago, 1890–1945* (New York: Oxford University Press, 2003).

14. Pierre Bourdieu, "Forms of Capital," 248.

15. Pierre Bourdieu, *The Social Structures of the Economy*, trans. Chris Turner (Cambridge: Polity Press 2005) 5.

16. Pierre Bourdieu, "Social Spaces and the Generation of Groups," 729.

17. For a fresh and disturbing look at the levels of repression experienced by southern "Italians" in the development of the nation-state, see Loreto Giovannone, *La Faccia Nascosta de Risorgimento* (Rome: Edizioni, 2020).

18. Lauren Berlant, *Cruel Optimism* (Durham, NC: Duke University Press, 2011), 4.

19. Ludwig Wittgenstein, *The Blue and Brown Books* (Oxford: Basil Blackwell, 1958), 17.

20. For a discussion of the game metaphor or more specifically the idea of "language games," see Ludwig Wittgenstein, *Philosophical Investigations*, trans. G. E. M. Anscombe (New York: Macmillan, 1958), 11–12. Bourdieu draws upon Wittgenstein's ideas of games throughout his discussion of social spaces. Specifically, he argues that social spaces are structured according to positions of domination and subordination, based largely upon one's access to capital. Those in the more dominant positions adopt more master strategies of *conservation*—that is, strategies aimed at maintaining the extant definitions and distribution of capital. Those in less powerful positions pursue more *subversive* strategies or practices that challenge the very legitimacy of those in power to define the standards and rules of the field. See David Swartz, *Culture and Power* (Chicago: University of Chicago Press, 1997) 123–25.

21. Beverly Santucci, " 'Against My Destiny': Reading an Italian Immigrant's Memoir in the Early 20th-century South" (2011). *University of New Orleans Theses and Dissertations*. 1344 (accessed January 8, 2020), https://scholarworks.uno.edu/td/1344.

22. Pietro di Donato, *Christ in Concrete: A Novel* (Indianapolis: Bobbs-Merrill, 1939), 18.

23. Food as an important form of symbolic capital has been a key theme in ethnic studies. For Italians, the social significance of food preferences seems especially significant. See Donna Gabaccia, *We Are What We Eat: Ethnic Food and the Making of Americans* (Cambridge, MA: Harvard University Press, 1998); Simone Cinotto, *The Italian American Table: Food, Family, and Community in New York City* (Champaign-Urbana: University of Illinois Press, 2013).

24. Interview Pasqua Sparvieri, box 7, folder 668, Italian American Collection Records (IACR), (1979–1980), Italians in Chicago, Department of History, University of Illinois—Chicago Circle Campus.

25. For an analysis of the connection between native whites, Blacks, and Italians in Spring Valley, see Caroline Waldron Merrithew, "Making the Italian Other: Blacks, Whites, and the In-Between in the 1895 Spring Valley, Illinois, Race Riot," (2003) *History Faculty Publications*. Paper 104, accessed December 10, 2022, http://ecommons.udayton.edu/hst_fac_pub/104.

26. Herman R. Lantz, with the assistance of J. S. McCrary, *People of Coal Town* (New York: Columbia University Press, 1958), 80. This was not the good fortune of 259 boys and men, most of them Italian, who died in the infamous Cherry Mine disaster in Cherry, Illinois, in 1909.

27. Pierre Bourdieu, *Distinction: A Social Critique of the Judgement of Taste*, trans. Richard Nice (Cambridge, MA: Harvard University Press, 1984), 194.

28. Pierre Bourdieu, *Outline of a Theory of Practice*, trans. Richard Nice (Cambridge: Cambridge University Press, 1977), 79.

29. Mangione and Morreale, *La Storia*, 224.

30. Louis Corsino, *The Neighborhood Outfit: Organized Crime in Chicago Heights* (Champaign-Urbana: University of Illinois Press, 2014), 56.

31. Richard Kozdras, "The Hill: The History of an Ethnic Neighborhood" (Chicago Heights: City of Chicago Heights, 1977), 15.

32. Robert Orsi, "The Religious Boundaries of an In-between People: Street *Feste* and the Problem of the Dark-Skinned Other in Italian Harlem, 1920–1990," in *Gods of the City*, ed. Robert Orsi (Bloomington: Indiana University Press, 1999), 266.

33. "Columbus Day," *Chicago Heights Signal*, October 19, 1911, 1.

34. Dominic Candeloro, "Italians: Immigrants, Ethnics, Achievers, 1850–1985," Illinois Periodicals Online, Northern Illinois University (accessed May 23, 2023), https://centurypast.org/great-lakes-states/illinois-social-history/.

35. See Swartz, *Culture and Power*, 125.

36. Rudolph Vecoli, "Chicago's Italians prior to World War I: A Study of Their Social and Economic Adjustment," (PhD diss., University of Wisconsin, 1963), 205.

37. Mangione and Morreale, *La Storia*, 159. As early as 1902, there was a sizeable number of socialist sympathizers in Chicago Heights. Thus, the Chicago Socialist Party had a local in the Heights and despite what the party called "trickery" on the part of Chicago Heights election officials, 188 citizens voted for the Socialist Presidential candidate in the 1902 election. See, *Chicago Socialist*, "The Revolt against Capitalism," November 15, 1902, 1.

38. Dominic Candeloro, *Voices of America: Italians in Chicago* (Charleston: Arcadia, 2001), 66.

39. Interview with Nick Zaranti, box 8, folder 668, Italian American Collection Records (IACR), (1979–1980), Italians in Chicago, Department of History, University of Illinois—Chicago Circle Campus.

40. La Cooperativa Italiana di Consumo di Chicago Heights, Ill., Casa Italia Cultural Center files, Stone Park, Illinois.

41. "Priests in Dread: Uneasy at Altar," *Chicago Tribune*, March 2, 1908.

42. "Matteson," *Chicago Heights Star*, July 13, 1911.

43. Interview with Joseph Giganti, box 92, Tamiment Library/Robert F. Wagner Labor Archives, Elmer Holmes Bobst Library (1983).

44. Jay Meadows, "The unsolved murder of famous anarchist Carlo Tresca," *New York Daily News*, August 14, 2017, accessed December 29, 2017, http://www.nydailynews.com/new-york/unsolved-murder-famous-anarchist-carlo-tresca-article-1.790137.

45. Letter Albert La Morticella to Nino La Morticella, courtesy Dominic Candeloro, Casa Italia Cultural Center files, Stone Park, IL.

46. "Socialists Bested by Loyal Italians," *Chicago Heights Star*, November 28, 1917.

47. "Statement of Dominick Mormile to Mr. August B. Loula, Special Agent, Bureau of Investigation, Department of Justice, Chicago, this tenth day of January, 1920."

48. "Statement of Dominick Mormile."

49. "Deportation Matter: Dominick Mormile," Bureau of Investigation, Department of Justice, December 7, 1919.

50. For an overview of this tumultuous period in American history, and in particular the antipathy on the part of the federal government toward the IWW, socialists, and Italians in the Chicago area, see Adam Hochschild, *American Midnight: The Great War, a Violent Peace, and Democracy's Forgotten Crisis* (New York: Mariner Books, 2022), especially, 159–70, 265–68.

51. Berlant, *Cruel Optimism*, 2.

52. Berlant, *Cruel Optimism*, 2. We are mainly speaking about the decisions and strategies of men. The habitus and practical definitions of Italian women, with notable exceptions, were circumscribed within a subset of social spaces—primarily, the family, the church, and other private venues. As such their hopes were more substantially restricted. Along these lines, see my "Gendered Spaces in an Italian Community," in *Italian Women in Chicago: Madonna Mia! (You Mean I have to Live HERE)*, ed. Dominic Candeloro, Kathy Catrambone, Gloria Nardini (Stone Park, IL: Casa Italia Cultural Center, 2013), 253–60.

53. Handlin, *The Uprooted*, 271.

54. Robert Orsi, *The Madonna of 115th Street: Faith and Community in Italian Harlem, 1880–1950* (New Haven, CT: Yale University Press, 2002), 20.

55. Handlin, *The Uprooted*. As Handlin suggests, "The idea was fully and clearly expressed in practice. The sense of being welcome gave people who had elsewhere been counted superfluous the assurance that their struggles to build a new life would be regarded with sympathy by their neighbors" (237).

56. Robert Wiebe, *The Search for Order: 1877–1920* (New York: Hill and Wang, 1967), 110.

57. Dick Hoerder. "From Dreams to Possibilities: The Secularization of Hope and the Quest for Independence," in *Distant Magnets: Expectations and Realities in the Immigrant Experience, 1840–1930*, ed. Dirk Hoerder and Horst Rossler (New York: Holmes & Meier, 1993), 11.

58. Robert Foerster, *The Italian Emigration of our Times* (Cambridge, MA: Harvard University Press, 1919), 395.

59. Robert Nisbet, *The Quest for Community* (London: Oxford Press, 1953), 226.

60. Handlin, *The Uprooted*, 271.

61. James Fraser, *A History of Hope* (New York: Palgrave, 2004).

62. Salvatore Mondello, "Italian Migration to the U.S. as Reported in American Magazines, 1880–1920," *Social Science* 30 (1964): 139.

63. Hana E. Brown, "Immigrant Body Incorporation" *Social Problems* 64 (2017): 15 (accessed December 19, 2022), https://www.jstor.org/stable/10.2307/26370888.

64. John E. Myers, "Do You Remember . . . ," *Chicago Heights Star*, July 31, 1980, 21.

65. David Efron, *Gesture and Environment: A Tentative Study of Some of the Spatio-temporal and Linguistic Aspects of the Gestural Behavior of Eastern Jews and Southern Italians in New York City, Living Under Similar as Well as Different Environmental Conditions* (New York: King's Crown Press, 1941), 150.

66. Chris Devatenous (Gregory), "Chicago Heights History" (Working paper, University of Chicago, 1924), 21.

67. Devatenous, "Chicago Heights History," 31.

68. David Roediger seems to be suggesting something like this when he wrote, "When new immigrant women insisted on having white curtains, they were claiming respectability and hope." *Working Toward Whiteness: How America's Immigrants Became White* (New York: Basic Books, 2005), 190. As these consumption processes relate to Italian Americans specifically, see the rich collection of articles in Simone Cinotto, ed., *Making Italian America: Consumer Culture and the Production of Italian Identities* (New York: Fordham University Press, 2014).

69. Evan Casey and Deirdre Clemente, "Clothing the Contadini: Migration and Material Culture, 1890–1925," *Journal of American Ethnic History*, 36 (2017): 17 (accessed January 11, 2020), http://dx.doi.org/10.5406/jamerethnhist.36.4.0005, With respect to "changing clothes," see Robert K. Fitts, "Becoming American: The Archaeology of an Italian Immigrant," *Historical Archaeology* 36 (2002): 5–6.

70. For a challenging and most thoughtful discussion of the relationship between architecture and hope, see Marina al-Sabouri, *Building for Hope, Toward an Architecture of Belonging* (London: Thames and Hudson, 2021).

71. San Rocco Oratory of the Archdiocese of Chicago, "Origins of the San Rocco Community" (accessed January 13, 2020), http://srocco.org/AboutUs/SAN-ROCCOPARISHHISTORYp1.html.

72. "Father Philip, Popular San Rocco Priest, Given Parish in Terre Haute," *Chicago Heights Star*, August 10, 1926, 1.

73. Personal Interview, Angelo Ciambrone, December 8, 2017.

74. Fred Deluca, "Our Neighbors in Heights—The Italian-Americans," *Chicago Heights Star*, May 8, 3.

75. Richard Juliani, "Italian Americans and Their Religious Experience," in *The Routledge History of Italian Americans,* ed. William J. Connell and Stanislao G. Pugliese, 197.

76. Dominic Candeloro, *Chicago's Italians: Immigrants, Ethnics, Americans* (Charleston, SC: Arcadia, 2003), 48.

77. Bourdieu, "Forms of Capital," 248.

78. Dorothee Schneider, "Naturalization and United States Citizenship in Two Periods of Mass Migration: 1894–1930, 1965–2000," *Journal of American History* 21 (2001): 50.

79. Schneider, "Naturalization and Unites States," 59.

80. John Gavit, *Americans by Choice* (New York: Harper & Brothers, 1922), 404, 408 (accessed January 19, 2020), http://www.gutenberg.org/ebooks/60576.
81. Gavit, *Americans by Choice*, 408.
82. Bourdieu, "Forms of Capital," 248.
83. Gavit, *Americans by Choice*, 9.

Chapter 2

1. Robert Foerster, *The Italian Immigration of Our Times* (Cambridge, MA: Harvard University Press, 1919), 47.
2. Jerre Mangione and Ben Morreale, *La Storia, Five Centuries of the Italian American Experience* (New York: Harper Perennial, 1992), 79.
3. Alan Kraut, *The Huddled Masses, The Immigrant in American Society, 1880–1921* (Arlington Heights, IL: Harlan Davidson, 1982), 41.
4. Humbert Nelli, *Italians in Chicago: 1880–1930, A Study in Ethnic Mobility* (New York: Oxford University Press, 1970), 3.
5. Maddalena Tirabassi, "Why Italians Left Italy," in *The Routledge History of Italian Americans,* ed. William J. Connell and Stanislao G. Pugliese, 119.
6. Edward Banfield, *The Moral Basis of a Backward Society* (Glencoe, IL: Free Press, 1958), 175.
7. Frank Cancian, "The Southern Italian Peasant: World View and Political Behavior," *Anthropological Quarterly* 34 (1961): 8.
8. Friedrich G. Friedmann, "Italian Letter: The World of La Miseria," *Partisan Review* 20 (1953): 220–21. Numerous other accounts also point out that hope was in short supply. For example, Peabody concluded that the economic and social conditions were so discouraging that "a feeling of hopelessness was therefore an inevitable result of such conditions." N.S. Peabody "Toward an Understanding of Backwardness and Change: A Critique of the Banfield Hypothesis," *The Journal of Developing Areas* 4 (1970): 384. Leonard Moss and Stephen Cappannari's "Estate and Class in a South Italian Hill Town," resulted in the observation that "the overwhelming problems of South Italy produces an apathy on the part of the general populace. This malaise . . . creates a futility on the part of the individual." *American Anthropologist* 64 (1962): 300.

At the same time, even if hope surfaced as a motivating force, larger social and economic forces may have shaped its expression toward or away from emigration. Rudolph Vecoli's reorienting critique of *The Uprooted* suggests such a varied response among the Italian peasantry at the turn of the last century. When peasants competed with one another as proprietors and tenant farmers, hope was organized in a self-interested, economically individualistic manner. It became a possession of the individual or the individual's family and freed the peasant to pursue emigration as a response to the social and economic misery. However, when land tenure policies favored communal agricultural collectivities, emigration rates, even in times of dire need, were low. Hope for the betterment of one's material conditions was expressed in "broad associative behavior," and economic aspirations were integrated with these broader collectives. Hope was bound up with the survival of the collectivity as a whole and anchored the peasant to the homeland or the *campanilismo*. See Rudolph Vecoli, "Contadini in Chicago: A Critique of the Uprooted," *Journal of American History* 51 (1964). Also, see J. S. McDonald, "Italy's Rural Social Structure and Emigration," *Occidente* 12 (1956): 454.

9. Foerster, "*Italian Immigration of Our Times*," 102.

10. James Henretta, "The Study of Social Mobility: Ideological Assumptions and Conceptual Biases," *Labor History* 18 (1977): 170. Also see Charles Stephenson, "A Gathering of Strangers? Mobility, Social Structure, and Political Participation in the Formation of Nineteenth-Century American Working Class Culture," in *American Working Class Culture: Explorations in American Labor and Social History*, ed. Milton Cantor (Westport, CT: Greenwood Press, 1979), 33–34.

11. James Henretta, *The Origins of American Capitalism* (Boston: Northeastern University Press, 1991), 75.

12. Henretta, *The Origins of American Capitalism*, 90.

13. David Montgomery, "The New Urban History," *Reviews in History* 2 (1974): 502.

14. Max Weber, *The Protestant Ethic and the Spirit of Capitalism*, trans. Talcott Parsons (New York: Charles Scribner's Sons, 1958), 60.

15. Peter Carravetta, "The Silence of the Atlantians: Contact, Conflict, Consolidation (1880–1913)," in *The Routledge History of Italian Americans*, ed. William J. Connell and Stanislao G. Pugliese, 135.

16. Joseph Senner, "The Immigrant Question," *The Annals of the American Academy of Social and Political Science* 10 (1897): 15.

17. See Daniel Okrent, *The Guarded Gate: Bigotry, Eugenics, and the Law That Kept Two Generations of Jews, Italians, and Other European Immigrants Out of America* (New York: Scribner, 2019), 147.

18. Vincent Cannato, *American Passage: The History of Ellis Island* (New York: HarperCollins, 2009), 94.

19. Phillip Rose, *The Italians in America* (New York: George H. Doran Company, 1922), 79.

20. Craig Calhoun, "Pierre Bourdieu," in *The Blackwell Companion to Major Contemporary Theorists*, ed. George Ritzer (Hoboken, New Jersey: Wiley & Sons, 2003), 277.

21. See Foerster, *The Italian Immigration of Our Time*; L. Villari, *Italian Life in Town and Country* (London: George Newnes, Limited, 1902); Jonathan Dunnage, *Twentieth Century Italy: A Social History* (London: Routledge, 2002), 4–37; Robert Lumley and Jonathan Morris, eds. *New History of the Italian South* (Exeter: University of Exeter Press, 1948).

22. As Dudley Baines suggests, a central question may be that given similar circumstances and the bleak realities, why is it that the vast majority of people did not depart for another country? To cite a lack of desire or hope shifts the explanation to a stream of unconscious, essentialist, and overly convenient psychological premises. See Baines, *Emigration from Europe, 1815–1930* (Cambridge: Cambridge University Press, 1995), 31.

23. Herbert Klein "The Integration of Italian Immigrants into the United States and Argentina: A Comparative Analysis," *The American Historical Review*, 88 (1983): 311; Dino Cinel, "Land Tenure Systems, Return Migration, and Militancy in Italy," *Journal of Ethnic History* 12 (1984): 55–76; Riccardo Fiani and Alessandra Venturini, "Italian Emigration in Pre-War Period," in *Migration and International Labor Market 1850–1939*, eds. T. J. Hatton and J. G. Williamson (London: Routledge, 1994), 72–90.

24. For example, see Antonio Margariti, *America! America!* (Casavelino Scalo: Galzerano, 1979); Ercole Sori, *L'emigrazione Italiana dall'unita alla Seconda Guerra Mondiale* (Bologna: Il Mulino, 1979); Pietro Borzomati, ed. *L Emigrazione Calabrese dall'unitá ad oggi* (Rome: Centro Studfi Emigrazione, 1982). Di Giuseppe De Bartolo, "L Emigrazione Calabrese a Chicago: Un Profolio Biografico," in *La Calabria Dei Migranti*, ed. V. Cappeli, G. Masi, and P. Sergi (Rivista Calabrese di Storia, 2014), 35–46.

25. Pino Arlacchi, "Perché si Emigrava dalla societá Contadina e non dal latifondo," in *L'Emigrazione Calabrese dall'unitá ad oggi*, ed. Pietro Borzomati (Rome: Centro Studi Emigrazione, 1982), 157–70.

26. Betty Boyd Caroli, "Recent Writing in Italy on Italian Emigration to the United States," *Journal of American Ethnic History*, 5 (1985): 70.

27. Berlant, *Cruel Optimism*, 2.

28. Charlotte Erickson, ed., *Emigration from Europe 1815–1914* (London: Adam & Charles Black, 1976), 90–104. In addition, see Mark Choate's detailed and innovative perspective on Italian *emigration* during this period. *Emigrant Nation: The Making of Italy Abroad* (Cambridge, MA: Harvard University Press, 2008), esp. 21–56; Also see the invaluable work of Donna Gabaccia, *Italy's Many Diasporas* (London: Routledge, 2000).

29. Grazia Dore, "Some Social and Historical Aspects of Italian Emigration to America," *Journal of Social History* 2 (1968): 112.

30. Alexander DeConde, *Half-Bitter, Half-Sweet: An Excursion into Italian-American History* (New York: Scribner, 1971), 80.

31. Betty Boyd Caroli, *Italian Repatriation from the United States, 1900–1914* (Ann Arbor: Center for Migration Studies, 1973), 156. Also, see Mark I. Choate, "Italian Emigration, Remittances, and the Rise of Made-In-America," in *The Routledge History of Italian Americans*, ed. William J. Connell and Stanislao G. Pugliese, 135.

32. Amoreno Martellini, "Il commercio dell'emigrazione: intermediary and agenti," in *Storia dell'Emigrazione Italiana: La Partenza*, ed. Piero Bevilacqua et al. (Rome, 2001), 297.

33. Torsten Feys, *Research in Maritime History, No. 50, The Battle for the Migrants: The Introduction of Steamshiping on the North Atlantic and its Impact on the European Exodus* (St, John's, Newfoundland: International Maritime Economic History Association, 2013), 81.

34. Gianfausto Rosoli, "From 'Promised Land' to 'Bitter Land': Italian Migrants and the Transformation of a Myth," in *Distant Magnets: Expectations and Realities in the Immigrant Experience, 1840–1930*, ed. Dirk Hoerder and Horst Rossler (New York: Holmes & Meier, 1993), 230.

35. Grazia Dore, *Some Social and Historical Aspects*, 116.

36. Grazia Dore, *Some Social and Historical Aspects*, 109.

37. Paolo Cresci Foundation for the History of Italian Emigration, Museo Dell' Emigrazione Italiana Online, "Guide for Emigrants" (accessed May 26, 2023), https://www.museoemigrazioneitaliana.org/dallitalia-nel-mondo/le-guide-per-gli-emigranti/.

38. Max Gallo, *The Poster in History* (New York: W. W. & Norton, 2002), 92.

39. Anita Pfeifer, "Their Memories of Ellis Island, USA," *Chicago Heights Star*, May 30, 1988, 8.

40. Torsten Feys, *Research in Military History*, 73.

41. Gunther Peck, "Divided Loyalties: Immigrant Padrones and the Evolution of Industrial Paternalism in North America," *International Labor and Working Class History* 53 (1998): 52.

42. United States Immigration Commission, 1907–1910, *Reports of the Immigration Commission: Abstract of Reports of the Immigration Commission, Vol. 2* (Washington, DC: Government Printing Office, 1911), 384.

43. Le Condizioni dei Contadini nel Veneto. Parte prima della relazione di Emilio Morpurgo sulla XI circoscrizione (Inchiesta Jacini) (Rome, 1882), 109. Quoted in Gianfausto Rosoli, "From 'Promised Land' to 'Bitter Land': Italian Migrants and the Transformation of a Myth," in *Distant Magnets*, ed. Dirk Hoerder and Horst Rossler, 227.

The promises made by the padrone rarely matched up with the reality of life in America. As one immigrant warned, "If you have to work investigate the person with whom you go very closely because you can be easily fooled." See Humbert Nelli, ed., "The Padrone System: An Exchange of Letters," *Labor History* 17 (1976): 410. At the same time, the *Bollentiino della Emigrazione*, the primary historical record of Italian immigration in Italy produced by the Commissariata Generale dell' Emigrazione, often spoke of the clandestine agents and the *fallaci promesse* these agents would offer to lure fellow countrymen to America. See "Publicazioni del Commissariato e Diffusione di Notizie Utili agli Emigranti," *Bolletinno dell' Emigrazione*, 7, no. 2 (1908), 185. Nevertheless, hope or the *fallaci promesse* was an effective ideological tool that immigrants adopted at least in these early stages of the immigration processes.

44. Dore, *Some Social and Historical Aspects*, 117.

45. See Cresci and Guidobaldi, *Partone I Bastiment* (Milan: Mondadari, 1980), 22. "Durante la navigazione la coperta era sempre affollata, se il bel tempo

lo permetteva. In coperta si lavavano i panni ad asciugare; si respirava una boccata d'aria, lontani dalle maleodoranti stive; si intrecciavano le prime le prime amicizie e si for mavano solidarieta di pena e di miseria specialmente con chi proveniva dalla stessa regione e parlava lo stesso dialetto. La coperta era ance l'unico posto dove—se non si soffriva il mal di mare—era possibilie avere spazio per consumare i pasta. La distribuzione del cibo era fatta in modo umiliante; una persona per ogni gruppo do sei lo ritirava in cucina e perico numererose erano le frodi e i reclami. La promiscuita, che l'affollamento e la mancanza, a bordo, di sale da pranzo rendevano impossibile qualsiasi norma igienica, tanto piu che in coperta veniva effettuata anche la macellazione degli animali e si rovesciavano tutte le immondizie volontarie o involontarie dei miserabili passeggeri." (During navigation the deck was always crowded, if the good weather permitted. On the deck they washed their clothes to dry; there was a breath of air, far from the foul-smelling holds; the first friendships were intertwined and solidarity of pain and misery was formed especially with those who came from the same region and spoke the same dialect. The blanket was also the only place where—if you didn't suffer from seasickness—it was possible to have space to consume pasta. The distribution of the food was done in a humiliating way; one person from each group of six collected it in the kitchen and there were numerous frauds and complaints. The crowding and the lack of dining rooms on board made any hygienic norm impossible, especially since the slaughter of the animals was also carried out on the deck and all the voluntary or involuntary garbage of the miserable passengers was overturned.)

46. Jason Francisco and Elizabeth Anne McCauley, "The Steerage and Alfred Stieglitz," *The Chautauquan: The Magazine of System in Reading* 48 (1907): 383–90.

47. Interview Olivia Kowalski box 24, folder 282. Italian American Collection Records (IACR), (1979–1980), Italians in Chicago, Department of History, University of Illinois-Chicago Circle Campus.

48. Personal Interview, Andy Corsino, March 13, 1993. The description of the treatment and the characterization of the immigrants themselves as somehow less than human was common. The immigrants often objected to their treatment as animals with respect to toilet facilities, sleeping arrangements, and feeding. The crews on the ships thought that the immigrants "crowded like swine." Barry Moreno, *Encyclopedia of Ellis Island* (Westport, CT: Greenwood Press, 2004), 228.

49. For example, the Italian Welfare League, the Society for the Protection of Italian Immigrants, and the Saint Raphael Society for the Protection of Italian Immigrants were among the most prominent aid societies focused on improving the conditions for Italian immigrants.

50. William Price, "What I learned By Traveling From Naples to New York in the Steerage," in *The Italians: Social Backgrounds of an American Group*, ed. Francesco Cordasco and Eugene Bucchioni (Clifton, NJ: Augustus M. Kelley, 1974), 108.

51. Alexander DeConde, *Half-Bitter, Half-Sweet*, 72.

52. In an ironic and foreshadowing manner, there was only one person who died in the construction of the Statue of Liberty. It was an Italian immigrant and laborer, Francis Longo. See Elizabeth Mitchell, *Liberty's Torch: The Great Adventure to Build the Statue of Liberty* (New York: Atlantic Monthly Press, 2014), 260.

53. Rudolph Vecoli, " 'Free Country': The American Republic Viewed by the Italian Left, 1880–1920," in *In the Shadow of the Statue of Liberty*, ed. Mariasnne Debouzy (Saint Denis, France: Presses Universitaires de Vincennes, 1986), 30.

54. Joseph Senner, Commissioner of Immigration at Ellis Island, would report that prior to 1900 only 5 percent of immigrants aboard ships from England or Scandinavia were detained for a special inquiry, and only a small number of these were denied admittance. The Italians did not fare as well. "We not infrequently have ships from Italian ports where 50 percent and more have been detained for special inquiry, resulting in the final debarring from landing of some 20 percent of such number." See "The Immigration Question," 10. And this was a period before the introduction of an education and literacy test at Ellis Island—challenges no doubt to the typical southern Italian peasant.

55. Curtis Swanson, "Life's Curveballs Didn't Faze Bruno," *Chicago Heights Star*, September 16, 1990, c-2.

56. Anita Pfeifer, "Their Memories of Ellis Island, USA," *Chicago Heights Star*, May 30, 1988, 8.

57. "Women Patriot Bodies Gather at Joint Meeting," *Chicago Heights Star*, February 24, 1928, 1.

58. Amy Fairchild, A. *Science at the Borders: Immigrant Medical Inspection and the Shaping of the Modern Industrial Labor Force* (Baltimore: Johns Hopkins University Press; 2003), 115.

59. Michel Foucault, *Discipline and Punishment* (Harmondsworth, UK: Penguin, 1991), 304.

60. "The Spectator," *The Outlook*, March 25, 1905, 731.

61. Amy Bernardy, quoted in Michael La Sorte, *La Merica: Images of Italian Greenhorn Experience* (Philadelphia: Temple University Press, 1985), 45.

62. Alan Kraut, *Silent Travelers: Germs, Genes, and the 'Immigrant Menace'* (Baltimore: John Hopkins University Press, 1994), 62. Along these lines. Nancy Carnevale suggests that the mannerisms and facial expressions of Italian immigrants played a significant role in deciding the suitability of Italian immigrants for entrance into the country. In an era and situation where language barriers were difficult to overcome, speech patterns and general body movements were often read as signs of mental health and potential grounds for deportation. See Carnevale's *A New Language, A New World* (Urbana and Chicago: University of Illinois Press, 2009), 79–86. Loreto Giovannone points out that in the inspection stations at Ellis Island something as simple as a look of sadness on the face of an immigrant, a look that conveyed a "faccia molte triste" could easily be interpreted as a sign of feeblemindedness and

serve as a basis for exclusion. See Loreto Giovannone, "Reconstructing the Risorgimento, Espresso, Italian-American Reflections 2020 Series," YouTube Video, 1:33.58, May 17, 2021, https://www.youtube.com/watch?v=CkVVlWqFMzw&list=PLkXrN-9HIqYpEZU8Q-jkKlAflkSxfXKuH-&index=32.

63. Kraut, *Silent Travelers*, 56.

64. Lorie Conway, *Forgotten Ellis Island* (New York: Smithsonian, 2007), 35–38.

65. David M. Brownstone, Irene M. Franck, and Douglass Brownstone, *Island of Hope, Island of Tears* (New York: Metrobooks, 2003), 161.

66. Interview with Nick Zaranti, box 52, folder 668. Italian American Collection Records (IACR), (1979–1980), Italians in Chicago, Department of History, University of Illinois-Chicago Circle Campus.

67. Pfeifer, "Their Memories of Ellis Island," 8.

68. See Catherine Clare Boland, *Spaces of Immigration: American Railroad Companies, the Built Environment, and the Immigrant Experience* (New Brunswick, NJ: Rutgers University Press, 2013).

69. Castle Garden's Monopoly: Cogent Reasons for the Abolition of the Emigration Commission," *The World*, 27 (1887): 5. Quote reprinted in Pamela Reeves, *Ellis Island: Gateway to the American Dream* (New York: Crescent, 1991) 26.

70. Theodore C. Blegen, "The Competition of the Northwestern States for Immigrants," *The Wisconsin Magazine of History*, 3 (1919): 12.

71. For a description of the padrone system in this morally objectionable form see Carol Wright, *The Italians in Chicago: Ninth Special Report of the Commissioner of Labor* (Washington, DC: US Government Printing Office, 1897), and "Padrone System as It Exists in the Italian Colony of Chicago," *Chicago Tribune*, November 14, 1897, 29.

72. Dominic Candeloro, "Suburban Italians: Chicago Heights, 1890–1975," in *Ethnic Chicago*, ed. Melvin G. Holli and Peter d'A. Jones (Grand Rapids, MI: W. B. Eerdmans, 1981), 191.

73. Personal Interview, Joe Nicastro, August 5, 1995.

74. Along these lines, see Grace Abbott, "The Chicago Employment Agency and the Immigrant Worker," *American Journal of Sociology* 14 (1908): 289–305.

75. Interview with Dominic Pandolfi, box 36, folder 449, Italian American Collection Records (IACR), (1979–1980), Italians in Chicago, Department of History, University of Illinois-Chicago Circle Campus

76. These percentages were compiled through a review of the Department of Commerce, Bureau of the Census, *Twelfth Census of the United States 1900, Population: Reports by States, with Statistics for Counties, Cities, and other Civil Divisions, Illinois, Chicago Heights Manuscripts* (Washington, D.C. Government Printing Office, 1901); Department of Commerce, Bureau of the Census, *Thirteenth Census of the United States 1910, Population: Reports by States, with Statistics for Counties, Cities, and other Civil Divisions, Illinois, Chicago Heights Manuscripts* (Washington, DC: Government Printing Office, 1911).

77. Jared Day, "Credit, Capital, and Community: Informal Banking in Immigrant Communities in the United States: 1880–1924," *Financial History Review* 9, no. 1, 2002: 67.

78. Interview with Theresa Giannetti, box 21, folder 239, Italian American Collection Records (IACR). Italians in Chicago, Department of History, University of Illinois-Chicago Circle Campus.

79. Department of Commerce, Bureau of the Census, *Thirteenth Census of the United States 1910, Population: Reports, Chicago Heights Manuscripts* (Washington, DC: Government Printing Office, 1901)

80. Rudolph Vecoli, "Chicago's Italians Prior to World War I: A Study of Their Social and Economic Adjustment" (PhD diss., University of Wisconsin, 1962), 205.

81. Richard Kozdras, "The Hill: The History of an Ethnic Neighborhood" (Chicago Heights: City of Chicago Heights, 1977), 7.

82. Michael *Piore, Birds of Passage: Migrant Labor and Industrial Societies (Cambridge: Cambridge University Press, 1979),* 64.

83. Robert Harney, "Boarding and Belonging," in *American Immigration and Ethnicity, Immigrant Institutions: The Organization of Immigrant Life*, ed. George Pozzetta (New York: Garland Press, 1991), 26.

84. "One Reason Why the 'Star' Opposes Mayor J.C. Mote," *Chicago Heights Star*, March 30, 1911.

85. Dominic Candeloro, "Suburban Italians: Chicago Heights, 1890–1975," 189.

86. John Wozny, *Growing up Polish: A History of the Polish Pioneers in Chicago Heights: Volume I, 1900–1930* (Steger, IL: Growing Up Polish, 1993), 109.

87. Letter Albert La Morticella to Nino La Morticella, courtesy Dominic Candeloro, Casa Italia Cultural Center files, Stone Park, Illinois, October 11, 1979.

88. Interview with Nick Zaranti, box 52, folder 668, Italian American Collection Records (IACR), (1979–1980), Italians in Chicago, Department of History, University of Illinois—Chicago Circle Campus.

89. Despite the deplorable and dehumanizing conditions in the factory and chemical plants in Chicago Heights, it is easy to gloss over the fact that these were considered some of the best jobs available. Indeed, many Italian immigrants came to Chicago Heights to escape jobs in the garment, construction, or mining industry that were less favorable and more dangerous. For example, jobs in mining paid less and had rates of accidents and death that were abhorrent. Betty Boyd Caroli reports that in Illinois in the period from 1883 to 1910, 180 men died each year in mining accidents, along with the number who suffered injuries and long-term ailments. Caroli describes how the miners "faced a particularly grim life." Whatever hopes lured these Italian men to America, it is difficult to see how they played out in the below-ground coal fields and mining communities. "Italians in the Cherry, Illinois Mine Disaster," in *Pane E LaVoro: The Italian American Working Class*, ed. George Pozzetta (Toronto: The Multicultural History Society of Ontario, 1980), 67–80.

90. "Mfrs. Association Annual Banquet," *Chicago Heights Star*, December 21, 1922.

91. Kozdras, "The Hill," 14.

92. "Woman Leads Aliens' Fight: Mrs. M.B. Spencer Wants East Chicago Heights Improvements," *Chicago Daily Tribune*, February 10, 1914, 3.

93. Interview with Nick Zaranti, box 36, folder 449, Italian American Collection Records (IACR).

94. Collen Newquest, "The Hill Boasts a 'Rich' Tradition," *Chicago Heights Star*, 1988, 3.

95. Personal Conversation, Celia Concialdi, March 7, 2021.

96. The environmental conditions on the East Side of Chicago Heights have changed little through the decades. See "Woman Leads Aliens' Fight," *Chicago Daily Tribune*; "City Seeks to Fix Blame in Grit Nuisance," *Chicago Heights Star*, August 26, 1938, 1.

97. Wallace Stegner's *geography of hope* provided the grounding for a broad understanding of the relationship between physical surroundings and the personal sentiment of hope. See Page Stegner and Mary Stegner, *A Tribute to Wallace Stegner: The Geography of Hope* (New York: Random House, 1996). David Harvey's *Spaces of Hope* (Berkeley: University of California, 2000) provides a more focused but distant understanding of how urban processes may generate or drain hope in a collective sense from the community.

98. Kozdras, "The Hill," 2.

99. There is no doubt that Italian immigrants and their children were geographically separated from the mainstream society in Chicago Heights for the first half of the last century. And this had consequences in terms of this geography of hope and where Italians fell in the immigrant hierarchy. The stories for the Mexican and Black populations in Chicago Heights were, and continue to be, even more dramatic and consequential. There is an unfortunate history of discrimination practiced by West Siders, now including a large segment of the Italian population. Thus, the dissimilarity index for Black–white populations in Chicago Heights stood at .068 in 2000, and for Latino–white populations at .063. Both indices suggest high segregation levels and are very similar to the Italian–Native White dissimilarity indicators in the first half of the century (See chapter 5 for this comparison). Maria Krysan, "Racial Residential Segregation and Exclusion in Illinois," *The Illinois Report*, 2009, https://igpa.uillinois.edu/sites/igpa.uillinois.edu/files/reports/IR09-Ch4-Segregation.pdf; also, see Ramon Garcia, *A History of the Mexican American People in the Chicago Heights, Illinois Area* (Chicago Heights: Prairie State College, 1976); Lolly Bowern, "Chicago Heights Overall Ordered," *Chicago Tribune*, February 10, 2006.

100. Rudolph Vecoli, "Prelates and Peasants: Italian Immigrants and the Catholic Church," *Journal of Social History* 2 (1969): 230.

101. Richard Juliani, "Italian Americans and Their Religious Experience," in *The Routledge History of Italian Americans*, ed. William J. Connell and Stanislao G. Pugliese, 197.

102. Interview with Dominic Pandolfi, box 36, folder 449, Italian American Collection Records (IACR).

103. Interview with Theresa Giannetti, box 21, folder 239, Italian American Collection Records (IACR).

104. Harold Colbert Jones Memorial Community Center (accessed November 10, 2011), www.jonescenter.org/.

105. Pierre Bourdieu, *Distinctions. A Social Critique of the Judgment of Taste*. trans. Richard Nice (Cambridge, MA: Harvard University Press, 1984), 466.

Chapter 3

1. James Henretta, "The Study of Social Mobility: Ideological Assumptions and Conceptual Biases," *Labor History* (1977): 172.

2. "Chicago Heights," *Chicago Heights Signal*, July 27, 1911, 2.

3. Louis Corsino, *The Neighborhood Outfit: Organized Crime in Chicago Heights* (Champaign-Urbana: University of Illinois Press, 2014), 76.

4. "Pressendo Story . . . A Story of Chicago Heights" *Chicago Heights Star*, July 13, 1951, 17.

5. "Too Much Speed; Car Turns Turtle; Two Lives Taken," *Chicago Heights Star*, September 22, 1917, 3.

6. This description glosses over the more robust and at times contentious social life that characterized these ethnic enclaves in Chicago Heights with its mixture of Italian, Polish Lithuanian, Greek, Mexican, and African American residents. For a more complete description, see Dominic Candeloro and Barbara Paul, *Chicago Heights: At the Crossroads of the Nation* (Charleston, SC: Arcadia, 2004); Genevieve Ford Reed, *Looking over Our Shoulders* (n.d.), 1, Chicago Heights History 1900–1930 (Chicago Heights Public Library Pamphlet File); John Wozny, *Growing Up Polish: History of Polish Pioneers in Chicago Heights* (Chicago Heights: Growing up Polish, 1993); Juan Ramon Garcia, *A History of the Mexican American People in the Chicago Heights, Illinois Area* (Chicago Heights: Prairie State College, 1976). There is also little discussion of the social life of Italian women in Chicago Heights. For a brief depiction, see my "Gendered Spaces in an Italian Community," in *Italian Women in Chicago: Madonna mia! Qui debbo vivere?*, eds. Dominic Candeloro, Kathy Catrambone, and Gloria Nardini (Stone Park, IL: Italian Cultural Center at Casa Italia, 2013), 247–54.

7. Oral History Interview with Anthony Scariano, Vol. 1, 7, 1988, Illinois General Assembly Oral History Program, University of Illinois at Springfield, Norris L. Brookers Library, Archives/Special Collections (accessed March 5, 2021), http://www.idaillinois.org/digital/collection/uis/id/5082/rec/8.

8. "I.W.W. Meeting Nipped in the Bud," *Chicago Heights Star*, June 20, 1918, 1, 2; "Socialists Bested by Loyal Italians," *Chicago Heights Star*, November 28, 1917, 1, 6.

9. "Council Stirred by Open Letter of Vice Situation," *Chicago Heights Star*, July 22, 1920. Indeed, many Italians themselves looked with appropriate disdain at the violence and organizational methods of these fellow Italians. The antipathy toward these organized crime figures was warranted on moral grounds. However, this may have also come about because the success of these men short-circuited the more grueling paths to mobility most Italians were attempting to navigate. As Louis Winnick pointed out, Italian gangsters created a "crooked ladder to achievement" and in the process put the socially sanctioned hopes and mobility aspirations of the typical Italians into doubt ("Yearning to be Free," *New York Times*, February 28, 1988). These sentiments were expressed by Dominic Candeloro. Candeloro said his father, Louis Candeloro, thought that those Italians involved in these criminal enterprises were "lazy and unwilling to do the hard work it took to be successful." Personal Interview, Dominic Candeloro, December 20, 2018.

10. On a personal note, I remember Luigi, my grandfather, asking me directly if I wore blue jeans to my job as a professor when I taught at the University of California, Riverside. I thought the question odd, for blue jeans have most always been my "uniform" as I made my way through the cultural maze of academia. When I responded that I did, he shook his head ever so slightly and in a grandfatherly way expressed his disappointment in my stylistic choices. It never occurred to me that I was disappointing him at a far deeper cultural level in terms of demonstrating that his grandson and namesake had in some part given away what he had worked so hard to achieve and never obtained—the ability to go to work dressed as a "white collar" worker.

11. Edward Pessen, "Social Mobility in American History: Some Brief Reflections," *The Journal of Southern History* 45 (1979): 177.

12. Specifically, Thernstrom's scheme places *high white collar* at the top (e.g., lawyers, manufacturers, merchants with sufficient property); followed by *lower white-collar* jobs (e.g., salesmen, foremen, small business proprietors); *skilled* occupations (e.g., masons, machinists, and tailors); *semi-skilled* (e.g., barbers, teamsters, and firemen); and *unskilled jobs* (e.g., laborers, porters, and gardeners). See Stephan Thernstrom, *The Other Bostonians: Poverty and Progress in the American Metropolis, 1880–1970* (Cambridge, MA: Harvard University Press, 1973), Appendix B. 289–302. Thernstrom's occupational scheme has not escaped sharp criticism from historians. See Patrick Horan, "Occupational Mobility and Historical Social Structure," *Social Science History* 9 (1985): 25–47; Clyde Griffen, "Occupational Mobility in Nineteenth Century America: Problems and Possibilities," *Journal of Social History* 5 (1972): 310–30; Bart Van De Putte and Andrew Miles, "A Social Classification Scheme for Historical Occupational Data, Historical Methods," *Journal of Quantitative and Interdisciplinary History* 38 (2005): 61–94, 10.3200/HMTS.38.2.61-94 https://doi.org/10.3200/HMTS.38.2.61-94.

13. To state that the information in this table captures "all" Italian immigrants in each census is not precisely accurate. We engaged in a systematic identification of

Chicago Heights Italians based on a review of the individual manuscripts for each of the relevant censuses. Though we methodically examined and double-checked our data-gathering processes, it seems inevitable that we may have missed some of the Italian males in the manuscripts. And the census takers themselves may have overlooked and underreported some fraction of this population for a number of understandable reasons. Still, we can state with considerable confidence that the numbers and percentages offered are an accurate reflection of the relevant populations.

14. Personal Interview, Marie Iafollo, November 8, 2017.

15. Interview with Frank Corradetti, box 13, folder 146 (IACR).

16. John Wozny, *Growing Up Polish: A History of the Polish Pioneers in Chicago Heights: Volume 1, 1900–1930* (Steger, IL: Growing Up Polish, 1993), 109.

17. Rudolph Vecoli, "Chicago's Italians Prior to World War I: A Study of Their Social and Economic Adjustment," (PhD diss., University of Wisconsin, 1963), 209.

18. Dominic Candeloro, *Italians in Chicago* (Charleston, SC: Arcadia, 2001), 68. The factories of Chicago Heights were indeed dangerous places to work. An ironically entitled *Chicago Heights Star* article, "Nineteen Twenty-Two; You Were Good to Us," could nevertheless report on "nearly a score of fatal accidents" in that calendar year alone, including George DeFrees who "burned to death" at the American Manganese Steel Company plant (May 6, 1922, 2).

19. For example, Baily points out in the larger, competitive market of New York City, Italian skilled workers made approximately twice as much as unskilled workers. Samuel Baily, *Immigrants in the Land of Promise: Italians in Buenos Aires and New York, 1870 to 1914* (Ithaca, NY: Cornell University Press, 1999), 119.

20. Chicago Heights Chamber of Commerce, "Industrial Survey," n.p., section IV, 1927, 7 (Chicago Heights Public Library Pamphlet File).

21. Interview with Frank Corradetti, box 13, folder 146, Italian American Collection Records (IACR), (1979–1980), Italians in Chicago, Department of History, University of Illinois—Chicago Circle Campus.

22. These patterns are roughly similar to the trends found in other communities. Thus, Perlmann's study of Italian immigrant "fathers" in Providence, Rhode Island, found a twofold increase in high white-collar occupations and an approximately one-third decrease in unskilled jobs in the period from 1910 to 1925. Joel Perlmann, *Ethnic Differences: Schooling and Social Structure among the Irish, Italians, Jews and Blacks in an American City, 1880–1935* (Cambridge: Cambridge University Press, 1988), 86–88. Josef Barton's study of Cleveland concluded that "between 1910 and 1930 a small proportion of manual workers began a slow but steady climb into white-collar jobs." Josef Barton, *Peasants and Strangers: Italians, Rumanians, and Slovaks in an American City, 1890–1950* (Cambridge, MA: Harvard University Press, 1975), 95. These incremental upward patterns may be explained, at least in part, by the gradual acquisitions of skills and experiences and by the structural transformations in the workplace whereby over time the number of white-collar jobs became more numerous, and the jobs in the industrial sector became more technologically and

organizationally advanced. Whatever the exact mix of personal and structural factors, if an Italian immigrant was to look toward fellow Italians then there would reasons to be encouraged (although one would have to look hard).

23. Baily, *Immigrants in the Land of Promise*, 113.

24. Melanie Archer and Judith Blau, "Class Formation in Nineteenth Century America: The Case of the Middle Class," *Annual Review of Sociology* 19 (1993): 29–30.

25. Barton concludes that Italian immigrants with menial or lower white-collar occupations had difficulty staying at that level throughout their careers and that most always went down rather than up (*Peasants and Strangers*, 99). For these "skidders," it is difficult to imagine how they may have maintained hope for success if "a man's occupation is the most important index of his social status" (91).

26. Pierre Lamaison and Pierre Bourdieu, "From Rules to Strategies: An Interview with Pierre Bourdieu," *Cultural Anthropology* 1 (1986): 112.

27. For a discussion of Weber's conceptualization of *paths* and *sociological loci*, see Stephen Kalberg, "The Rationalization of Action in Max Weber's Sociology of Religion," *Sociological Theory* 8 (1990): 58–84; Stephen Kalberg, *Max Weber's Comparative Historical Sociology* (Chicago, 1994), 46–49.

28. This "linked sample" is again based upon the identification of 1,453 male Italian immigrants who were ten years or older in the 1910 census of Chicago Heights. Overall, we were able to find 559 matches in 1920 (39 percent), 476 matches (33 percent) in 1930, and 310 (21 percent) in 1940. The procedures engaged in to create the sample give considerable confidence that the matches found were in fact matches of the same immigrants across the various censuses. In other words, we do not believe the problem of "false matches" to be significant. However, issues remain. Thus, simply finding enough of these matches across ten-year census cycles was daunting. As numerous other studies have pointed out, life experiences tend to work against this dedicated linking of an individual in these different population censuses. People die, they move outside the designated area of study (especially back to the old country), they escape enumeration for a variety of reasons. As such, the number of matches varies inversely with the length of the period under study.

Studies of immigration in the later part of the nineteenth century generally place "persistence" or the identification of the same individual over a ten-year cycle within a range of 25 to 45 percent. However, Parkerson also argues that under enumeration in the US Census, and hence low persistence rates, may be structured in such a fashion as to discriminate against "foreign-born boarders in smaller households who worked as laborers for low wages in large, crowded, developing urban centers with rapid population growth, and who were clearly out of the political mainstream." See Donald Parkerson, "How Mobile Were Nineteenth Century Americans?" *Historical Methods: A Journal of Quantitative and Interdisciplinary History* 15 (1982): 99–109. This certainly seems to have had a potential impact upon our sample result, for the 1910 Chicago Heights census lists 740 "lodgers," "boarders," and "roomers" (or 51 percent) among the 1,453 adult Italian males in our original population. And an overwhelming number of these boarders were low-wage laborers and out of the political mainstream. As such, some unknown percent of these immigrants were never identified in subsequent census enumerations even though they may have been present in Chicago Heights or the surrounding communities. At the same time, the high probability that few of these boarders were married or owned property (factors highly associated with persistence) may have also contributed to the difficulty in finding these individuals in 1920, 1930, or 1940. For a discussion of how such factors may impact persistence, see William Toll, "Ethnicity and Stability: The Italians and Jews of South Portland, 1900–1940," *Pacific Historical Review* 54 (1985): 161–89. Finally, the high rate of return migration among Italians may have also undercut our ability to locate immigrant Italians in subsequent censuses. Thus, Cinel suggests that nearly half of the Italian immigrants to America returned home. The majority of these were males of working age, unskilled laborers from the southern regions of Italy, with stays in the United States of less than five years. See Dino Cinel, *The National Integration of Italian Return Migration, 1870–1929* (Cambridge: Cambridge University Press, 1991), 103–11. This typology of emigrant Italians very closely matches the demographics of the Italian population in Chicago Heights.

29. A legitimate question in this comparison of native born, Polish, and Italian concerns the relative age of these populations. For example, one could argue that Italians had higher rates of unskilled and semiskilled workers because they had a younger population just at the beginning of their careers. Or conversely, the native-born citizens in our sample had lower rates because they had matured into advanced stages in their careers. On an individual basis there may have been some of this. However, overall, the average ages of each group in our sample were remarkably similar such that the majority in each group were arguably in the early part of their mature occupational journeys. Specifically, the average age for the native born in 1910 was 31.5, for the Polish 29.1, for the Italians 30.3.

30. John E. Myers, "Special Events Mark Anniversary of Parish Group," *Chicago Heights Star*, June 3, 1962, 4.

31. Howard Aldrich and Roger Waldinger, "Ethnicity and Entrepreneurship," *Annual Review of Sociology*, 16 (1990): 116.

32. Peter Catron, "Made in America? Immigrant Occupational Mobility in the First Half of the Twentieth Century," *American Journal of Sociology*, 122 (2016): 325. Catron carried out an in-depth study of three firms in America, one of which was the Pullman-Standard Manufacturing Company, located just several miles from Chicago Heights (accessed July 22, 2020), https://www.journals.uchicago.edu/doi/abs/10.1086/688043.)

33. Letter, Albert La Morticella to Nino La Morticella, courtesy Dominic Candeloro, Casa Italia Cultural Center files, October 11, 1979. It should also be pointed out that Italians also practiced this form of occupational hoarding in a more limited fashion when the opportunity presented itself. Specifically, Italians often favored hiring workers from their own province or region in the old country.

As Dominic Candeloro points out, Alberto Spina held an influential management position at the American Manganese Steel Company for a number of years. In this position, Spina "began a chain employment that made the large steel company a virtual Marchegianna institution." Dominic Candeloro, "Mostly Melted/ Still Connected: The Marchigiani in Chicago Heights 1893–1997," Casa Italia Cultural Center, Chicago Italian Archives, https://docs.google.com/document/d/1VeaUFTIXEKv6k9SXcEkOe0cqaSw45fjMPTtWou-DF4w/edit.

34. Wozny, *Growing Up Polish*, 109.

35. Interview with Mario Bruno, box 21, folder 239, Italian American Collection Records (IACR), (1979–1980), Italians in Chicago, Department of History, University of Illinois-Chicago Circle Campus.

36. Vincent Parrillo, "Italian-Americans," in *Encyclopedia of Race, Ethnicity, and Society*, ed. Richard Schaefer, 2 (Thousand Oaks, CA: Sage, 2008), 770.

37. Richard Sutch, "Immigrant Homeownership, Economic Assimilation, and Return Migration During the Age of Mass Migration to the United States," paper offered for discussion in the Economic History Seminar Economics 211, University of California, Berkeley, March 11, 2013, 18 (accessed April 7, 2022), https://eml.berkeley.edu/~webfac/eichengreen/Sutch.pdf).

38. Chris Devatenous, "Chicago Heights History" (working paper, University of Chicago, 1924), 22, 19.

39. Richard Dyer, *White* (London: Routledge, 1997), 15.

40. Adam Hochschild, *American Midnight: The Great War, a Violent Peace, and Democracy's Forgotten Crisis* (New York: Mariner Books, 2022), 296–314.

41. Chicago Heights Chamber of Commerce, "Industrial Survey," n.p., section IV, Chicago Heights Library, Pamphlet File, 1927.

42. US Industrial Commission (vol. 8, 415) quoted in David Gordon, "Capitalist Development and the History of American Cities," in *Marxism and the Metropolis: New Perspectives in Urban Political Economy*, eds. William Taub and Larry Sawers (New York: Oxford University Press, 1984), 41.

43. For example, see James Welch, Striker Shot, *Chicago Daily Tribune*, June 28, 1900, 2; "Chicago Heights Factory Owners Call for Protection," *Chicago Daily Tribune*, June 18, 1909, 3; "Gov. Towsend Says No to Plea for Soldiers," *Chicago Daily Tribune*, June 1937, 1.

44. Wozny, *Growing Up Polish*, 113.

45. Neil Fligstein and Roberto Fernandez, "Workers Power, Firm Power, and the Structure of Labor Markets," The *Sociological Quarterly*, 29 (1988): 17 (accessed July 9, 2020), www.jstor.org/stable/4121570.

46. Elizabeth Cohen, *Making a New Deal: Industrial Workers in Chicago, 1919–1939* (Cambridge: Cambridge University Press, 2014), 169.

47. Elizabeth Cohen, *Making a New Deal*, 170. What one African American factory worker put succinctly, "hope on the job." See Mark Hendrickson, *American*

Labor and Economic Citizenship: New Capitalism from World War I to the Great Depression (Cambridge: Cambridge University Press, 2013), 243.

48. "Mfrs. Association Annual Banquet," *Chicago Heights Star*, December 21, 1922.

49. Sanford Jacoby, "The Origins of Internal Labor Markets in American Manufacturing Firms, 1910–1940" (PhD diss., University of California Berkeley, 1981). 38, Quoted in Elizabeth Cohen, *Making a New Deal*, 70.

50. Interview with Mario Bruno, box 21, folder 239, Italian American Collection Records (IACR).

51. Interview with Frank Corradetti, box 13, folder 146 (IACR).

52. Lauren Berlant, *Cruel Optimism* (Durham, NC: Duke University Press, 2011), 2.

Chapter 4

1. See the discussion and review by Gordon Kirk and Carolyn Kirk, "Home Is Where the Heart Is: Immigrant Mobility and Home Ownership," in *Immigrant America: European Ethnicity in the United States*, ed. Timothy Walch (New York: Garland, 1994), 67–88.

2. US Immigration Commission (1907–1910), *Statements and Recommendations Submitted by Societies and Organizations Interested in Immigration* (Washington, DC: Government Printing Office, 1911), vol. 26, 103.

3. Edith Abbott, *The Tenements of Chicago, 1908–1935* (Chicago: University of Chicago Press, 1936), 378.

4. Michael Doucet and John Weaver, *Housing the North American City* (Montreal: McGill-Queen's University Press, 1991), 188.

5. Stephen Thernstrom, "Socialism and Social Mobility," in *Failure of a Dream? Essays in the History of American Socialism*," eds. John Laslett and Seymour Martin Lipset (Garden City: Anchor, 1974), 523, 521.

6. "Suddenly the Town Grew into an Industrial Giant," *Chicago Heights Star*, September 23, 1982.

7. Indeed, as early as 1915, Chicago Heights was identified by social reformer Graham Romeyn Taylor as one of a new breed of "satellite cities" that would model industrial development well into the future. *Satellite Cities: A Study of Industrial Suburbs* (New York: D. Appleton, 1915), 320.

8. "Chicago Heights," *Chicago Daily Tribune*, May 29, 1982, 20.

9. "Real Estate Notes," *Chicago Daily Tribune*, May 15, 1892, 29.

10. "Women Leads Aliens' Fight: Mrs. M. B. Spencer Wants East Chicago Heights Improved," *Chicago Daily Tribune*, February 10, 1914, 3. Also, see, "Debolt Reports on Pollution Case," *Chicago Heights Star*, September 20, 1927. 1; "Com-

missioners Disagree on Refuse from Albert David Chemical Plant," *Chicago Heights Star*, March 27, 1924, 1.

11. Weston Goodspeed and Daniel Healy, eds. *History of Cook County* 2 (Chicago: Goodspeed Historical Association, 1909), 347–48.

12. Doucet and Weaver, *Housing the North American City*, 163.

13. Richard Sutch, "Immigrant Homeownership, Economic Assimilation, and Return Migration During the Age of Mass Migration to the United States," Paper offered for discussion in the Economic History Seminar Economics 211, University of California, Berkeley; Monday, March 11, 2013m (accessed March 25, 2022), https://eml.berkeley.edu/~webfac/eichengreen/Sutch.pdf.

14. For a detailed discussion of homeownership as a significant strategy employed by immigrants in Chicago's working-class neighborhoods during the first decades of the last century, see David Hogan, "Education and the Making of the Chicago Working Class, 1880–1930," *History of Education Quarterly* 18 (1978): 227–70.

15. US Department of Commerce, *Fifteenth Census of the United States, 1930 Census: Manufactures, 1929, Volume 3, Report By States, Illinois*. While data is not available for Italians or other ethnic groups per se, the average salary was certainly lower as these second-wave immigrant groups assumed positions in the lower ranks of these factories and plants

16. Personal Interview, Nick Digiovanni, April 9, 2022.

17. "Chicago Heights Suspends All Trade for Week," *Chicago Daily Tribune*, July 1, 1932, 30.

18. Genevieve Ford Reed, *Looking over Our Shoulders* (n.d.), 1, Chicago Heights History 1900–1930, Chicago Heights Public Library Pamphlet File.

19. Interview with Theresa Giannetti, box 21, folder 239, Italian American Collection Records (IACR), (1979–1980), Italians in Chicago, Department of History, University of Illinois-Chicago Circle Campus.

20. "Rid the City of Tenements," *Chicago Heights Star*, September 30, 1938, 8.

21. Interview with Mario Bruno, box 21, folder 239, Italian American Collection Records (IACR), (1979–1980), Italians in Chicago, Department of History, University of Illinois-Chicago Circle Campus.

22. Elizabeth Cohen, *Making a New Deal: Industrial Workers in Chicago, 1919–1939* (Cambridge: Cambridge University Press, 2014), 234.

23. Doucet and Weaver, *Housing the North American City*, 339.

24. Virginia Yans-McLaughlin, *Family and Community: Italian Immigrants in Buffalo, 1880–1930* (Urbana: University of Illinois Press, 1977), 177.

25. Oscar Handlin, "The Shock of Alienation: From 'The Uprooted: The Story of the Great Migrations that Made the American People," *Race/Ethnicity: Multidisciplinary Global Contexts* 1 (2007): 13.

26. Vincent Cannato, *American Passage: The History of Ellis Island* (New York: HarperCollins, 2009), 12.

Notes to Chapter 4 | 163

27. "Keep the Gates Closed," *Chicago Daily Tribune*, March 27, 1923, 27.

28. Sarah Churchwell, *Behold America: A History of America First and the American Dream* (London: Bloomsbury Publishing, 2018), 106.

29. "Better Government," *Chicago Heights Star*, April 3, 1924, 1.

30. Illinois Legislative Investigation Commission, "Ku Klux Klan: A Report to the Illinois General Assembly," October 1976 (accessed February 23, 2023), https://www.ojp.gov/pdffiles1/Digitization/46433NCJRS.pdf

31. "Men Set Ablaze Ku Klux Klan Tent," *Chicago Heights Star*, July 24, 1924, 1.

32. Knights of the Ku Klux Klan. Advertisement. *Chicago Heights Star*, February 21, 1924; February 28, 1924; March 6, 1924.

33. "Immigration Propaganda," *Chicago Heights Star*, August 11, 1927.

34. "Europe Take Notice," *Chicago Heights Star*, May 15, 1924, 1.

35. Gwendolyn Wright, *Moralism and the Modern Home: Domestic Architecture and Cultural Conflict in Chicago, 1873–1913* (Chicago: University of Chicago Press, 1980), 45.

36. Gwendolyn Wright, *Moralism and the Modern Home*, 234.

37. Henry Demarest Lloyd, "In New Applications of Democracy," *Congregationalist*, January 5, 1901 (as cited in Wright, *Moralism and the Modern Home*, 336–37).

38. "The Joys of Home Ownership," *National Real Estate Journal*, 9 (1914): 421.

39. Adna Ferrin Weber, *The Growth of Cities in the Nineteenth Century: A Study of Statistics* (Ithaca, NY: Cornell University Press, 1963), 467.

40. Gwendolyn Wright, *Building the Dream: A Social History of Housing in America* (Cambridge, MA: MIT Press, 1983), 151.

41. "Home Comforts Reflected Here, Make Good Citizens," *Chicago Heights Star*, February 7, 1924, 1.

42. Wright, *Building the Dream*, 150.

43. "Bolshevism on Trial," *Chicago Heights Star*, May 29, 1919, 1; "Political Ownership," *Chicago Heights Star*, April 26, 1927, 4; "The Changing World," *Chicago Heights Star*, January 24, 1924, 4; "Bolshevism and Religion," *Chicago Heights Star*, July 22, 1927, 4.

44. "The Right Welcome," *Chicago Heights Star*, July 9, 1927, 2.

45. "Indian Speaker Raps Communism," *Chicago Heights Star*, May 4, 1934, 10.

46. "A Misconception of Communism," *Chicago Heights Star*, September 26, 1938, 6.

47. "Home Comforts Reflected Here, Make Good Citizens," *Chicago Heights Star*, 1.

48. Margaret Garb, *City of American Dreams: A History of Home Ownership and Housing Reform in Chicago, 1871–1919* (Chicago: University of Chicago Press, 2005), 146.

49. Garb, *City of American Dreams*, 2.

50. "Home Comforts Reflected Here, Make Good Citizens," *Chicago Heights Star*, 1.

51. Wright, *Moralism and the Modern Home*, 83.

52. Natalie Walker, Chicago Housing Conditions. Greek and Italians in the Neighborhood of Hull House, *American Journal of Sociology* XXI (1915): 285.

53. Graham Romeyn Taylor, *Satellite Cities: A Study of Industrial Suburbs* (New York: D. Appleton and Company, 1915), 29.

54. Josiah Strong, *Our Country, Its Possible Future and Its Present Crisis* (1885, rep. ed., Cambridge, MA: Harvard University Press, 1963), 177.

55. Wright, *Moralism and the Modern Home*, 294.

56. For a more general discussion of these efforts, see Richard Sutch, "Before the American Dream: The Early Years of Urban Home Ownership, The United States, 1850–1940," Paper presented at the Social Science History Association's 36th Annual Meeting, Boston, November 19, 2011.

57. "'The Great Idea' Tells You How to Own Your Own Home," *Chicago Heights Star*, April 17, 1924, 1.

58. A. J. Klyczek, & Co. Advertisement, *Chicago Heights Star*, March 27, 1924, 8.

59. McEldowney & Co, Real Estate, Loans, and Insurance. Advertisement *Chicago Heights Star*, April 17, 1924, 18.

60. Frank McEldowney, "Realtor Talks on Home Subdivisions: Real Estate Men Perform an Important Service by Urging Home Building," *Chicago Heights Star*, April 24, 1924. 1.

61. McEldowney & Co, Real Estate, Loans, and Insurance. Advertisement *Chicago Heights Star*, December 28, 1922, 8.

62. Richard Kozdras, "The Hill: The History of an Ethnic Neighborhood," (Chicago Heights: City of Chicago Heights, 1977), 15.

63. Personal Interview, Diane Melchiore, March 1, 2018.

64. Interview with Aldo DeAngelis, courtesy of Dominic Candeloro, Casa Italia Cultural Center. Stone Park, IL. March 1, 1997.

65. Personal Interview, Marie Iafollo, November 8, 2017.

66. John E. Myers, "Special Events Mark Anniversary . . ."*Chicago Heights Star*, June 3, 1962, 4.

67. James M. Whelan & Sons: Real Estate, Advertisement. *Chicago Heights Star*, May 1, 1928, 4.

Chapter 5

1. Ran Abramitzky, Leah Platt Boustan, Elisa Jácome, and Santiago Pérez, "Intergenerational Mobility of Immigrants in the US over Two Centuries," NBER Working Paper No. 26408, October 2019, JEL No. J15,J61,J62,N30, accessed, March 17, 2020. http://www.nber.org/papers/w26408.

2. Andrew Greeley, "The Italians," The American Experience Series, Public Broadcasting, Boston, 1973.

3. Ran Abramitzky and Leah Boustan, *Streets of Gold: America's Untold Story of Immigrant Success* (New York: Public Affairs, 2022).

4. Abramitsky and Boustan, *Streets of Gold*, 69, 57.

5. Ran Abramizky, Leah Boustan, Elisa Jácome, and Santiago Pérez, "Intergenerational Mobility of Immigrants in the US over Two Centuries," NBER Working Paper No. 26408.

6. Joel Perlmann, *Ethnic Differences: Schooling and Social Structure among the Irish, Italians, Jews and Blacks in an American City, 1880–1935* (Cambridge: Cambridge University Press, 1988), 86; see also Leonard Covello, *The Social Background of the Italo-American School Child* (Leiden, Brill, 1967); John Briggs, *An Italian Passage: Immigrants to Three American Cities 1890–1930* (Princeton, NJ: Princeton University Press, 1978). Nancy Foner, *From Ellis Island to JFK: New York's Two Great Waves of Immigration* (New Haven, CT: Yale University Press, 2000).

7. Humbert Nelli, *Italians in Chicago, 1880–1930: A Study in Ethnic Mobility* (New York: Oxford University Press, 1970), 66–67. Along these lines, Matteo Pretrelli relays the writings of Jerre Mangione, well-known Italian American scholar, who revealed that his mother was fearful that "reading too many books could eventually lead to madness." "Italian Americans, Education, and Italian Language: 1880–1921," *Quaderni d'italianistica* 38 (2017): 63.

8. Joseph Bodnar, *The Transplanted: A History of Immigrants in Urban America* (Bloomington: Indiana University Press, 1985), 73–74.

9. Robert Orsi, "The Fault of Memory: 'Southern Italy' in the Imagination of Immigrants and the Lives of Their Children in Italian Harlem, 1920–1945," *Journal of Family History* 15 (1990): 143.

10. Paul Campisi, "Ethnic Patterns: The Italian Family in the United States," *American Journal of Sociology* 53 (1948): 447.

11. David Riesman, *The Lonely Crowd: A Study of the Changing American Character* (New Haven, CT: Yale University Press, 1950), 40.

12. Jerre Mangione and Ben Morreale, *La Storia, Five Centuries of the Italian American Experience* (New York: Harper Perennial, 1992), 232–34.

13. "Umberto La Morticella" in *Voices of America: Italians in Chicago* (Charleston, SC: Arcadia, 2001), 66.

14. Interview with Theresa Giannetti, box 21, folder 239, Italian American Collection Records (IACR), (1979–1980), Italians in Chicago, Department of History, University of Illinois-Chicago Circle Campus.

15. Personal Interview, Marie Iafollo, November 8, 2017.

16. Interview with Theresa Giannetti, box 21, folder 239, Italian American Collection Records (IACR).

17. Campisi, "Ethnic Patterns: The Italian Family in the United States," 448.

18. Orsi, "Fault of Memory," 140.

19. F. S. Beeson, "History of Chicago Heights, Illinois, 1833–1938," 1938 (Federal Writers' Project, Chicago Heights Public Library Collection), 71.

20. Robert Orsi, *The Madonna of 115th Street: Faith and Community in Italian Harlem, 1880–1950* (New Haven: Yale University Press, 1985), 107–89.

21. Allan Schnaiberg and Sheldon Goldenberg, "Closing the Circle: The Impact of Children on Parental Status," *Journal of Marriage and the Family* 37 (1975): 946.

22. Pierre Lamaison and Pierre Bourdieu, "From Rules to Strategies: An Interview with Pierre Bourdieu," *Cultural Anthropology* 1 (1986): 113.

23. Lamaison and Bourdieu, "From Rules to Strategies," 113.

24. See Mariam Slater, "My Son the Doctor: Aspects of Mobility among American Jews," *American Sociological Review* 34 (1969): 367.

25. Leo Rosten, *The Joys of Yiddish* (New York: McGraw-Hill, 1968), 434.

26. Richard Alba and Nancy Foner, "The Second Generation from the Last Great Wave of Immigration: Setting the Record Straight," Migration Information Source (October 2006) (accessed April 30, 2022) https://www.migrationpolicy.org/article/second-generation-last-great-wave-immigration-setting-record-straight.

27. For an in-depth look at the subtle ways in which parents' hopes may be invested in their sons by creating "future priests," see Joseph Sheley, *Preordained: Boys as "Future Priests" During Catholicism's Minor-Seminary Boom and Bust* (Sacramento, CA: Byron Laredo, 2020).

28. Herbert Gutman, *Work, Culture and Society in Industrializing America* (New York: Vintage Books, 1976), 234–60.

29. Lamaison and Bourdieu, "From Rules to Strategies," 112.

30. Stephen Steinberg, *The Academic Melting Pot* (New Brunswick, NJ: Transaction Books, 1977), 10.

31. Department of Commerce, Bureau of the Census, *Fifteen Census of the United States 1930, Volume II, Population: General Report, Statistics by Subject, Illinois* (Washington, DC: United States Census Bureau, 1932).

32. Department of Commerce, Bureau of the Census, *Fifteen Census of the United States 1930, Volume III, Reports by States, Showing the Composition and Characteristics of the Population for Counties, Cities, and Townships and Other Minor Civil Divisions, Illinois* (Washington, DC: United States Census Bureau, 1932).

33. At the same time, the educational accomplishments of Italian girls were rarely seen as objectified embodiments for hope on the part of parents. See US Immigration Commission, *Reports: The Children of Immigrants in Schools* (Washington, DC: Government Printing Office, 1911), 29–33.

34. Richard Kozdras, "The Hill: The History of an Ethnic Neighborhood" (Chicago Heights: City of Chicago Heights, 1977), 17.

35. Personal Interview, Marie Iafollo, November 8, 2017.

36. Personal Interview, Pasqualina Pancrazio, March 8, 1997.

37. Perlmann's data on Italian school achievement and occupational attainment in Providence, Rhode Island, at the beginning of the last century is instructive.

While school achievement is significantly less than that of other ethnic groups in the study, the occupational attainment of Italian children did not differ significantly from these other groups. There are a number of possible explanations. It may be that the accomplishments within the educational system (i.e., academic grades, conduct grades, promotions) were more foreign to parents who themselves had little formal, school training. See Perlmann, *Ethnic Differences*, 96–100. In Bourdieu's words, these accomplishments were not seen as a "collectively recognized credit," as opposed to a paycheck or job title, that parents could use to certify hope. Pierre Bourdieu, *Outline of a Theory of Practice*. trans. Richard Nice (Cambridge: Cambridge University Press, 1977), 121.

38. Committee on Field Services, Department of Education on the University of Chicago, "Field Course and Survey Greater Chicago Heights Area," Boards of Education Districts 170 and 206, Chicago Heights, Illinois, 1942, 24.

39. Committee on Field Services, "Field Course and Survey Greater Chicago Heights Area," 24.

40. The occupational data for sons was gathered from available sources (for example, US Census materials, marriage records, military records, obituaries) in the period from 1930 to 1940. This, presumably, was at that critical juncture when sons were experiencing their prime career years. The average age of the sons in this sample was thirty-one in 1930. Overall, there were 218 fathers in the original 1910 population of 1,420 Italian male immigrants. These fathers had 708 children as of 1910, 306 daughters and 403 sons. We were able to locate the occupational statuses of 320 (or approximately 80 percent) of the sons, from a total of 157 fathers. Of course, sons born after 1910 may have theoretically impacted the ability to objectify hope. However, most of these sons would not have matured into their occupations until the late 1940s or 1950s, and the case mortality of the sample would have been substantially higher.

41. C. Wright Mills, *White Collar: The American Middle Class* (New York: Oxford University Press, 1951), 74. Perhaps, this comes rather late here and is not adequately recognized, but the "native born" referred to in this study also came from immigrant backgrounds wherein their acceptance in Chicago Heights was fraught with a host of challenges. The Irish and the German immigrants in particular were often placed, for different reasons, at the lower rungs of the immigrant hierarchy. I am indebted to Garrett Paul for this helpful reminder (Garrett Paul, email message to author, September 5, 2022).

42. Alejandro Portes and Rubin G. Rumbaut, "Introduction: The Second Generation and the Children of Immigrants, Longitudinal Study," *Ethnic and Racial Studies* 28 (2005): 985.

43. Elizabeth Cohen, *Making a New Deal: Industrial Workers in Chicago, 1919–1939* (Cambridge: Cambridge University Press, 2014), 213.

44. Elizabeth Cohen, *Making a New Deal*, 241.

45. Fred De Luca, "Our Neighbors in Heights—The Italian Americans," *Chicago Heights Star*, May 1, 1936.

46. Chris Wright, "Popular Radicalism in the 1930s: The History of the Workers' Unemployment Insurance Bill," *Class, Race and Corporate Power* 6 (2018) (accessed March 14, 2023), https://digitalcommons.fiu.edu/classracecorporatepower/vol6/iss1/4; also for a thorough look at the problems and organizing efforts to address the ravages of the Depression in the Chicago area, see Chris Wright, "Down But Not Out: The Unemployed in Chicago during the Great Depression" (PhD diss., University of Illinois at Chicago, 2017).

47. Robert Heinsen, "The Economic and Industrial History of Chicago Heights" (MA thesis, University of Iowa, 1937).

48. Interview with Dominic Pandolfi, box 36, folder 449. Italian American Collection Records (IACR), (1979–1980), Italians in Chicago, Department of History, University of Illinois-Chicago Circle Campus.

49. Collen Newquest, "The Hill Boasts a 'Rich' Tradition," *Chicago Heights Star*, September 8, 1988, 2.

50. Genevieve Ford Reed, *Looking over Our Shoulders* (n.d.), 2 (Chicago Heights Public Library Pamphlet File).

51. For an in-depth discussion of the various tactics and inducements used to turn "aliens into citizens" and refiguring hope in World War I, see Richard Juliani, *Little Italy in the Great War Philadelphia's Italians on the Battlefield and Home Front* (Philadelphia: Temple University Press, 2020).

52. For personal accounts of Italians forced to relocate as a result of this executive order, see Lawrence DiStasi, ed. *Una Storia Segreta: The Secret History of Italian American Evacuation and Internment during World War II* (Berkeley: Heyday Books, 2001).

53. "Alien Registration," *Chicago Heights Star*, August 23, 1940.

54. "A Timely Suggestion," *Chicago Heights Star*, December 12, 1941, 1.

55. Dominic Candeloro and Barbara Paul, *Chicago Heights: At the Crossroads of the Nation* (Charleston, SC: Arcadia, 2004), 122–123.

56. Paul Rabinow, "Introduction" in Michel Foucault, *The Foucault Reader* (New York: Pantheon, 1984), 21.

57. "Alien 'Census' Gaining After a Slow Start," *Chicago Heights Star*, August 30, 1940, 1; "1603 Aliens Registered at Post Office," *Chicago Heights Star*, December 27, 1940.

58. DiStasi, *Branded*, 18.

59. John Wozny, *Growing up Polish: A History of the Polish Pioneers in Chicago Heights, Volume 1, 1900–1930* (Steger, IL: Growing Up Polish: 1993), 137.

60. Dominic Candeloro and Barbara Paul, *Chicago Heights: At the Crossroads of the Nation* (Charleston, SC: Arcadia, 2004), 125.

61. Personal Interview, Marie Iafollo, November 8, 2017.

62. Dominic Candeloro, "World War II Changed Everything," in *The Routledge History of Italian Americans*, ed. William J. Connell and Stanislao G. Pugliese (New York: Routledge, 2018), 377. Also see Tommaso Caiazza, "The Impact of World War II on San Francisco's Italian-American Community Continuity and

Change," in *What is Italian America?*, ed. George Guida, Stanislao Pugliese, Alan Gravano, Peter Vellon, and Jennifer Kightlinger (New York: Italian American Studies Association, 2015), 81–97.

63. Juan Ramon Garcia, *A History of the Mexican American People in the Chicago Heights, Illinois Area* (Chicago Heights, IL: Prairie State College, 1975), 85.

Conclusion

1. Emile Durkheim, *Suicide: A Study in Sociology*, trans. John Spaulding and George Simpson (New York: Free Press, 1951), 248.

2. Emile Durkheim, *The Division of Labor in Society*, trans. George Simpson (New York: Free Press, 2014), 251.

3. Charles Lindholm, *Charisma* (Oxford, Blackwell, 1990), 33.

4. Richard Alba, *Italian Americans in the Twilight of Ethnicity* (Englewood Cliffs, NJ.: Prentice-Hall, 1985).

5. Richard Alba, *The Great Demographic Illusion: Majority, Minority, and the Expanding American Mainstream* (Princeton, NJ: Princeton University Press, 2020), 9.

6. Alba, *Great Demographic Illusion*, 167–68.

7. Jerre Mangione and Ben Morreale, *La Storia, Five Centuries of the Italian American Experience* (New York: Harper Perennial, 1992), 451.

8. Stefana Vaccara, "Italian Americans and The Impact of Their Five Centuries of History in America: Our Interviews with the historians William J. Connell and Stanislao G. Pugliese, editors of the essential volume, 'The Routledge History of Italian Americans'" VNY La Voce di New York, May 17, 2020 (accessed December 26, 2020),https://www.lavocedinewyork.com/en/people/2020/05/17/the-italian-americans-and-their-five-centuries-history-in-america-thats-it/.

9. Robert Foerster, *The Italian Emigration of Our Times* (Cambridge, MA: Harvard University Press, 1919), 101.

10. J. S. McDonald, "Some Socio-Economic Differentials in Rural Italy, 1902–1913," *Economic Development and Cultural Change* 7 (1958): 67.

11. Peter Thompson and Slavoj Žižek, eds., *The Privatization of Hope: Ernst Bloch and the Future of Utopia, SIC 8* (Durham, NC: Duke University Press 2013).

12. Jerome Krase, "Whatever Happened to Little Italy?" in *The Routledge History of Italian Americans,* ed. William J. Connell and Stanislao G. Pugliese (New York: Routledge, 2018), 527.

13. Vincent Scully, *American Architecture and Urbanism* (San Antonio: Trinity Press, 2013), 16.

14. William Egelman, "Italian Americans, 1990–2000: A Demographic Analysis of National Data," *Italian Americana* 24 (2006): 9–19.

15. Over the years a number of studies suggest that the social mobility experiences among Italian Americans have not been uniform and in ways replicate the

historical division between northern Italians and southern Italians. For example, see Herbert Gans, *Urban Villagers* (New York: Free Press, 1962); Micaela di Leonardo, *The Varieties of Ethnic Experiences: Kinship, Class and Gender Among California Italian-Americans* (Ithaca, NY: Cornell University Press, 1984); Karl Bonuti, "Economic Characteristics of Italian-Americans," Center for Migration Studies 7 (1989): 62–79; Tom Verso, Italian Americans by the Numbers—Income, Earnings, and Poverty," *i*-Italy, November 25, 2009 (accessed December 26, 2020), http://iitaly.org/magazine/focus/facts-stories/article/italian-americans-numbers-income-earnings-poverty#:~:text=For%20example%2C%20the%20raw%20data,that%20of%20Italian%20Americans%20%2464%2C4 71. Frances X. Femminella's analysis of the 1980 census reveals that Italian Americans generally had lower rates of divorce, single parent families, congregate living arrangements for the elderly, and mental illness than the general population. Nevertheless, these rates were beginning to mirror those of the general population as the "external press of the American value system" impacted each succeeding generation. "Italian American Family Life," *Center for Migration Studies: Special Issue*, 7 (1989): 60. Also, see Dominick Carielli and Joseph Grosso, eds., *Benessere Psicologico: Contemporary Thought on Italian American Mental Health* (New York: John D. Calandra Italian American Institute, 2013).

16. See Stout et al., "Study of an Italian-American Community in PA; Unusually Low Incidence of Deaths from Myocardial Infarctions," *Journal of the American Medical Association*, 188 (1964), 845–49. Also Egolf et al., "The Roseto Effect: A 50-year Comparison of Mortality Rates, *American Journal of Public Health* 82 (1992), 189–1092.

17. John Bruhn and Stewart Wolf, *The Roseto Story, An Anatomy of Health* (Norman, University of Oklahoma Press, 1979), 41.

18. Bruhn and Wolf, *The Roseto Story*, ix.

19. Personal Interview, Caroline Giovannini, June 15, 2023.

20. Bruhn and Wolf, *The Roseto Story*, 80.

21. Bruhn and Wolf, *The Roseto Story*, 79.

22. Bruhn and Wolf, *The Roseto Story*, 37.

23. Bruhn and Wolf, *The Roseto Story*, 39.

24. Personal Interview, Adriana Trigiani, May 10, 2023.

25. Bruhn and Wolf, *The Roseto Story*, 138.

26. Personal Interview, Caroline Giovannini, June 15, 2023.

27. Along these lines, stories of the horrible conditions in Italy at the turn of the last century served to buttress the commitment to hope in America. This provides an interesting contrast to Orsi's discussion of the ways Italian immigrants built a fanciful, idealized "southern Italy" as a proper way of being in the world in the face of assimilation challenges posed by their children in America. So, too, descriptions of the miserable conditions in southern Italy on the part of many immigrants, tied to realistic experiences no doubt, may have nevertheless served as "public performances" justifying the way of being for those who achieved a measure

of success in the American context. Robert Orsi, "The Fault of Memory: 'Southern Italy' in the Imagination of Immigrants and the Lives of Their Children in Italian Harlem, 1920–1945," *Journal of Family History*, 15 (1990): 135–36.

28. Colleen Newquest, "The Hill boasts a 'rich' tradition," *Chicago Heights Star*, September 8, 1988.

29. Robert N. Bellah, Richard Madsen, William M. Sullivan, Ann Swidler, and Steven M. Tipton, *Habits of the Heart: Individualism and Commitment in American Life* (Berkeley, University of California Press, 1985), 153.

30. William Foote Whyte, *Street Corner Society* (Chicago: University of Chicago Press, 1967).

31. Edward Shils, "The Virtue of Civil Society." *Government and Opposition* 26 (1991): 14.

32. Anthony Giddens, *Modernity and self-identity: Self and Society in the late Modern Age* (Stanford, CA: Stanford University Press, 1991).

33. Bellah et al., *Habits of the Heart*, 154.

34. Richard Alba, *Italian Americans: Into the Twilight of Ethnicity* (Englewood Cliffs, NJ: Prentice Hall, 1985), 10.

35. Richard Alba, "Italian Americans and Assimilation," in *The Routledge History of Italian Americans*, ed. William J. Connell and Stanislao G. Pugliese (New York: Routledge, 2018), 498.

36. US Census Bureau, Quick Facts: Population Estimates, American Community Survey, Chicago Heights, Census of Population and Housing, 2021 (accessed May 19, 2022), https://www.census.gov/quickfacts/fact/table/chicagoheightscityillinois/LND110210.

37. Bellah et al., *Habits of the Heart*, 292.

38. Max Weber, "Class, Status, Party" in *From Max Weber: Essays in Sociology*, ed. H. H. Gerth and C. Wright Mills, with new preface Bryan S. Turner (Oxford: Routledge Press, 1991), 189.

39. For a discussion of the "communities of memory," see Bellah et al., *Habits of the Heart*, 152–55, 282–83. Also, Durkheim thought long and hard on how to promote social structures that would appropriately ground desires outside the individual and the family but also exist below the more distant and anomic nation-state. A class or caste system, or in Bourdieu's terms a hierarchy of social spaces, was too stratified. Instead, the formation of intermediary groups or secondary associations would provide communal values and hopes that were civil yet relevant. The key, however, was not to form homogeneous organizations that demanded solidarity, for then communal hope or the integration of hopes would be preordained. Instead, these previously "unconnected coexistences" of ethnic associations should be created in a fashion that differences be allowed and encouraged. There should be a multiplicity and crisscrossing of interests and experiences and in the process hopes become broadened and contextualized. For a discussion of these ties between individual and communal hopes in civil society, see Edward Shils, "Civility and

Civil Society: Good Manners between Persons and Concern for the Common Good in Public Affairs," in *The Virtue of Civility: Selected Essays on Liberalism, Tradition, and Civil Society*, ed. Steven Grosby (Indianapolis: Liberty Fund, 1997): 63–103.

40. Ben Joravsky, "Blue Collars among the Blue-Bloods: A History of Highwood, the North Shore's Island of Italian Immigrants," *Chicago Reader*, September 10, 1987, https://www.chicagoreader.com/chicago/blue-collars-among-the-blue-bloods-a-history-of-highwood-the-north-shores-island-of-italian-immigrants/Content?oid=871105; Also, see Adria Bernardi, *Houses with Names: The Italian Immigrants of Highwood, Illinois* (Urbana: University of Illinois Press, 1990).

41. Josiah Royce, "Provincialism," in *Race Questions, Provincialism, and Other American Problems* (Freeport, NY: Books for Libraries Press, 1967 [1908]), 1069.

42. Josiah Royce, *The Problem of Christianity* (Washington, DC: Catholic University Press, 2001), 248.

43. Kieran Setiya, *Life is Hard: How Philosophy Can Help Us Find Our Way* (New York: Riverhead Books, 2022), 178.

Index

Alba, Richard, 3, 108–109, 124, 131
American Dream, 56, 59, 67, 96, 100, 126–127

Bellah, Robert, 17, 131, 132
Berlant, Lauren, 3, 44, 84
Black residents, 14–15, 82, 112, 119
boarders, 56–59
Bourdieu, Pierre, 5; on social spaces, 21–22, 30, 108, 120, 130

cultural capital: definition, 5; embodied, 23, 34–36; institutionalized, 24, 38–39; objectified, 23–24, 36–38
Chicago Heights: history, 88–90; racial and ethnic residential patterns, 62, 131; social characterization 12–13

Durkheim, Emile, 7–8, 123, 126–127, 134

Ellis Island, 2, 51–53
emigration brokers and agents, 45–49

Foucault, Michael, 6, 117

Great Depression, 81, 93, 94, 115–116

Gugliemo, Thomas, 11, 15, 24

habitus: definition, 24–25, 27
Handlin, Oscar, 2, 27, 94, 144n55
hope: characterization of, 1–2, 5; communal hope in Italy, 125–126, 146n8; definition, 135n2; individual versus communal hope, 126–127; Royce and community of hope, 133; as sacred object, 123; as shared experience, 141n6; as social practice, 33–34, 130; sociological conceptualization, 21

Italian immigrants: as enemy aliens, 116–118; dissent practices, 29–32; reasons for emigration, 141–145; resignation practices, 27–28; working conditions, 59–61, 68, 73

Latino residents 82, 119, 120; early Chicago Heights experiences, 139n54

Marx, Karl, 7, 9, 75

nativism, 94–95, 97
Nelli, Humbert, 10–11, 41, 105

173

occupational mobility, 71–84 passim; sons from fathers, 113–115; in other communities, 157n22
organized crime, 4, 69–70, 156n9
Orsi, Robert 106, 107

padrone system, 49, 54–56
Polish immigrants, 14, 76, 77, 78
provincialism, 25, 26

renters, 96, 97, 99, 100
residential segregation, 93–94, 154n99
Roseto, Pennsylvania: communal hope and medical outcomes, 127–128; transformations in Roseto culture, 128–129

schooling, 36, 63, 105, 109–112, 166n37
socialist/socialism, 60, 69, 82, 96–97, 143n37
social mobility, 3–4, 42–43; comparison immigrant and native-born children, 104–105; personal consequences, 170n15
steamship travel, 50–51, 149n45

Thernstrom, Stephan, 3, 72, 156n12

Vecoli, Rudolph, 11, 63, 73

Weber, Max, 8, 71, 132, 158n27
Wittgenstein, Ludwig, 5, 142n20
women, 110–111, 125, 136n18, 144n52